DR. RUTH'S GUIDE FOR MARRIED LOVERS

Dr. Ruth Westheimer

WINGS BOOKS
New York • Avenel, New Jersey

This 1992 edition is published by Wings Books,
distributed by Outlet Book Company, Inc., a Random House Company,
40 Engelhard Avenue, Avenel, New Jersey 07001,
by arrangement with Warner Books, Inc.

Printed and bound in the United States of America

Library of Congress Cataloging-in-Publication Data
Westheimer, Ruth K. (Ruth Karola), 1928-
Dr. Ruth's guide for married lovers / Ruth Westheimer,
        p.   cm.
Originally published : New York : Warner Books, c1986.
Includes Index.
ISBN 0-517-63174-1 : $6.99
1. Sex in marriage.   2. Sex instruction.
I. Title.   II. Title : Doctor Ruth's guide for
married lovers.   III. Guide for married lovers.
[HQ31.W493 1992]
613.9'6—dc20
92-18893
CIP

8 7 6 5 4 3 2 1

"Sex is a foretaste of the world to come"
—*Talmud Brachot 57-B*

In addition to dedicating this book to my husband, Fred, my son, Joel, and my daughter, Miriam, I would like to welcome my new son-in-law, Joel Einleger, to our family!

Acknowledgments

As time goes on, the list of names of those people who have shared their friendship, have encouraged and constructively criticized me grows by leaps and bounds. What a very fortunate person I am!

I will list only some representing the many—otherwise another chapter would have to be added to the book!

Heartfelt thanks to my clients, listeners, viewers, and readers for sharing their concerns with me and permitting me thus a glimpse into their lives!

Here is my partial list—thank you all:

The terrific professional and technical staff of my television and NBC Radio Entertainment program; KFI Radio; and King Features.

Ron Alexander	Stuart Cattell
Larry Angelo	Frank Ciarkowski
	Father Finbarr Corr
Ruth and Howard Bachrach	Marie Cuadrado
Susan Brown	
	Georgia Dullea

Betty Elam
Cynthia Fuchs Epstein, Ph.D.
Howard Epstein

Vincent Facchino
Avi Feinglass
Jack Forest, M.D.

Harvey Gardner
Jon Glascoe
Dean Gordon
David Goslin, Ph.D.

Frederick C. Herman
Martin Herman

Alfred Kaplan
Helen Singer Kaplan, M.D., Ph.D.
Else Katz
Harold Koplewicz, M.D.
Richard Korman
Evelyn and Nathan Kravetz, Ph.D.
Bill and Marga Kunreuther

Lani Lehman
Joanne Lehu
Hope Leichter, Ph.D.
Lou Lieberman, Ph.D.
John and Ginger Lollos

Paul Noble

Deborah Offenbacher, Ph.D.
Dale Ordes

Asa Ruskin, M.D.
Francine Ruskin, Ed.D.

Ira Saker, M.D.
Elaine Silver
Fred Silverman
Olena Smulka
Arthur Snyder, M.D.
Hannah Strauss
William Sweeney, M.D.

Mildred Hope Witkin, Ph.D.

Fred Zeller

Bernard Shir-Cliff, my editor, and Margery Schwartz, my managing editor.

Rabbi Leonard Kravitz and Rabbi Selig Salkowitz, who generously shared their knowledge with me and co-authored an article with me about sexuality and the Jewish tradition.

Rabbi Robert Lehman and Pierre Lehu who continue to provide me with their counsel and friendship and John A. Silberman, my attorney and special friend who "protects me."

Contents

1

*Why
a New
Marriage Manual?*

A CHILDHOOD memory. I am too small to reach up to the book that I am so curious about. I am sure my parents put it on that high shelf so that I can't reach it. But they are both out of the house now, and I am determined to peek at its mysterious pages.

To a grown-up a bookshelf is a fine place to keep and display books, and the highest shelves are a good place for certain volumes—nice editions that are better without tiny thumbprints on the pages, and books that are...for grown-ups. But to a small child a bookcase is an Everest to conquer. Up I climb to get that fascinating green clothbound book they don't want me to see. In a moment I am on the clean, *clean* carpet (this is Frankfurt, Germany) and looking into the first sex book of my life. Van de Velde's *Ideal Marriage.*

I don't remember what I thought of the staid text of that famous manual. Nor the outcome of my stealthy adventure. Was I caught? Spoken to? If so, it was no traumatic experience. My parents were gentle with me. Maybe I got the book back in its place again before anyone came home; maybe someone sagely put it back without saying anything to me about it. Which is what I would do, as long as the child had not torn a page or spilled jam on the binding.

I am fond of the memory, and it comes to me often when I talk to groups about children's natural curiosity about sex.

That book was the great sex manual of my parents' generation, back in the late 1920s. Thoughtful couples used to read it together before marriage. Often it was put in their hands by friends or elders who knew that sex, especially for those who went as virgins to the marriage bed, could be awkward and could cloud over those first months of what should be married happiness.

Since those days sex books of many varieties have come to crowd bookstore shelves, to be massed boldly in window displays. Many are more advanced than the dear old Van de Velde book; certainly, many are more raucous in spirit. (Van de Velde approached the subject reverently for the infinitely more convention-bound readers of his time.) But, in the age of AIDS, sex manuals should place an emphasis on making stable relationships more exciting so as to reduce the temptation for one to stray because of dissatisfaction.

Those readers and listeners who have followed my books, columns and shows know that I rarely say "should" to people. "Should" statements usually reflect values and morality that not all readers and clients share with a sex therapist and educator. But, because of the AIDS epidemic, the use of the phrase "married lovers" in the title is not merely to define a population of readers. More importantly, it suggests an emphasis on ideas for maintaining a more stimulating sex life within all on-going and stable relationships, of which traditional marriage is only one type. And so I now say that people *should* try to remain in their stable relationships, heterosexual or homosexual, because the singles scene these days—with all the casual sex and all-too-often unprotected sex—is not a safe place to be.

MARRIAGE MAKES A COMEBACK

Back in the late 1960s and early 1970s, we would often

hear from self proclaimed experts and media sensationalists that the "family is dead" and that traditional marriage is obsolete. Why bother with a piece of paper called a marriage certificate? Let us experiment with group marriages, corporate marriages, entire commune marriages—anything except the age-old two-person lifetime commitment sealed by a legally sanctioned ceremony. But that tough old institution known as marriage is, by the 1990s, stronger than ever. It is so strong that even homosexual couples are arguing and petitioning for recognition to become legally married in the eyes of community, church and state.

This growing popularity in marriage may be a move back to more traditional times, but I'm for it—wedding parties are my favorite kind. But the news about the marriage comeback doesn't surprise me because I never had a strong impression of marriage really being on the way out. The disaffected young people were trying to reinvent marriage, or design a new pattern. They were seeking "relationships." What they didn't realize is that they were looking for deep emotional commitments of a marital and familiar nature— that the experimentation with communal life was actually a search for family and that the sexual experimentation was more often than not the search for depth in relationships. The swingers were coming to my office because they were losing interest in wide-open sex. And the majority of clients were married people who felt something was missing. Many homosexual clients were in permanent relationships or wanted to be. Most of my friends and neighbors were married, and I was married. It wasn't that so many people were against marriage—they were really, unconsciously, for better and stronger marriages. With all the media noise about marriage disappearing, I had the feeling it would last long past my lifetime.

A friend theorized that marriage would come to be something practiced by a kind of elite—people with a higher capacity for sustained relationships. But I thought that people in general would always seek meaningful and permanent relationships even when they called them by another name.

The day came when my editor said, "Do a book for married people."

"People in sustained relationships," I said.

"Married people," he said.

He didn't have to work too hard to persuade me.

But remember, this book is also for all of you in those sustained relationships, even when you won't—or can't—call what you have a marriage.

WHY PEOPLE WANT TO MARRY

People marry for many reasons. Children: there are still people who feel the need to be parents and who marry with that in mind. And people marry seeking that ideal connection with another human being. Also, people marry to get away from the parental home, for a kind of recognition as adults or as substantial people—not the best of motivations, but unfortunately true. Some people marry for protection, others for money or convenience—even less justification for marriage. But the underlying human reason is a need for closeness with other human beings and a special closeness with a particular human being. We have this need as babies, and it stays with us to the end.

In babies the need is linked with the need for food. We get both food and closeness at the breast, and in nurturing families the child gets closeness and sustenance at the family table. Very early in life we hardly know other people except as existing to feed and comfort us. Then we grow up into a world of other people with their own interests, who don't exist only to gratify our needs. As grown-ups, we have strong sexual needs, linked with the need for closeness.

The satisfaction of this need for sex and closeness is generally seen as the very substance of happiness. That is why fairy tales often end in marriage.

In real life the story begins with marriage. The rigors of marriage—sometimes compared unfavorably with the pleasant solitariness of single life!—are more than made up for by the comfort and convenience and support that marriage brings. But the sex life and the intimacy of the couple can very easily be overwhelmed by other things. Earning money and keeping part of it, tending to the details of a household, supplying the needs of children, meeting the insatiable demands of a career or two careers, meeting the ego demands of husband and wife in a challenging and competitive society—all of these things intrude on the sexual closeness of the couple unless they guard it.

And then the real-life husband and wife are not perfectly matched like the fairy tale couple, who exist only to marry each other. No, they aren't! When you see a couple who seem meant for each other, you are looking at two individuals, with common and conflicting needs, who have taken care to keep the seams of their union in good repair.

Perhaps there are couples who care for their marriages easily, who learn the need for that care with little difficulty. But you and your mate may not be like that, and you don't have to be. Yours may be a marriage with unavoidable struggle, a marriage of strong, somewhat opposing wills, and still be a splendid marriage! Probably for you a life of endless sunny days, serene as the high white clouds of August, would be too damn tame! But you will need ways to reconcile daily, and you can learn those ways early in marriage and save a lot of emotional pain.

With some couples, every quarrel ends in bed. That isn't the kind of foreplay we sex therapists recommend. We suggest other forms of sexual excitation! Still, that may be your way. It seems wearing to me, too stressful for healthy living, but here I express a personal preference.

WHAT KEEPS MARRIAGES TOGETHER

Many things work to maintain a marriage. A shared interest in the children, the life that has grown up around the couple. A belief in the steadiness of the other partner. A stubborn unwillingness to admit failure. A sense of duty. Support from a religious belief. Shared interest in a business, a cause, a hobby. A sense of perspective, a sense of humor (people with these qualities tend to make molehills out of those emotional mountains that wreck many marriages). I will even give credit to a certain amount of laziness, an unwillingness to "break up and start all over and go through all that." I mention all these things to show my head is not in the clouds. A strong binder in a marriage is good sex—darling intimacy and the memory, the afterglow, of the first intimacy two years or thirty or fifty years ago.

No two marriages are quite alike, and I think you should not think of yours as something that should meet all the standards of some outside authority, but as your own odd but absolutely charming marriage, an owl-and-the-pussycat marriage, with its own quite individual story unfolding. Now that's a pleasant idea, and it will account for some peculiarities that might otherwise cause you to panic. A husband who forgets all appointments, who likes his feet sticking out from under the blanket...A wife who likes peanut butter on toast and Coca-Cola for breakfast...A mate who hates parties, who dresses oddly, who may have to be washed or have his nails cut like a child, or who always leaves her gloves or handbag wherever she goes, who always sleeps in a fetal position. A person of good abilities who needs to be told again and again that he or she is not a failure. Who has to be tactfully persuaded to bring his or her ideas about sex into line with yours, or whose sexual needs demand concessions from you. These things don't make your marriage a disaster. They just make it your particular marriage.

Loving a real person means loving things like that. Some good marriages include extreme accommodations to the other person's peculiarities. Your mate's brilliance may impress the world at large as eccentricity. Your mate may even refuse, he or she, ever to wash the dishes. I say, make a list of your mate's better qualities, and put red circles around those that appeal to you, personally, without undue regard for the standards of the people next door.

You wanted this union. You loved the other person or had a high opinion of him or her in the beginning. Please, I am not a fool; some marriages will end in divorce. But what you wanted you really ought to be willing to try to preserve, to repair, or even to consider trying to rebuild entirely. Because sometimes the old happiness does come back, or a new and better kind replaces it after a period of wretchedness. So many people have honestly thanked God that they didn't break up when they wanted to so badly.

WHY MARRIAGE IS SO POPULAR

G. B. Shaw said that marriage is popular because it offers the maximum of temptation with the maximum of opportunity. He meant sexual temptation and sexual opportunity, and it was a shocking, daring, pleasing thing to say because in those days sex was unmentionable.

The detractors of marriage say, "What temptation?" Marrying somebody strips him or her of sexual interest. "What opportunities?" He's working late or she has a headache. Sex gets to be on a level with household chores. Marriage produces the sexual blahs.

If familiarity and the pressures of an orderly life can produce sexual boredom, that is only one side of it. The other side is that the married couple can create between them a sex life geared just to their needs. And supportive partners can help each other through sexual difficulties with a patience casual pickups seldom display. If the sexual wanderer, the one-night-stander, develops a sexual difficulty, he or she is much more likely to get stuck in it.

AIDS—SOME SOBERING THOUGHTS FOR THE MARRIED COUPLE AND THE NOT-SO-MARRIED

People who live together often have the same problems as those who are married. It also works the other way around: married couples may have the same concerns as those who live together even for short periods of time. This may seem obvious to some people but I raise this now because in talking to many young married couples I have found that because they married the "nice boy—or girl— next door" AIDS is of no concern to them. They are far from right for two main reasons:

> • The incubation time from exposure to the appearance of the virus called HIV (human immune deficiency virus) may vary from a few months to eight years or more—so, unless you are absolutely positive that your partner has never had any sexual contact with a person who is HIV positive or who has AIDS, you and your partner might consider being tested.

> • As disconcerting as the thought might be, all too many married persons have extra-marital sex at some point in their marriage. Even though you may believe in forgiveness and reconciliation or consider yourself sexually liberated and tolerant of such behavior, your spouse's exposure to someone with AIDS is a possibility. In these circumstances, you too should consider being tested.

Why be tested? After all, if you get AIDS there is no cure so why not be fatalistic about already having it? First there is the moral reason: the absolute injustice and despicability of transmitting this disease to an innocent person when it probably could be prevented by various means, such as effective condom use and avoidance of the transmission of body fluids to the other person.

Second, if you are tested HIV positive but have not yet developed any of the AIDS-related diseases, your quality of life, as well its length, may be enhanced by some of the available medication. In addition, there are many support groups to help you through this difficult period.

Maybe you think your chances of contracting AIDS are small. If you or your partner has had sex with another person during the past eight years or more, how many persons are there from whom you might have been exposed? According to the Centers for Disease Control, through

March 1992, 218,000 cases of AIDS had been reported (with 139,000 deaths) and *one million* Americans are infected with HIV, the virus that causes damage to the body culminating in AIDS. The C.D.C. also said that about 45,000 people will die of AIDS this year and that the rate will climb to 50,000 per year by 1994. And if you think that this is limited to male homosexuals and drug addicts, you are wrong. Anyone can get AIDS, so if you have even the slightest hint of a suspicion that you or your partner may have been exposed, please discuss it with him or her and consider going for a test. In most states, there are many good places to go that will assure you the anonymity and confidentiality you would want. You can locate these "Anonymous Testing Sites" by checking with the Department of Health in your area. You can get the locations anonymously by phone and be tested anonymously.

If you have been tested at any time, should you be tested again? Yes—authorities I have spoken to tell me that to be tested every six months for a number of years is not too often, if you think you might have been exposed to someone at risk. Certainly, do not wait more than a year between tests.

If you test negative—the tests are more than 99 percent accurate—and you practice safer sex, you can still have a joyous sex life without anxiety and with a clear conscience. Because the practice of safer sex varies with different persons and situations, we cannot go into it in depth in this book—although I will touch on it from time to time—so I had to write an entire book on the subject, *Dr. Ruth's Guide to Safer Sex.* Practicing safer sex is wise in order to reduce the possibility of AIDS. Remember, there are many other sexually transmitted diseases that can also be avoided by these practices. Let us hope that one day, with all of us supporting the medical and scientific research underway, such a reminder will not have to be stated so strongly.

DIFFERENT AND DELICIOUS

Before we end this chapter on why we need a new marraige

manual, let me discuss something different—something different and delicious. How often do you hear, "Let's eat something different and delicious." That's a tempting proposition when people think about lunch. And, from time to time, a pleasing suggestion for sex. In most marriages, it's better to vary the sex a little rather than the sex partner— certainly, in light of the previous discussion on AIDS, it is the only sensible thing to do.

Something different and delicious. Some people say I'm always comparing sex to food. That's because I'm brilliant and notice that each feeds a hunger! I have no intention of trying to stop making that comparison. So I end my program sometimes saying, "Have good sex!" So I sound like Grandma Chickensoup saying "Eat, eat!" I come by that honestly.

One evening when I was starting to write this book I was walking past a lot of neighborhood stores where they sell food—fruit, vegetables, pastries, meat, delicatessen. It was that hurrying-home time of the day, and I began to think what fun it is being married and taking something home to share, some unplanned, impulse-bought treat. Young couples hurrying home after a day's work are thrilled by this new sharing. It's fun for old married folk, too. That fun lasts a lifetime.

I knew that I wanted to contribute to the joy people get out of marriage with sudden little acts of intimacy, fresh and unexpected. How nice to think of something like that when you ride homewards, something surprising and sly to do with your chosen one. And, on the way, why not stop at the bakery?

2

Your Sexuality and You

*T*HAT may sound silly—"Your Sexuality and You."
Like a book they sell in a pet shop—*Your Pekinese
and You*. Perhaps I am going to tell you how to
housebreak your sexuality and make it walk on your left.
But before I say anything about it, I want to get straight
what a person's sexuality *is*. Some very bright people are
confused about that. I see the startled look in their eyes
when I speak of their sexuality. They ask questions. What is
it? Where is it? And so on.

WHAT IT IS

Your sexuality is made up of your physical male- or
femaleness, your responses to stimulation through touches,
sights, sounds, odors, thoughts. Your readiness to become
erect in the penis or lubricated in the vagina. The frequency
and nature of your sex thoughts, your involvement in sex,
your sexual preferences. Your ability to take part in sexual
encounters, to continue satisfactorily to orgasm and to bring
your partner to satisfaction, and to enjoy orgasm, fulfillment

11

and the drifting away that follows. And your sexuality includes the quality of your involvement in sex—the variety or narrowness of your sexual habit and the way you integrate it with your affections and your general feelings about life. Your understanding of your own needs and of your partner's needs, and the way you and your partner are developing together sexually.

SEPARATING YOUR SEXUALITY FROM YOU

If you are imaginative, it may be hard to try to separate your sexuality from the rest of you. It is of your very flesh, and it is so much mixed up with your view of life. It looks out at the world with the same eyes you use. If you look at some fruit—oranges, pears, bananas, bunches of grapes—it all may look sexy to you on certain days. Is it you or your sexuality that makes fruit sexy? Have you ever picked a sun-warmed red tomato off its vine, held it in your sensitive hand, gazed on it with your appreciative eyes and wondered, "Is it I or my sexuality that makes this seem like a breast, a buttock, a pregnancy?" Probably not. More likely you thought, "Wow, all I think about is It!" Or maybe, "Some days everything, *everything*, is sexy."

I think it is useful to have a concept of Your Sexuality. With such a concept you can take stock now and then. Are you taking good care of your sexuality? What have you done for it lately? What has it done for you? I don't mean that periodically you have to go on a sex rampage from a sense of duty! More, just see where you seem to be going and perhaps make a little correction, like somebody steering a boat. Or at least take stock and understand what your present sexuality is and how you feel about that.

RECOGNIZING YOUR SEXUALITY

One amusing young woman told me she wouldn't know it if she met it coming down the street. She rather pictured it

THE BRADFORD EXCHANGE ADVANTAGE

• A hand-numbered limited-edition plate with a correspondingly hand-numbered Certificate of Authenticity

• A complete plate story introducing you to the artist and detailing the significance of this recommendation

• The potential for appreciation—like 1988's "Elvis at the Gates of Graceland†" which last quoted on the Bradford Exchange at $73.00** 184% of its $39.75 issue price

• An unconditional, no-questions-asked, 365-day guarantee—so you risk nothing

Date Ordered _____

†Elvis and Elvis Presley are trademarks of Elvis Presley Enterprises, Inc.

**Reflects last quote on the exchange as reported in the Canadian Bradford Exchange *Current Quotations,*® Vol. 21-1.

The Bradford Exchange: Recommending Tomorrow's Treasures Today™

IMPRESSIVE ARTISTRY: With offices in twelve countries, the Bradford Exchange is often first to find the hot artists—like Charles Fracé, Lena Liu, and Thomas Kinkade— as well as the up-and-coming artists—like Donald Grant, Robert Richert, and Lily Chang.

MARKET POTENTIAL: Exceptional Bradford Exchange-recommended plates have historically posted price increases.

AUTHENTICATED: Each hand-numbered plate arrives with a Certificate of Authenticity, your assurance that it is part of a strictly limited edition.

GUARANTEED: With all Bradford Exchange plates, you have 365 days to change your mind. And if you do, we'll refund every cent you've paid, including postage—no questions asked.

TEAR OFF
and keep for your records

as something electrical attached to her by a long cord—so long that her sexuality could go right around the block and meet her going the other way.

A fellow told me, "I didn't know I *had* a sexuality. I didn't think it was a thing you *had*. I thought it was something people went in for or didn't go in for, like golf."

I tried to be helpful. What else am I here for? "Don't you say in English, 'How is your golf?'"

"Ah!" he said. "It's like *that*."

I said it was something like that, but not so competitive.

It is good to recognize your own sexuality in the sense of knowing and acknowledging to yourself that you are a sexual being. You were born that way, like everyone else, and finding your own way through life can be smoother and happier if you realize it. And knowing that your particular sexuality is not exactly like everyone else's, any more than your face is just like everyone else's, is useful in choosing the way you live and in resisting pressure to live in ways that are not best for you. Knowing that you are sexual and also that your sexuality is an individual thing can let you decide that you never have at any time an obligation to fall into step with prevailing sexual fashions. It can let you negotiate with your partner for changes you want in your shared sex life—without feeling guilty. You need not feel guilty about wanting more sex, more often, nor about liking sex less frequently than your partner. Consideration for the other's needs and feelings need not make you violate your own—not within the framework of a reasonably good relationship. There are grounds, sometimes, for divorce because of sexual incompatibility, but whether you can reach a loving agreement with your partner or not, you need not feel that your greater or lesser appetite, wider or narrower sexual tastes, are of themselves wrong and deserving chastisement or suppression. Recognizing the quality of your own sexuality as a part of yourself, a mark of your individuality, absolves you of any such blame.

This is good to know as well—that your sexuality grows and changes, and may come closer to your partner's with the passage of time.

A TIME FOR EVERYTHING

Sex, like all things in life, should not become all-consuming. I think often of the man who could keep his erection for hours without climaxing. He was so sure he was the world's greatest sexual athlete! He could keep a woman pinned to the mattress for hours—long after her vagina had dried up and sex was a painful bore for her and she wanted to dress and go for a walk. Or of the woman who thinks of her husband only in terms of sex and tries to keep him in a sexual prison. He might be wanting to read a book about Central America, but this woman keeps at him, making a bore of herself and of sex.

I happen to believe in religion as an important part of life. People do not all follow the same religion, but everyone is religious and finds some outlet for religious promptings. But I do not think sexuality makes a good religion. I am sure someone will be surprised to read that, because when I talk on the radio or write a piece for a magazine, it is about sex. I only hope that a lot of people listen carefully and hear me say that sex has its time and place, and living for sex alone is not good living and really quite bad for sex.

So—a time and place for sex. But not always the same time and place!

DEVELOPING SEXUALITIES

A person's sexuality is a developing thing. As a baby, a male has no notion of his own sexuality—but he has it. Lying back to be dried, or changed, he may gurgle happily with a hard little erection. As innocently as he may, a minute later, send a clear little parabolic stream of urine into the air in full view of Mother, Auntie, visiting friends or clergy. Later he will masturbate, with increasing and changing awareness of what he is doing. Still later he tries to make sexual contact with young women, perhaps more interested in sex than in the women. At thirty he has acquired more skill in sexual encounters and has developed strong preferences in sex. The more mature man usually establishes an emotional bond first, before engaging in sexual activities.

A woman's developing sexuality follows approximately a similar course. But in our culture, learning to achieve orgasm is often more complicated for her than for the average male. With any luck she learns how to reach orgasm and how to guide a male to help her reach it. She too will grow stronger in sexual knowledge about pleasing and being pleased, something she is more likely to do in prolonged relationships with men she finds companionable.

These are the general lines of developing sexuality, by no means guaranteed to be strikingly similar in all people. Some will reach a highly and broadly developed sexuality; some will live on and on in a restricted sexuality. Satisfaction may come for some in mild periodic sexual encounters; others may require daily sex to meet a stronger hunger. The need for more sex may be from bodily needs or from those of the emotions or the mind—it is unwise to picture the slenderer sexual nature as always existing in a weakened or less vigorous body. Overwhelming concentration on other concerns in life, expending huge energies on work or mental interests, may crowd out sexuality even in a very strong person.

If you look about at other people, a wide variety of sexualities will be obvious. You will see people you may think of as lecherous, timid, uninterested, contented, devoted to a single sex partner, straight or gay. Or, by your standards, freakish.

Other people are assessing your sexuality in the same way. This may be done in a polite or restrained manner, by people who keep their notions pretty much to themselves, or rudely, by those who try to intrude on what is your business. But, if you are a woman, men will look at you in movement and in repose—and women will do so as well. They will form notions of your sexuality. If you are habitually slow or languorous, or lively as a cricket, either may lead others to think of you as very, very sexy—and their view may differ from yours. And may be very inaccurate. By the way, women look at men too—it's a two-way street.

A certain way of glancing at people may be indicative of sexual interest, of course, but it may just be a matter of heavy lids and long lashes, a certain size or color of pupils. A woman shaped like Venus encourages men to think of her as having a sexual nature equal to what she arouses in them—often very mistakenly. And a demure exterior, a restrained manner, quiet clothing may disguise a strong and insistent sexuality. This picture that others form of your sexuality may help or hinder you in attracting just the kind and amount of attention you want. But knowing your real sexuality, at any stage of development, is really up to you alone.

It is best and wisest to know your own sexuality long before you go into a relationship in which you want to find long-lasting happiness. Not to try to be what you are not in order to match the other person's needs and preconceptions about you. In a good relationship the two of you will slowly explore and build a common sexuality, bringing both ardor and patience to each other. At the outset, try to assess where you stand with each other sexually, to set a way of sexual exploration pleasing to you both for the present. And promising long excitement and mutual satisfaction.

Asserting your sexuality does not mean confronting your mate with an angry bill of particulars! That is a terrible idea. On the contrary, it means getting a clear understanding at the beginning of what each of you expects—not in every detail, but in general. It doesn't mean saying, "I demand your whole attention to my urgent sexual needs or I'll picket the house!" It may mean expressing your present uncertainties about sex, as well as your hopes for a happy marriage warmed by sexual enjoyment.

Understanding your own present sexuality and your hopes for the future should prevent certain catastrophes that you have heard about in marriages. If you are ignorant of your own sexual state at the beginning of a relationship, you may soon be outraged by what your mate demands or expects of you! If you know well what you expect sexually at present, at least understand that this may be quite foreign to your chosen one in his or her present development.

Don't go into a relationship where incompatibility and conflict seem to be a dead certainty. Do I have to tell you this? Perhaps you don't need such primitive counseling, but hear me—every week I see people who have gone blindly into unions that were doomed from the beginning. They always feel, naively, that they can change their mate. Each partner would have been happier with someone more suitable.

People don't need to match each other perfectly. They need not be mirror images of each other sexually or in other respects. It is as wise to hope for a good growing together, where there are no enormous omens of disagreement, as it is to use prudence in forming a marriage. It may damned well be better to live singly than to have a rotten marriage—keep that clearly in mind! But reasonable risk taking is not only fun, it is probably necessary. Who can give you a blueprint of the future?

There are times when two people in a sexual relationship have different sexual needs and desires. And, sexual needs and desires grow and change. Know what your sexuality is right now so that you can communicate this to your partner—whether it is a partner of three months or thirty years. Be prepared for some negotiating about what goes on in the bedroom, to do some talking in order to bring two individual sexualities together as lovingly and harmoniously as possible.

Don't make well-matched sexualities or mutual sexual attraction your only criterion for considering a marriage. There *are* other things in life and marriage. A vast number of things—like religion, background or youthful idealism and ardor that sweep aside other differences. How you feel about having children. About fidelity (not what you feel is fashionable to feel about it, but what you honestly feel). How you like to spend leisure time and vacations. What level of housekeeping suits you. And how you like people to leave the tube of toothpaste! Ideas about good conduct and the goals of human existence. Of course, as unpleasant or embarrassing as it may be, it is wise to bring up the subject of AIDS. If either of you has had previous sexual partners maybe you should consider taking a test for AIDS. Even if you test negative, maybe you will want to consider using condoms for several years if there is any possibility that you might not know if a previous partner was exposed to AIDS. In any case, talk to someone in your community who is knowledgeable about the AIDS problem, such as the people from an AIDS crisis hotline.

People who hear me speaking on topics which other people pay me to talk about—the specifics of sexual behavior in human life—sometimes say, "She knows only about the plumbing; she speaks only of sensations and the gratification of lust." Well, I am not a poet or a rabbi; people don't come to me to hear me talk about Shakespeare or for spiritual counsel! I answer questions that people ask. I try as often as I can to put sex in a human context. To show it as part of the human experience, which also includes paying the bills and rendering unto God that which is God's. I was raised in a religion that sees sexual contentment, in the man and in the woman, as strengthening the life of the temple we call a home. So.

3

Marriage Fantasies

*D*EAR *Dr. Ruth: I have too many imaginings about my intended. When we are making love especially, but also at other times. For instance, I might be looking forward to meeting him but I pretend he will be different, more like some kind of hero. It makes me wonder if I really want him to be my husband. Why do I keep pretending he is someone else very different from the way he is? I imagine him as being black sometimes. Sometimes I pretend he is a pirate or highwayman, very forceful sexually. He is quiet and sensible and I think I love him. Should I marry somebody I have to keep changing to somebody else in my mind? Will I want to be unfaithful or to leave him after we have been married awhile?*

You are asking two different questions. One, how do I know I love this man enough to commit my future to him? Two, what danger is there in daydreaming about him as some more romantic kind of guy?

Answering the first question—how do you know you love him enough to marry him? I think you should be sure that you have a clear picture in your mind of what it would be like to be married to this man as he is by full daylight, not

19

in the moonlit world of your fantasies. You say he is a quiet, sensible person. Terrific—that kind of man makes a good husband. A very good husband. Not the only good sort of husband, but a very good sort. But unfortunately, a woman often says a man is good and kind meaning ordinary and boring. So I believe you should try to form a very realistic picture of your fiancé and see if it fits him as he carries on for a reasonable period. But don't up and marry him with nothing more definite in your mind than "quiet and sensible."

I am definitely one for making lists, and I suggest that you sit down and make a list of his good points and his bad points. I am not going to give you a list of points to look up, like one of those magazine tests or quizzes. The idea is for *you* to think up the good and bad aspects of the fellow, so that they are *your* points, not someone else's. While you are thinking about your feelings toward this man, keep the list and go over it now and then and add observations to it and maybe correct some ideas that begin to seem wrong. This will help you to form a picture of him as a person responding to your needs in life—to discover good points you perhaps hadn't noticed and to give you time to consider the bad points that you have written down. These bad points may, after you have thought about them, seem to have been unjustly attributed to him. Or they may seem, balanced against some very pleasing quality, not so important after all. But above all, this list, and the examination of the fiancé it facilitates, will get you into the habit of thinking about the real fellow, of thinking about real fellows in general as opposed to movie and TV images.

I say to keep the list around for a while, but I do not say to leave it where he, or your mother, can find it. Some people have a way of keeping things like that private, but if you are careless about leaving things around, I would keep the list in my head. Every now and then sit down, write out the list with any changes that have occurred to you, look it over and destroy it. The writing down and rereading will help keep the points in your mind.

This listing and considering over a period of weeks should bring you to a point where you know your feelings and your most practical assessment of the man. I have seen this process turn a very lukewarm engaged person into a happy and enthusiastic one—it doesn't just work to throw cold water on love. I know sometimes a lover hears, "It pays to wait a little while and think things over calmly," and the lover *knows* the advice-giver is cold, hostile, unromantic, boring and has no idea what it is to find life lovely and enthralling! And the advice only makes the lover more impatient and impulsive, so cold and ugly is the viewpoint the advice came from. But when the lover is in doubt as to her own feelings, she needs to explore them.

As to the danger or value of having fantasies about your fiancé, you should know that for you they are inevitable; if you try to disapprove of them it will do no good, because you will have them anyway. It is an unusually unimaginative person who has no fantasies about a loved one. And when the relationship is good, the fantasies are helpful, they enhance it.

Most women want pirates, or something like pirates, with a part of their minds. I think women tend to want pirates and to marry sensible guys. If they succeed in marrying sensible guys, they dress them up in pirate clothes in their fantasies. This is fair enough, because there is a certain amount of wild man in every quiet fellow. There's no harm in dressing him up a little in your imagination, either while he is away at work or while you are having sex with him. You are not thinking of someone else while your husband is inside you—you are thinking of *him* in his bold, untamed aspect. This helps him and you.

Here is a good marriage fantasy—to imagine that your nice steady husband, who never inconveniences you by being arrested or a fugitive, is really a dangerous criminal from the 1700s. In this life he is going straight! He is hiding his dangerous old-time self-because he is tired of running from the hangman and he wants to live with you and look after you. Only you and he know his secret past. That's called having your cake and eating it too! Who doesn't want that? A solid citizen during business hours, a highwayman at night in bed.

If you try to stamp out girlishly romantic daydreams they won't die anyway, so make them fit into your more sensible plans!

I have a job and I lust after prestige and power as a career woman, but about my impending marriage I keep thinking I am a traditional Jewish bride, like those in the stories of Isaac Bashevis Singer or Shalom Aleichem. This seems to suit two sides of my character, and I think I can be a modern woman and enjoy the traditional feelings about being a wife. I am sure I can have everything I want out of this marriage—sometimes. Other times, not so sure. . . .

I wouldn't dream of getting in the way of a woman who is sure of things, if I were you. Let the sure side of yourself have her way. Of course, you may be encouraging that fiancé of yours to think of you as more submissive than you really are, and this may lead to some power struggles in your marriage. But the traditional wife has a need for power too. And probably your fiancé really likes your dual role of dynamic woman and sweet, comforting wife. "To the world, a tigress; to me, a pussycat." That may be *his* little fantasy. If by any remote chance you two should ever have a little domestic power struggle, be ready to negotiate with him as soon as things quiet down. A day or two, or maybe five minutes, after all the angry words.

Good marriages are good for both parties to them. Most good marriages are between imperfectly compatible people who give love and comfort to each other, learning both to love better and to negotiate better as the years go by. I think your little daydream about being a storybook Jewish bride is cute. A good marriage fantasy—that is, a dream about being a wife instead of being out of the house in a torn nightgown and being given a runaround by King Kong. Don't be afraid of being sweet and loving and ready to yield on occasions. Would you want him to be afraid of being strong and protective when you could use it?

I was away in the service and I kept fantasizing about being married to my girl. I would go to sleep pretending to be holding this plump young woman close, with my hands on her big tits and her fat ass against my groin. When I got home she had lost fifteen pounds! When I left she was cute and fat. Now she's gorgeous—a movie star. This doesn't make me jealous because she isn't the kind who would make a guy jealous, but sometimes I wonder about how I wanted a cute fat wife for so long and got a gorgeous one. . . .

This may be one of those things you just have to be a man about. After all, if instead of fat and cute she is only gorgeous, well, there could be worse things. Try to live with it.

Here's a tip: When you get into bed with this gorgeous woman who is so nice to walk into a room with, pretend she's fat after the lights are out. She'll still feel fat in the dark! And think of this: In time she may weaken and eat a few fattening things between meals and put on weight. Then you will have had a cute fat girl, a gorgeous woman who looked like a star wherever she went, and a voluptuous mature woman. That would make you one lucky guy. All in one lifetime.

I have a fantasy of living on an island with my future wife and she goes around naked or with just a leaf over her crotch. I grab her and do everything to her out in the open air. I want to marry her very much, but I wonder if she would like this kind of thing, because I would really like that kind of physical sexy action without any restraints very much.

Maybe you could tell her about it sometime when you are talking intimately and maybe a little foolishly, the way people do who are on very close terms with each other. I can't see why any woman would not like that fantasy you have about your future wife. No, let me correct that statement—I have known only a few women who wouldn't like that fantasy, and a lot of women who would be delighted that a man had had such daydreams about them. Still, you are fairly safe about confiding some fantasies to a loved one because they are only fantasies. They are in the realm of imagination, where you make up jokes and playful ideas, and compliments. Some couples can share fantasies, and some can share *some* of their fantasies, each of them keeping certain reveries under wraps, even from their soulmate. Being wild and unfettered in a wilderness is such a pretty fantasy that many couples share it, and turn their bedrooms into Tarzan-and-Jane country. It is part of their private life.

I have the idea that you just may think your fiancée would not like your outdoors fantasy for some good reason. She has, although she is very desirable to you, impressed you as straitlaced or not playful. If you are terribly attracted to her, and she has wholeheartedly agreed to marry you, I would not worry about a little mental rigidity of this sort, because women do change, with regard to what is acceptable or desirable sexually, as they share a sex life with a man. Right now there may seem to her to be something too literal, specific, uncouth or juvenile about your fantasies of desert islands; later she may understand them better as part of the 90 percent of sex that takes place from the neck up.

It also happens that a bride who wants the lights out in the early weeks of marriage may herself have a yearning to run naked on a beach or through the trees, if she is put in the right sort of scenery. Keep an eye out for vacation spots where you just might live out a little of your shipwreck fantasy. An island, some sort of wilderness camp. If you ever do get to such a place, remember that Tarzan and Jane are not real human beings. They never get poison ivy rash. Tarzan never even needs a shave. Be sure that your jungle love set has off-camera conveniences such as a blanket to lie on at the very least, and good contraception supplies!

I have been faithfully married to the same woman for forty years, but my roving eye still lights on strange women and I have fantasies about being intimate with them in very marital ways. A while ago I went into a bakery and there was a very sensible woman in a blue smock putting pastries into boxes and tying them quickly and deftly with that thin bakery string. Suddenly I imagined myself upstairs over the shop, in one of those old-fashioned live-over apartments, full of a kind of furniture suitable to such a place. I am undressing the bakery woman, who is not a Hollywood goddess but a plump little creature. . . . I saw a black woman on a bus, and right away I was with her in a falling-down sharecropper's shack. After seeing the movie The Deer Hunter *I daydreamed about a Slavic wife in a mill town near roaring blast furnaces. These daydreams don't make me erect—not at my age. Just a little excited and uneasy. I am always in a marriage situation in my fantasies. I seem to have a marriage fixation. . . .*

Both in life (married faithfully forty years) and in your fantasies, your daydreams disturb you, as they often do men who feel they should have passed the age for daydreaming, especially about sex. You seem to feel that you have reached the time when your sexual and romantic inclinations should either have been met or their defeat have been philosophically absorbed, and the fact that you are still having sexual fantasies, you see as a sign of frustration. Now, as nearly as I can make out, to be really alive is still to have unfulfilled desires. And yours seem to be so humane, to show so much interest in the stories of people quite different from yourself! I think your interest in other kinds of people is very outgoing and generous. The stirrings of sexual desire and an interest in the world around one do seem to go together. So at the least you can congratulate yourself on being very much alive and interested, in your mature age. I think you show a great interest in life that might be directing you into something like recording the changing times with a camera, taking courses in sociology, doing a lot of directed reading on your own, doing volunteer work with some social agency or religiously sponsored group, etc.

With your wife of forty years you might find it harmlessly exciting to make love to her in one of those odd scenes that presents itself to your imagination. Either by finding places to stay on car trips that come close to scenes you have imagined, or by fantasizing these scenes in your own bedroom.

A contented spouse often wonders, "Do I love this partner of mine, or do I love *marriage*?" One is entitled to wonder anything, but the distinction here is very nearly a useless one.

I am pregnant for the first time, and I keep thinking the baby inside me is my husband in miniature. I have to remind myself that it will come out looking like a baby and that it will be a totally new person, very likely a girl. Recently I thought of taking my baby's penis in my mouth (once again picturing it as a male). I don't do that even with my husband. These thoughts make me feel a little weird. I have also thought of breast-feeding my husband.

Just being pregnant is enough to make you feel a little weird. Think, a real human being growing inside you! Just because it happens all the time doesn't mean it isn't strange and wonderful. And it never happened to *you* before. As for thoughts and mental pictures, it is practically impossible to prevent the human brain from thinking and picturing every sort of oddity, all harmless if left in the realm of fancy. A woman will picture herself harming her baby sometimes; it is as unavoidable as thinking you might break some fragile expensive gift you have been given. As for thinking the baby is your husband, it *is* half him, and in *your* uterus, isn't it? And I suppose you have thought of taking his penis in your mouth at some time. Sometime, in the middle of excited lovemaking and full of love for your husband, you may do that—it is done all the time and considered very normal behavior. Your new feelings and imaginative confusions are both beautiful and full of deep personal symbolism of a kind that grown women come to understand.

If you need some thoughts to make you feel less disoriented, try these. Always be a mother to your husband when he needs that. It is part of being a wife. Love your child as being part of your husband as well as being a new person. And consider that your husband at this time is having "funny" thoughts come to him, such as taking your milk from your newly maternal breasts sometime. Men not only think of that, they do it sometimes.

There is fear of incest here—but real incest is acting out certain urges in a way that makes a bad confusion of reality, not a fleeting thought in the amazingly fertile human brain. Any fear of being erotic with a child or maternal with a mate is to be noted but not to be given exaggerated importance. Real incest consists of certain definite acts that are to be avoided, but a confusion of feelings toward either mate or child is quite usual, normal, ordinary, natural, etc. The feelings do overlap one another. Exaggerated fear of incest can lead to being cold and unparental to the child, cheating it of what it needs.

Marital sex feelings are of the stuff of life and creation, and not merely an entertainment—though of course marital sex is sometimes very entertaining! But it is for grown-ups, who respect but do not fear the heat or darkness.

I include this chapter about marriage fantasies—which differ from erotic fantasies in general by being about the real spouse, about marriage, about marital business, rather than about outside people borrowed from stories, pictures, movies or the neighborhood—because such fantasies can strengthen the marital union.

Sometimes a therapist urges people to strengthen sexual activity with fantasies and there is resistance. Because a wife does not want to be like Scarlett O'Hara, thinking of a man she loves while having sex with her husband. Or the husband has compunctions about thinking of a raunchier sort of woman while physically engaged with his wife. For such people, who can't feel easy with mentally exaggerating the exciting aspects of the spouse by using imagination, by fancifully dressing the spouse in secret disguises, very good use can be made of strong fantasies about the marriage itself.

Strong love unions need the imagery and poetry of passion. Human sex is 90 percent in the head, we say—and that is not a scientific percentage but a poetic one. Ninety percent in the head and the feelings, at least! A sex urge may begin in the body, but it burgeons in the mind.

Sometimes I have a hard time getting clients to imagine *anything* while they try to make love! They are not unimaginative by nature, but they find it hard to use imagination just when it would be most helpful. And I have to ask such people to borrow fantasies from explicitly sexual movies, books, pictures, assuring them that there is no harm in this.

There is no harm in clothing your physically naked partner with fantasy. It is not so much pretending that he or she is someone else, but enjoying that partner in another, secret side of his or her many-faceted being. In the marital bedroom, people-within-people are turned loose for the full experience of passion.

4

Honeymoons

*I*WANT to clear up some confusion about virgins and
honeymoons in the present era, because you may have
heard that there are no virgins and that nobody goes on a
honeymoon anymore. By "honeymoon" for the time being
let us mean the *honeymoon* honeymoon, on which the
couple depart from the wedding party still virgins and come
back nonvirgins.

VIRGINS: A FACT OF LIFE

That isn't a fairy-tale happening, as any sex therapist can
tell you. If you think so, then you seem to be unacquainted
with any strictly brought-up religious people. Perhaps you
are too worldly to believe in virgin brides and bridegrooms,
but I say your circle of acquaintances is very narrow!

For myself, I was orphaned at a tender age and I have
lived through two wars at close range. I have been an
agricultural worker, a soldier, a combat casualty. I have
been down-and-out in Paris and have supported myself as a
housemaid, and the sexual scene of the past forty years has

29

not been screened from my eyes. I am a sex therapist and sex educator, and I talk about the specifics of sex on the radio to people who phone in about every sexual matter you ever heard of or imagined, and I say there are still lots of virgin honeymooners, male as well as female, and they consult me about their honeymoons both before and after. So let us hear no more about how there are no more marriageable virgins!

The story goes that whenever a virgin walks by the stone lions in front of the library at Fifth and Forty-second in New York they stand up and roar. But, they say, this happens very, very seldom.

The reason it doesn't happen more often is not a shortage of virgins. The reason is the laziness of male lions, especially stone ones. If they stood up and roared whenever a virgin passed by they would be worn out by opening time every morning. The workload would be too heavy for them.

People believe everything I say except that there are virgins. If I say in print, on radio, or on TV that there are swingers, one-night-standers, sadomasochists, fetishists, people who make love to their close relatives, who use abortion as a means of contraception, the whole world believes me. But if I say a boy or girl is a virgin because of religion or bashfulness, suddenly I am a naive old Auntie Ruth and I should teach sex only to the primary grades.

Ha!

WEDDING NIGHTS AND HONEYMOONS

We Judeo-Christians traditionally believe in the ardent bridegroom joyfully "taking" the bride's virginity on the wedding night. It seems to be something a guy can take. "And some day for my sake / She may let me take / The bloom from my wild Irish rose."

We like to joke about something so far back we can only read about it, the local nobleman's having the *droit du seigneur*, the right to "take" every local bride on her wedding night, leaving seconds, thirds, fourths and the rest to the bridegroom.

Our traditions call for no fumbling or bumbling in the initial stages of mutual sex between the newlyweds. This has led to some newlyweds' thinking things are really like that, and that if they aren't perfect lovers from the first, why, then they just aren't up to being married. Of course the tradition has simply misled them, but when will they find that out?

A little history: In certain old countries the bloody sheet would be hung out the window to show all the world that the bride was pure and the bridegroom a hero. The bride's mama, also according to tradition, gave the girl a phial of chicken blood to take into the bedroom. Look, the sheet was for show; what went on in the bedroom was private business.

In a certain Middle Eastern country the custom was to post an old woman at the bridal chamber door to observe the goings-on. To those watching her she would pass on, by well-understood gestures, what was happening in the chamber. She would wave a certain way when the deed was done, and a man in the street would fire his musket into the air! And the whole neighborhood would cheer.

For the old woman it was a nice way to pick up a little pin money and invitations to parties. How much in demand would she have been if she started to report wedding-night failures?

The wedding-night consummation is like the little bride and groom on top of the wedding cake, or throwing the bouquet, or wearing something old, something new, something borrowed, something blue. It is a cute idea, but nobody should make a terribly serious issue of it.

Oh, it happens. And it also happens that a coin lands on edge instead of coming up heads or tails. But it should not be regarded as more than a pretty possibility.

I say the wedding night is a happy night when the virgin couple get in bed together and get closer to each other than they ever did before. They hug and kiss and touch each other intimately. And find out what cuddling up to a spouse all night is like.

It is not to be expected that the couple will not attempt intercourse—but what they do privately from now on is *their own married business*. If they have evaded pressure to have premarital sex, they can now wave away any pressure to consummate in a hurry. Let the honeymoon, not the short hours of darkness after the wedding's hurly-burly, be the time to court each other, invite each other to come closer and closer, until they have performed the marital act the best they can in their charming awkwardness and inexperience.

I have counseled nervous premarital couples to go to bed that wedding night and rest quietly in each other's arms, to sleep, and not to begin the attempt at intercourse until they are well rested.

Before an act of intercourse, we sex mavens tell you, the woman should be aroused and wanting to have intercourse. Wise men do not force themselves into dry loins! This is especially true the first time a couple try intercourse. Any couple, even two nonvirgins, should approach the first mutual sex with mutual consideration, looking for the joy of intimacy more than for the most intense sexual pleasure, which only comes after some practice.

Of course the virgin honeymooners are not the sexual performers they will be in a few weeks, months or years. But they are a great romantic pair—as great as any pair can be. They are naked in bed together, with no more barriers between them than those they impose themselves as they touch and invite touching more and more intimately.

To grow into the way of touching each other erotically, of approaching coitus, effecting intromission ("getting in"), of giving and taking pleasure, is the business of a long honeymoon. And that honeymoon can extend well past the couple's arrival at their permanent home.

THE IMPATIENCE OF NEWLYWEDS

Our tradition calls for a groom bursting with desire and being at the same time an angel of patience. The bride has to be demure though she may be a storm of conflicting feelings inside. Each has a tough role to play—a Jekyll-and-Hyde role, in fact. It is best if each partner is let off the hook and made to understand that nobody has to feel anything that is not sincerely felt.

Suppose you are the bride, for instance. Are you truly going to be pleased by his showing the iron self-control that some teachers tell him to show? Or will that make him seem cold, unmoved by your desirability, or more timid than you want him to be? Generally, when talking about the wise defloration of virgin women, we assume a girl who is wavering between wanting to have her hymen done away with and fear of doing it. Or one who is simply terrified of the coming invasion of her body and needs lots more wooing to bring her to the point of permitting it. That is the bride.

As for the male about to try his first defloration, we presume that he is prone to great erections and almost uncontrollable urges to thrust into the female rudely.

It is nearly always true that the male is powerfully aroused, and he *may* believe that blundering is the rule of the day. But it is not true that every virgin female is petrified with fear of defloration. Some brides care nothing for the idea of a little pain, and some are so determined to get the business over with, to be done with virginity, that they may cry out, like Lydia in *Love for Lydia*, "Hurt me! I want you to hurt me!"

There is nothing about the bride's fear or lack of it on which to base any prediction of her future sexuality. The bold bride may prove to be much less voracious as an experienced woman than the one who was overfearful on the wedding night.

A CALM APPROACH AND HOW TO HAVE IT

Let's call it hymen stretching. Stretching is much closer to what typically happens. Well, about the fear of stretching this membrane: There have been girls so scared of it they didn't realize it when the bridegroom had made an entrance.

It was all over before they knew it. Sometimes the hymen gives way like wet facial tissue. And, once she is initiated, many a girl makes fun of virginal fears, I am sorry to say.

I mean, of course, that the fear is sometimes a greater barrier to commencing married sex than the hymen itself. But both are to be treated with respect. If sometimes a frightened bride is amazed at how easily she lost her virginity, brave women have learned that a hymen can be tougher than they are, and a difficult thing to get rid of.

But the *fear* of undoing hymens, at least, can largely be eliminated if the bride and groom have a prior agreement. Let them agree to this: to try it as calmly and cooperatively as possible, and, if it proves too discouraging, simply to turn to the many other forms of erotic play until the time comes, in a moment of high sexual excitement, that the bride insists on the penetration.

The groom must not blame himself for any difficulty to be found in getting inside the first time, nor must he allow resentment to grow against the bride. Nor should the bride let herself think that the difficulty is his fault. In particular, he is not to be made to feel that, by being cautious and considerate, he has made her think that he is inadequate, not forceful enough, a "wimp." That is not the right reward for "being gentle with her." We have wisely spent much time urging young men to use restraint and to consider the woman's feelings; it would be a mistake to hold such gentleness against him.

Any attempt to push through the hymen should be brief. If it resists one insistent push, give up for that night. Return to comforting embracing and kissing.

Van de Velde, the classic author on marital love, suggests that if after four nights there is no success from mutually agreeable efforts, then the couple should consult a good gynecologist, who can give psychological aid and advice or, painlessly, with his scalpel, make the desired opening. That is still reasonable advice, especially since knowing that there is a sure end to this problem can lower tension, often making a home defloration possible.

IF THERE IS NO HYMEN

Certain American Indian tribeswomen used to do away with their own hymens before marriage so that the braves would not be inconvenienced by it. And in some pagan cultures hymens were parted ritually by priests using stone phalluses. It has been suggested that in this way the bride would not associate the groom with an unpleasant initiation.

Today there are virgins with no hymens. Some are born with so little that it makes no barrier at all; some are broken rather easily in the rough-and-tumble of childhood or in sports incidents. Some are done away with by gynecologists in order to make vaginal examinations. These are all real happenings, not just fibs to tell suspicious suitors and bridegrooms!

If your virgin bride has little or no hymen, count yourself lucky and believe whatever she tells you. Believing her about this is the most honorable, sensible, practical and self-comforting thing you can do, all in one little act of faith.

FEARLESSLY, NOT BLINDLY

"We were hugging and kissing and suddenly there was an unspoken signal between us, and then there was a soft, warm mist and when it cleared away I wasn't a virgin anymore. I felt a little sore down there but I was very pleased."

Well, I don't say it never happens that way. Nor that it shouldn't happen that way. Only that you can't count on it.

The girl quoted above went at it the First Time blindly and fearlessly. I prefer that they do it fearlessly, yes, but not blindly.

Fearlessly from knowing that if something goes wrong it is no tragedy.

Let us consider some things that can spoil a first attempt.

WHEN THE BRIDE BEGS OFF

The hymen resists and the bride begs off. So? Stop and

try it again sometime when she is ready, and always understand that nobody has to go through terrible pain to become sexually active. Help is at hand from the friendly gynecologist. To comfort the man, let the woman show all the appreciation she can of his restraint, his kindness and lovingness, his possible doubts of his own performance, and his deep disappointment.

A bride who is a "technical virgin"—that is, who has engaged with the groom in sexual activities short of intercourse before the wedding—can bring him to orgasm now as she has done in the past. Having established intimate behavior to fall back on can be very helpful on the honeymoon.

The bride may be too wrought up to do this. The groom may be unwilling, right now, to accept "kid stuff" when he wants the marital act so badly. Let each leave the other alone, or offer touching and holding, as the mood of the other indicates. Avoid anger or tears. If they come, take them understandingly.

THE MAN LOSES CONTROL

The hymen resists, but the all-worked-up male can't control his thrusting even though he wants to.

I say he *can* control it if he carries the idea in his mind. But if he loses control, let both understand that playing with sex has its dangers. That is why it is a grown-up thing to do. The sooner the male feels regret and shows it, the better. Remember, thousands of marriages have survived this.

COMING TOO SOON

The groom, approaching the hymen with his penis, ejaculates prematurely and can't force the opening.

Premature ejaculation is very common at this point. Let the couple giggle and pet for twenty minutes or an hour and try again.

I know that there are people who feel too solemn to

giggle, but how I wish they didn't! It is so good for a marriage, and gets people past so many obstacles.

Because you giggle at a sexual mishap doesn't mean you will giggle when things are going right, after you have acquired experience. When passion takes hold, in the course of a full sexual flight, the giggling stops. But a giggle is a marvelous release when attempts to fly become ridiculous.

FEAR OF DYSFUNCTION

Don't think because he comes too soon a few times in the early sex tries that the man is a chronic premature ejaculator. This problem often goes away as the couple develop their knack for Doing It. And remember—premature ejaculation, if chronic, is the most easily overcome performance problem. So don't let fear of it bother either party.

LOSS OF CONCENTRATION

The groom is erect and ready, but when he puts on the condom and anoints it with K-Y jelly the erection goes down.

This is caused by loss of concentration. With experienced couples I recommend making the putting on of the condom part of foreplay. The woman arouses the penis by petting it, puts on the condom, makes it her responsibility to keep the penis erect by teasing and touching. Few penises can resist this kindness. But a shy virgin with her own fears to contend with may not be up to doing this well. So maybe the groom has to make a few tries before he can bring a hard penis to the task.

Perhaps with increasing boldness, with getting used to being naked with this naked man and his amazing penis, the bride can begin to play with the penis, bring it to erection, dress it and practice making it hard by kind attentions.

At least she can behave encouragingly and show how she is cheering for the groom in this event.

LUBRICATION: A GREAT HELP

I have mentioned K-Y jelly. This is a very good thing to take along on the honeymoon because lubricating the penis with it can make entering a virgin orifice so much easier. K-Y is good for use on condoms because it does not eat into the rubber, making the condom less reliable as contraception. Petroleum jelly, which is most famously sold under the brand name of Vaseline, is marvelous stuff but I'm told it may harm rubber.

When having first intercourse with a virgin, the contraception of choice is the condom—because how can a diaphragm be inserted when there is a hymen? The pill, of course, is a possibility but its use must always be checked with a gynecologist first.

Honeymooners who plan to have children as soon as possible will of course ignore advice about contraception.

It once was the practice for the groom to try to slip on a "rubber" and lubricate it without attracting the bride's attention to all this activity. I am definitely against making the contraceptive activity a backstage business that isn't supposed to be noticed. For one thing, it *will* be noticed, and any fumbling will be likely to make the groom even more nervous than he is. Let everybody present be aware that there is contraception, and that there is a pause for it to be put on. It is, of course, put on a hard penis, and there may have to be some loss of erection in putting it on. The erection can be restored by returning to pay attention to the bride's waiting body, by petting and stroking the penis, and then the intromission can be tried.

If the erection goes way down and the condom comes off, start over with a new condom. One that has been donned and doffed is no longer a good barrier to impregnation.

Here is something that is not absolutely necessary, but it makes the first intromission easier, so why not use it? I refer to putting a pillow under the bride's buttocks. This makes inserting the penis into the vagina a much simpler business. I like to have the bride guide the penis to the opening of the vagina. She is much likelier to know where that is than an inexperienced man; I rather hope that before the wedding she has at least explored down there enough to know where the vaginal opening is.

Many people who don't know the territory believe that the external genitalia of the woman, that slit between the legs, is one generous funnel into the vagina. In fact, the vaginal opening is concealed about halfway down from the top of the slit, considerably below the clitoris. It is to *this* opening that the bride guides the penis. If she will not do this, then the groom had best have a good idea where he is supposed to be going.

When the bride guides, she has control over the direction and the force of the thrust. Knowing this can give her much better confidence.

Once the groom does make an entry into the vagina, let him not try to make this first event a marathon. Let him thrust away and come as soon as he can and withdraw from this tender area. This first entry is symbolic intercourse, and not ever the greatest lovemaking of any lifetime.

A VERY READY VIRGIN

There are virgins who are really ready to Do It. There she lies, hymen intact, vaginal juices flowing, wanting him inside. As he inserts his penis between the labia and against the little opening in the hymen, she thrusts! He is in! Let him finish quickly and withdraw. But this eager former virgin wants more gratification—she is aroused and not satisfied. Let him caress her clitoris, not touching the vaginal entrance, as gently or vigorously as she indicates, until she sighs happily and relaxes.

I would not have him insert his penis in her vagina again until the following night at the earliest. Perhaps he should let the soreness down there heal for two or three nights—or, like the Orthodox Jewish groom, for a full seven nights!

I say to stay out of there at least twenty-four hours, but *she* may say otherwise!

DON'T WORRY, IT'S JUST A LITTLE BLOOD

Stretching the hymen doesn't always entail bleeding. When there is blood, the best first aid is just to stay away from the vagina. Bleeding will stop. If it does not, of course check with a gynecologist.

A lady who manages a select New York hotel informs me that some years back there were certain brides who would take the chambermaid aside and arrange to buy the sheet. To take home and give proudly to an old-country mama, who no doubt showed it to certain relatives and acquaintances so she could hold her head up among them.

Don't worry about the stained sheet—hotels are in the sheet-cleaning business, and not in the business of insulting guests who may stain linen in any number of ways.

I like to tip chambermaids, although the custom has all but disappeared. Whether or not I spill borscht on the sheet! In the 1980s, five dollars is enough, more than ten is ridiculous. Ten is indicated after a stay of a week. Tipping the maid after making a mess of the sheet may make you feel better. To her a bloody sheet is part of the day's work, hardly worth noticing.

A SCENARIO FOR THE BRIDAL SUITE

When the bellman has taken his tip and left (with an order for iced champagne? Your choice) you are alone at last. What happens next? Here are the ways some certain couples conducted themselves.

"I said, 'First of all, kiss me!' He was glad to do that. Then I said, 'I know you are a great big man, but I am nervous, so if you are a little nervous, I don't mind. Let's pretend we are a real married couple and unpack our things and put them in drawers and on hangers and chat brightly about this and that as we get ready for beddy-bye.'

"So we did that, or rather I did because he was tongue-tied. 'Cat got your tongue?' I asked, and my voice was trembly. He took me in his arms in my slip and stocking feet, standing up, and I began to cry and he kissed my tears.

"I told him to undress me. I was scared, but I wanted to stay in charge and keep things moving along. So pretty soon I was stark naked and he still had his pants, shirt and shoes on. 'I have to brush my teeth and stuff. You don't want a wife with rotten teeth, do you?' I said, and went into the bathroom and showered and everything and came out again and said, 'Your turn.' And he went in and showered and came out naked and I turned my eyes away and turned out the light.

"Then he slipped in next to me and I was nervous, so I climbed all over him to push the scared feeling away, and he began feeling me and I encouraged him. Then we tried to Do It and thank God it worked. It didn't hurt, and I was so glad it was over I cried, so he thought he had hurt me a lot, but I kissed him while I was blubbering and we curled up. After a while I took hold of his penis. The idea just came to me. And we drifted off to sleep. We were really pooped."

LET'S DO THIS GRADUALLY

Another couple's nuptial flight.

"We were so nervous, and I had read about first times, so I said, 'I want to go into this by degrees.' He said all right. 'Let's undress in front of each other and then take a shower together,' I said. I made him wash me all over and I washed him. I thought his penis would frighten me, but it didn't—it just didn't look the way I thought it would. When I washed it, it was hard, and he said, 'That thing's loaded, you know.' I said I knew and it went off while I was washing it.

" 'How long will it take to get hard again?' He said it usually took a week, but it got hard almost at once. I had read about that. We dried each other, and I was partly happy to be naked with him and still scared, so I hugged him tight. If that makes any sense. And we got in bed and he held me tight and I was wet down there already, but he sort of 'did' the foreplay like in the books, and then he tried to get in but I was tense so he quit. And I whispered that I'd like to wait until morning.

"So we slept spoon-fashion, and in the morning he tried but it hurt, so he stopped. I then wanted to be a good egg about it so I tried to masturbate him, but I was clumsy, so he rubbed against me and he came. I put my finger in the come and sniffed it and tasted it, and he went down on me and his tongue felt wonderful, and I began saying, 'Mmm!' Because it felt good. I didn't know if it was an orgasm or not. It wasn't—but it was exciting! He kissed me all over and rubbed against me again and went to sleep in my arms.

"We got up at quarter to eleven and the dining room was closed, so we walked around the waterfront and had a burrito and coffee and went back to the hotel. The bed was all made up. We lay down and played with each other until lunch. That night we got each other very excited and he tried again and I got tough and pushed hard and he was in.

"So that time he got inside me and we officially Did It. After that he rubbed me hard with his hand and I had an orgasm, which I guess was pretty good luck. We couldn't keep our hands off each other, but he wouldn't have intercourse for a couple of days and then we Did It again. We did all the sightseeing things in the daytime, and we were very happy and proud of ourselves for not being virgins anymore but licensed lechers."

I WOULDN'T LET HIM

Another bride reports, "He said, 'How do you want to do this?' and I said I wanted to touch first in the dark and look after. We petted and petted, and I liked it but wouldn't let him try for three nights. We kept laughing. I made him come and he kept trying to make me come, and finally I got wild and told him to try Doing It. But it took so long getting the rubber on and arranging the pillow under my butt that I was frigid and clamped my thighs together. I said I loved him, and he said he knew it. I put my nightie on and he hugged me all night. Then we tried and he came too soon and he said, 'Shit!'

"That was only the second time I ever heard him say it. The other time he got dust in his eye in New York and he said, 'Excuse my French.'

"I said, 'Let's stay in bed. Put the Do Not Disturb sign on the door.' We tried again and it hurt, and he said, 'That's it for today.' So I said, no, let's wait and try again. He said we should wait a while; Dr. Ruth said to. I said never mind Dr. Ruth this time. I was mad, and I really pushed onto him and he stayed hard. And he got in! He thought I was upset, that *he* had been the one to get rough! And he thought that because I just lay there and didn't respond to his loving. But I was exhausted. It hurt but I was glad to have Done It. So he got up and showered and shaved, and when he came back in I was looking at the bed. I took his hand and I pointed at the blood. I said, 'That's more like it.' Then I showered and we went out to a matinee and held hands all the time."

I asked the husband in the last story how he was feeling while all that was going on, and he said that it was frustrating and he was wondering if they shouldn't take a full-semester course in marital sex, but at the same time he enjoyed all the intimacy with a real female even if it wasn't perfect sex. And the struggles to get the sex started made their first success all the more triumphant. "And I really learned a lot about women from her," he said.

WHEN THE HONEYMOON IS OVER

The honeymoon is a time of pleased intimacy—and usually something of a trial. Even if sex is easy, they find that in other ways, being part of a pair is hard at first. The honeymoon, Part One, ends when they go to their new home the first time. Part Two goes on until each one has thought in turn, "This is being really married."

They say "the honeymoon is over" when some new condition becomes ordinary and boring. I hate that! Not that there isn't something to it, but *I hate it*! I say, let the honeymoon be over because being really, solidly married is better than honeymooning.

People speak of second honeymoons that are better than the first. That can mean all sorts of things—better sex, more time for the vacation, more money for it, all sorts of reasons for more security about it. But I say that the excitement, novelty and adventure of the first honeymoon, the *honeymoon* honeymoon, is a wonderful trip into grown-up love. There is a hot-and-cold venturing into the desired unknown that is unrepeatable. I have in my files many more honeymoon stories—some avoidably disastrous, some definitely to be blamed on the wrong people coming together. But brave young people long to take the big chances. Sometimes the sex does not work out at first. But very often I hear—from people who live out months of sexual frustration—that the time of trial was a bittersweet period in the story of their love, when they found strength and sweetness in each other that a happier beginning might have hidden. I mention their stories only to do them honor, not to say that bittersweet honeymoons are the only kind.

TRYING NEAR-COITUS

It may be wise to do some near-coitus for a while. Let the couple become aroused, dress the penis, and let him thrust to orgasm on top of the mound, that furry hill above the vulva, the external genitals of the woman. Until the penis is accustomed to functioning with the thin sheath in that neighborhood! Then it will be more likely to hold its erection for a careful try at the hymen.

The worst attitude at this time is to expect an inexperienced partner to behave like a past master at sex. That is what each of you will become in time, as you learn together—but you can't be that now.

YOU TWO AGAINST THE WORLD

Remember that nonsexual hugging is a strongly wanted and needed thing, and now is a time for lots of that.

And *this*. The dynamics of this relationship, particularly at this time, set the couple together, apart from and, to a considerable extent, *against* all the rest of the world. So neither of you will betray the other's private sexual behavior to outsiders, and each of you knows that. This is important for egos and for good sex.

To the world, look like the happiest of lovebirds. To each other, be encouraging and confident of sexual success very soon.

5

A Wise Wedding Present

I THINK of this present as one that a clever auntie gives to her niece on her wedding, because the lady I got the idea from gave such a present to her niece. When the niece unwrapped it there was a very nice leather address book with quite a few entries already made in the auntie's firm, clear handwriting. A note tucked inside explained that life is largely made up of little emergencies, most of which can be dealt with right away if you only know the right phone number to call.

You may think, "Some rich aunt; some rich niece. All they have to do is pick up the phone." But even if you find yourself in very modest circumstances, even if you boast of being really *poor*, you still need phone numbers. Maybe not for wall-to-wall carpet dryers, since you live on linoleum. Maybe not for caterers who work in caviar, but still you need a gang of phone numbers suited to your needs. You don't actually need a clever aunt, or a costly leather address book—you can start your own listing of phone numbers in a sturdy plastic-back book.

The aunt listed the following in the little book: family doctor, dentist, gynecologist, urologist, police, fire department, hospital emergency room, electrician, plumber, the number to call to report a gas leak, the poison control center, the animal hospital, a clergyman in case a friend wanted to get married suddenly, places to order good meat, fish, cheese, pastry, different kinds of clothes and a special kind of homemade chocolate mints! A nice mix of necessary, helpful, useful, pleasant-to-know and just-plain-frivolous numbers.

Naturally the aunt hoped the book would set a pattern of collecting useful numbers and of sensing that a grown-up is one who has useful handholds all around, and is a source of helpful information at all times.

The bride-to-be saw at once the usefulness of a book like this with numbers covering so many problems that her aunt had faced in the past. And she saw the value of each person's keeping a record of peculiar disasters and how they were met—which number proved to be the right one. For future reference, for passing on to the next generation.

WHY A SEX THERAPIST IN YOUR BOOK?

You could add a sex therapist's number to your book, or at least a human-sexuality clinic. Why not? You might never need either, but it couldn't hurt!

A married couple may get by for a lifetime without expert advice on their private sex life. I don't advise looking for trouble in this department. But knowing where to turn in case of problems is the way to avoid long periods of private anguish and uncertainty. *That* is certainly avoidable. So the couple who have an active sex life who may be called on by friends for help should know what certain specialists are for and how to reach them at once: the gynecologist, the urologist, the obstetrician, the marriage counselor, the sex therapist, the source of contraception information of the very latest date, the VD clinic.

The gynecologist is the woman's doctor for problems of the womb and the vagina and connected problems, the man goes to a urologist for anything to do with his sexual and urinary parts and functioning.

The obstetrician is of course the doctor for women who are definitely pregnant.

Customarily the family doctor recommends the gynecologist, urologist and obstetrician, but it is wise to know that you can choose these specialists for yourself, because you may not like the treatment you get from a certain one.

Don't wait for emergencies to drive you into making a choice suddenly. Be ready to dial the doctor you want the moment you want him or her.

The marriage counselor is a professional who helps people through problems of perpetual disagreement, of withdrawing from each other, all kinds of two-person difficulties that the pair can't seem to cope with on their own. Many a good marriage that seemed headed for the rocks has been saved by the marriage counselor.

The sex therapist is a specialized therapist who helps couples or individuals with problems of sexual functioning. The help to be had from this kind of professional fills a need that is not usually filled by related professionals such as psychologists, gynecologists, urologists. Psychosexual therapy, as sex therapy is formally called, is not supposed to go on for long. Psychoanalysis is by its nature long-term and goes on for years, but sex therapy deals with specific problems of sex functioning and it often happens that one visit is enough. Very often all that is needed is a bit of sex education. Sometimes it happens that the gynecologist or urologist also has training as a sex therapist. Or, as in my case, that the sex therapist is also a marriage counselor.

In my own practice, I often send a client to a gynecologist or urologist in the beginning, to learn if the client has a problem that is physical. Or to assure the client and myself that the problem is *not* physical.

Sometimes I stop the sex therapy for a while and turn to marriage counseling because the marital sex difficulties are aggravated by other things that are wrong in the marriage. It might be conflict over money or in-laws, old angers over past injuries, any number of things gone wrong.

BEING READY TO HELP

The agency that offers the latest contraception information may not be of great use to the couple themselves, who have probably settled on a contraceptive method they find best for them, but a handy thing to know about so that they can send other people to the most authoritative source.

A friend may approach the husband or the wife privately and in great turmoil over a suspected infection—a venereal disease, as it used to be called (VD), or sexually transmitted disease, as we prefer to term it at present (STD). The thing to do in that case is to look up the nearest clinic for that problem right away, write down the number and put it in your friend's hand. He or she must contact that service right away. No sense in wasting time.

The phone numbers of all these sexual specialists should be in every family phone book. If you are old enough to have a sex life, you are old enough to approach having it in a grown-up way.

6

Openness

*T*HIS book is not about open marriage, open relationships, allowing sex with outsiders. Why not? Well, I have a strong prejudice against the idea! And the book can't be about everything. This book is for people who are interested in monogamous behavior in today's world.

The openness under consideration here is between the wife and the husband. Ideally these two can turn to each other with great frankness, knowing that this partnership is where the most personal support is to be found. If you have a full heart, you can pour it out to your spouse and get love and counsel. You don't have to be on your guard with your spouse, no matter how close to the vest you must play it with the rest of the world. Isn't that what marriage is for?

I say it is, but that you have to judge your spouse's strength when you load your troubles on his or her back. Perhaps you should keep some of your troubles to yourself when you think your spouse is carrying enough. That involves holding something back, or less than total openness. I suggest this kind of restricted or selective openness, even though I know the suggestion will horrify some readers!

Here are some things a spouse might wisely swallow and absorb rather than being totally open about them.

Suppose people you work with show a sexual interest in you. Unless this is so troublesome that it becomes a crisis in your life, if it is something you can brush off or cope with lightly, don't bother your spouse about it. In most marriages the couple must be separate many hours of every day. They have to trust each other when they are apart so that each is free to do the task of the day. This trusting means believing not only that the other will not carry on as soon as the way is clear, but also can be trusted to treat flirtatiousness as a mere compliment, and deal firmly and quickly with more forceful advances. People trying to get it on with married people is a common part of ordinary life, in every workday scene. It isn't just in show biz. It's in offices, hospitals, factories, college faculties. What minister or rabbi has no women making advances? And these men in particular must be discreet, because they must look after the good of the congregation and each member of it, including the wayward ones. So they have to fend off some advances without telling their wives. A clergyman must be free to say, "Look, this never happened. The matter is closed." And not betray the would-be seducer to anyone.

On my radio talk show, men phone in and say that sisters-in-law have put the make on them. Women tell how fathers and brothers and friends of their husbands have behaved treacherously. I advise telling the interloper to cut it out, with a threat to tell the spouse if it doesn't stop. But not to tell the spouse. Because if the thing can be stopped and kept quiet, the whole family will be better off for it.

Lies—I am very shy of telling people to lie, though even a rabbi will tell you that certain fibs are not lies in the sense of disobeying the commandment. A fib to a mad person, for instance. But you don't have to blurt out a truth that will do much more harm than any good it can possibly do.

At fairly predictable intervals I will hear a certain question from a likable young woman who sounds very much like the last one who asked it. She has been living with a young man for a year or two according to rules they have designed to promote an honest, open, unhypocritical relationship that can be ended any time either one is unhappy in it. Either one is free to become involved with other people as the fancy strikes. Neither need ever hide any inclination toward other people, nor the fact of sexual contacts with other people. That is the background of her question. The question, asked in many different ways, is always essentially this: Has she any right to ask her honest, open, unpretending lover to cut it all out and be faithful to her?

I always say that she has every right to ask for a change in the rules of the relationship. And, if she doesn't get agreement to the revision she wants, to walk out of the relationship and go through a period of heartache and then pull herself together and look for a new man and an agreement that suits her better. Obviously this is her privilege in the relationship she has accepted.

There is a surprising amount of pain in walking out of an open relationship. It was supposed to be easy, but when the time comes there is a bond that has to be severed. A dependence to overcome. A strong habit to break. People then turn to a search for a relationship with great commitment and stronger restrictions. Living without walls has proved to be lonely, scary and hurtful. People find out that heartache is a real pain in the chest—and they had thought it was just poetic mush. Okay, so I did talk a little about open relationships.

No matter what you may feel about open relationships as far as the morality and emotional aspects go, there is a reality that must not be ignored. You see, once your spouse or partner—even with your agreement—has sex with someone else, you have really lost the security you might have had in a strictly monogamous relationship that he or she will not pick up a sexually transmitted disease. Especially in light of the terrible consequences of acquiring AIDS, we believe that old-fashioned monogamy is the wisest course and as liberated as you may want to imagine yourself to be, let us not be foolhardy for the sake of sexual excitement. Let's find it inside a stable—and monogamous—relationship.

Modern marriage, which used to be called Anglo-Saxon or American but is now spread all over like Coca-Cola and fast-food places, is based on this idea: A couple meet freely and go into the euphoria of love, often with sex. They want to keep it forever, so they bind themselves together with a contract. Then the first stage of love, that terrific high, diminishes, and either the marriage goes to pot or the couple wisely care for it, like a house and garden where they can live in safety, taking comfort and pleasure from each other.

The wise couple do many active things to enhance their marriage, and they abstain, as they promised, from doing wounding things. And from saying them.

The talking to each other is of first importance; it might be called the substance of the marriage. The more good, helpful, amusing, comforting words you put into the marriage, and the fewer damaging ones, the better the long conversation becomes.

"My husband and I are totally open with each other," babbles a woman, who hasn't let anyone get a word in edgewise through this little dinner party where three couples have sat around the table for an hour. And now five little smiles grow on the faces of her audience, the slowest smile to appear being her husband's. Everyone is thinking that one member of that couple is less open than the other, maybe only because she never stops talking. But of any two people talking to each other, whether they are married or have only met five minutes ago, one is more open than the other.

The lady appears to be one of those who believe in total openness. It is a belief that sex therapists and marriage counselors run into a good deal, but ordinary citizens get an earful of it too. A man tells me that a middle-aged lady, a total stranger, sat next to him on the train and told him all about her daughter's menstrual troubles. That was another case of one person being open and the other getting the whole load.

It is not always the female of the pair who is open while

the other is cool and reserved. A wife who gets home a few minutes before her husband each evening says she desperately needs half an hour of quiet time, but her husband begins telling her all about his day the moment he comes in.

I think openness between the marriage partners is a wonderful and beautiful thing but that it is an accomplishment, not just a matter of two people running an openness contest and one of them winning.

Real openness begins when one of the pair begins to listen attentively to the other.

As a sex therapist and marriage counselor, I find openness in my office very helpful, but at other times and places I have found it very tiresome, I assure you. I meet people who made their most private business mine, and sometimes I long for a little old-fashioned reticence. It isn't even as though the wide-open one is looking for help with a private problem at the wrong time, when I'm resting up from being a professional helper. I expect a certain amount of that—it goes with being known as a counselor. I don't expect to be paid in dollars for every tidbit of information I pass on to perplexed friends and associates. But I can sense it like any other citizen when someone is obsessed with every minor symptom or always looking for unimportant half-feelings and half-faked reactions to minor events, and expecting you to pay close attention. It is low-grade egotism to tell others about your itches, sneezes, bowel movements, vaguely erotic inclinations, fears about the size of your penis, or oral sex you had fifteen years ago with someone or other, without the slightest shyness, as though there were no danger of boring people. As for telling everything to a spouse or lover, who can be badly hurt by pointless exposure to misguided episodes from your past, that can poison a relationship that really didn't have to be poisoned.

A young woman who had a few homosexual involvements as a teenager asks if she has to tell her boyfriend. She is afraid that if she has sex with him he can tell that she is lesbian.

Don't laugh—for all she knows it might leave some mark on her. She has heard that having sex with a boy leaves her so that every boy after that can tell she's not a virgin. That if she has a baby she will have stretch marks on her belly that tell she has had a baby. That masturbating enlarges the clitoris. So this girl, who is not a physiologist or sex expert, wants to know if something in her behavior or in her physical makeup will show that she has shared sexual experiences with girls.

I tell her it won't. That's all there is to that, it just doesn't show. And she doesn't have to tell him about it, especially in the initial stages of their relationship. I counsel her against telling anyone about it. It was a juvenile phase, something that happens to some people before they become openly interested in the opposite sex.

Particularly in the initial stages, neither the man nor the woman has to advertise prior experiences, as though wearing a scarlet letter. Doing that is like saying, "Stay away from me, don't find out what I am like, don't pay any attention to anything you like about me right away. Just look at this tag I've hung on myself."

The present era of permissiveness is not necessarily a time for aggressive frankness. You don't have to say, "I lost my virginity when I was thirteen," or "I've had two abortions," or "Last year I let the whole team have me after the big game." Just coming on like that is obnoxious, like saying, "My father has fifty million dollars," or "You might as well know, I'm a virgin and I mean to stay that way." If you come on like that, you're just asking people to say "Congratulations!" and walk away.

During the entire relationship, whether it lasts a week or fifty years, you don't have to reveal things that are buried for keeps unless you want to dig them up. And if you are part of a well-publicized story, you don't have to be the one who keeps retelling it. Say you are the girl who let a certain senior boy pressure you into having sex, believing he loved you and would fall ill if you were so cruel as not to go all the way, and then found out that he had bragged all over school about it. Now a story like that may live forever, and if you think it will reach your permanent man someday, you don't want to live in fear of that day coming. But I don't say that you have to challenge your fiancé with it before you marry him. What you have to do is decide what you will say and do if he ever confronts you with the story.

A wife in that position has every right to say, "You're talking about something that happened before I met you. You had plenty of time to interrogate me about my past if you wanted to, before we got married. What happened was the most cruel thing anyone has ever done to me. It was partly my fault, but I was very young."

It is reasonable to suppose that a man who accepts that his wife had sex with others before him also accepts that she has had misfortunes and disappointments. If he never asks her, then he is tacitly letting bygones be bygones.

It may be wise to say, before the wedding plans are set, that now is the time to ask any questions about the past. Not later.

PROTECTING YOURSELF BY SILENCE

A certain accountant of the Bronx (to start my tale in the style of Boccaccio) used a crystal bowl to catch cigar ashes. Knowing that his wife would be annoyed at this, he washed it later but managed to break it in the sink. This was terrible—the bowl had been given to his wife by a sister who had died, and she treasured it. He took the largest piece, wrapped in paper, to a very expensive Fifth Avenue store and told the clerk he would pay a fortune to replace it with an identical bowl. The clerk said a fortune would not be necessary, but that forty-five dollars would do the trick as they had that bowl in stock. Our accountant sneaked the new bowl back into his apartment, and over the years that followed he observed his wife looking at it and touching it with love and reverence as a gift from her sister. What can be said of a man who is a coward, a cunning knave and a loving husband all in one? I confess that I am all for him.

Let us take his action as a deception used to keep certain important feelings intact.

Dear Dr. Ruth: I slept with my sister-in-law and the

*burden of this is intolerable. My sister-in-law and I have
agreed never to touch each other again and to keep the
matter a secret, but I feel so deceitful to my wife. We have
always been totally open with each other....*

What did I tell him? I said to button his lip! He and his
sister-in-law were the guilty ones. Why should his wife and
the rest of the family suffer when they were innocent? To
commit adultery with a sister-in-law is one wrong thing; to
explode a bomb in his marriage and the whole family would
be another. Keep his pain to himself.

As a marriage counselor I'm not often asked to give
advice to practiced adulterers—they are hardened and they
seldom seek advice from the likes of me. But I often have to
counsel people who have been foolish, weak or self-
indulgent—and now they want to be more weak, foolish and
self-indulgent and confess to their spouses, putting the
burden of the wrongdoing on the injured one. If you have
sinned against your marriage you have done yourself an
injury. You have spoiled your image of yourself and your
precious marriage for yourself. Let the pain of this be yours
as far as you can. In almost every case I would say that to be
the one who tells the injured spouse is to do wrong.

A husband who was a client told me the following. He
had been unfaithful to his wife and had forced himself to be
quiet about it although he wanted to confess. Being deceitful
caused him pain, and besides, he worried about her finding
out and wanted to get that worry off his mind by being the
one to tell her. Now, this is human because it is human to
act like a baby and treat your wife like a baby's mama. But
it led to his feeling abused by his wife! Every time she was
cross or nagging or used him unfairly, he thought, "If only
you knew what pain I go through to protect you from pain!"

I said to him, "Look, you are letting yourself get sore at
your wife just because she feels a little off and isn't always
perfect. Because you did something unwise, she has to be
perfect! This thing is gnawing at you and it's spoiling your
common sense. That's because you carry around in your
head a monstrous picture of three people. All you see in
your wife is a woman you wronged but whom you saved

from disaster. Suffering in silence, you protect her. Yourself you see as a wrongdoer and a silent sufferer. The other woman, no matter what else in her life, you see as your fellow sinner. I want you to change the picture you carry around of these three. Yourself: List all the good things you do and are. I don't mind if you lay it on a little thick. But leave out this wonderful thing you are doing by being silent. As for the other woman, think of her as entirely apart from this one episode with you. Think up ten good things about her and three bad things, all without reference to you. Do the same for your wife. Then whenever you think of one of these three, be sure to think of some of these aspects of them that have nothing to do with this foolish episode that happened. It's over, and should be forgotten by the two who know about it. Put a label on each of these people for reference. Call yourself, for instance, the executive and the guy who cleans out the car on weekends. Call the other woman, if this is the case, the tennis player. Call your wife the librarian and bird-watcher. Tag them that way, call those tags to mind when you think of them. Forget about The Injured Wife, The Betrayer, and The Other Woman. Practice forgetting this thing that must be forgotten."

"And if my wife finds out?"

"She'll remind you. Leave that to her, don't you be the one. But she probably won't find out, and if she does she may say nothing about it. But in any case, you will be seeing these characters as they truly are, and not as they were at one short period in time. You must make the ordinary daylight truth push out this monstrous exaggeration."

One wife complained that her husband always bragged about how women fell for him. He had this silly notion of himself as the universal sex symbol that made women act crazy. He was so open with his wife that he shared this with her. In the course of a session he told me and his wife that this was only an amusement to him, just a fantasy he liked to air. He didn't mean for his wife to take it seriously, just to be amused at him and by him. He agreed to stop amusing her in this way. His openness about these daydreams was doing harm to his real-life marriage. He was painting for his wife a picture of his life away from home that upset her badly, and one of himself as a low-grade Lothario—not actually having affairs but certainly obsessed with the idea.

Here is something else to hold back—intimate moments from the past, before you met your spouse. A spouse can live with the idea that you have had other loves, and had sex with previous spouses or lovers—if all that is kept fairly vague. But in the cozy confidence-sharing of marriage, people may easily go beyond what is acceptable. In the morning the talker may well wish he or she had been more reticent with the other about certain things. I think of a case where the wife foolishly told the husband what cute names her former husband had called her genitals and his own. Another giddily supplied details of a camping weekend she had gone on with three guys. However, there is one thing you must not be vague about and that is the possibility that any partner either of you had may have been at a higher risk for AIDS. Once you both are aware of this possibility that a former lover may have been at risk, then even though you have tested negative for AIDS, you may want to practice safer sex for several years of your relationship until you feel secure that you are past the time period during which the HIV virus may appear.

Every good marriage survives mistakes. When you have said what you should have held back, or heard what you wish you had never heard, the best thing to do is look forward a week, when the revelation will have assumed a smaller place in the grand scheme of things, and be balanced against the better impressions you and your spouse have of each other.

WHEN YOU CAN'T GET OUT OF IT

You can't get out of it when you have caught herpes at the office party. Your spouse has to know why you are avoiding sex, keeping your genitals out of sight and making a fuss about having your own towel that nobody else must use. He or she has to know what precautions must be taken in the future when you two have sex. You can't dodge this, and the best you can do is to try not to make things worse by the way you break the news.

With other sexually transmitted diseases you may be able to get past the infectious stage, to a point of recovery where you are infection-free, without telling your spouse. Syphilis and gonorrhea are usually curable and do not recur.

If you are being blackmailed, you had best tell your spouse why and let the blackmailers slink away.

There is a way to break the news. It will still take courage and cause you both pain, but it minimizes the effect. Tell your spouse that you want to have a serious talk in private. A good place to have it is in the car, in a place where neither of you is known—parked. Don't break the news while one of you is driving. This way, away from other people, such as strangers in a restaurant or the children at home, your spouse has the privilege of shouting, or crying, or whatever is needed, to let go without being observed. Don't take a drink to get your courage up—you need your cold-sober emotions and thoughts to get through this.

This thoughtfulness may not save your marriage (though marriages outlive crises like this all the time), but it will be the most considerate way to tell the ghastly truth.

If you can't arrange the scene in a parked car, you may have to do it at home—but not in front of children, and preferably with no children in the house.

FINDING A CAREFUL OPENNESS

Marriages take place in the real world; there has to be talk about difficult things, and disagreement occurs between any two people. So it is best to start working out disagreements from the beginning, establishing a way for doing it. Letting your feelings be known and hearing the other partner's feelings. By all means, let yourselves be known to each other.

But it is wrong to make a fetish of brutal frankness, to overdo "kidding," to play the dozens with a spouse. That is not "modern," it is only juvenile. A grown-up is not afraid to be kind and loving with words.

Openness means above all openness to the flow of warmth and tenderness between husband and wife. While you're being open, say something sweet!

Finding the right mixture of frank intimacy and careful tact in marital conversation takes time. The do's and don't's are different with each couple, and they change from year to year within each marriage. But be prepared for surprises. Be ready to learn that your loving spouse can flare up when you dig into a nerve, just as if you were a stranger.

When you first visit a married couple, the easy talk between them may startle you. You can see they are a comfortable, contented couple—but the way they tease and play with fire in their easy chatter!

The fact is that they are steering confidently through familiar waters, avoiding dozens of dangerous places. Avoiding subjects they never approach except carefully, and only when alone with each other. They have learned the territory.

7

What Am I Doing in Your Bedroom?

IN bedrooms all over the country, I happen to know that my name comes up in a funny way.

The woman says, "Not yet."

"Why?"

"Not yet."

"You're ready."

"I know if I'm ready"

"You're wet down there. Your Bartholin's glands are pumping enthusiastically. You're ready but don't know it."

"Dr. Ruth says men think women are ready if they are wet. But that isn't necessarily so."

"*Aiee! I'm* ready! If I wait I'll lose my erection. Or I'll explode."

"You'll get another one. You won't explode. Dr. Ruth—"

"Dr. Ruth! A telephone should grow from her ear!"

Now, I'm not the only sex maven who gets into other people's bedrooms. The couple might be talking about any one of a crowd of other psychosexual therapists. Dr. Good, Dr. Wise, Dr. Wonderful, any number of them. Is this good? Shouldn't the couple be alone in that bedroom?

Remember the ill-fated sexual encounter when the wife

asked, just as the husband was coming, "Did you remember to wind the clock?" Her husband felt that the moment was ruined by this intrusion of mundane matters. That she should have had her mind on having sex with him at that sacred moment when they might be starting another human life. And many a lover, without thoughts of impregnation, may resent the inclusion of outside things at a moment that should be sheer intimate beauty.

For myself, I don't mind being in the bedroom with them as long as I'm not there in person! But if couples are thinking about me at that intimate moment, what harm? Basically, I think of myself as a friend with some good information that lovers can use. That thought pleases me!

But some people who want to find something wrong with sex education and sex therapy will always be around to say that I interfere in the lives of other people—I make sex too mechanical, too hedonistic, denying the spiritual side of it.

PARTLY GUILTY, YOUR HONOR

Right away I plead guilty to a certain kind of interfering. Unasked, uninvited, I will take any opportunity to shout certain ideas that I want people to take with them into their most private moments. If a boy and girl are together and find themselves overwhelmed with desire, what if one of them hears a certain voice in the ear saying, "Contraception!" And the great event they were about to stage is halted until contraception is installed—in a few minutes, or in a day or two, who cares?

Good! Terrific! And there are other ideas I am very glad to put into the heads of lovers, even if they didn't ask. Because probably they didn't ask because the questions never occurred to them. That's sex education, whether in the classroom, the lecture hall, on the radio, wherever.

And let me bug you once again. Even if you were confident that you couldn't get pregnant because "it is the wrong time of the month," or your lover had a vasectomy—and he has a very low sperm count anyway, you should still use a condom to protect yourself against many of the sexually transmitted diseases and particularly from AIDS. To make sure you are using the best possible type of condom, speak to a pharmacist about which ones are best—you can always tell him that you are inquiring for a friend.

YOU'VE GOT TO KNOW WHAT YOU'RE DOING

Let me say something about making sex too "mechanical." That means too physical, too much attention paid to physiology. Well, sex *is* physical and has its learned technique. You see what happens when zoo keepers try to get animals to mate and to care for their young in captivity. A she-ape or panda will fail to mate with the male provided by these human marriage brokers. Or, having been impregnated artificially, will not care for her baby when it comes as a good animal mother should. In the wild these animals learn mating and caring for young by watching others of their kind doing these things. By being brought up isolated, like prisoners, they don't learn what their own kind will ordinarily teach them.

In human society teaching sex and child care is needed too. I don't like too much comparing human beings to animals, because the old Jewish feeling that we are unique in God's creation is very strong in me. But I think that, as very bright human beings, we can learn from animals. We should not be too proud to learn from simpler creatures than ourselves.

SEX AND RELIGION

Doesn't sex teaching, being too hedonistic, too much a teaching of self-indulgence, make sensuality the main issue in human life instead of parenting and goodness to our fellow beings and obedience to God? I think that good sex is good for the home, where the man and woman have a right to feel safe and happy, the children have a right to live with happy parents and to learn human happiness and wisdom. All the pleasures of this existence that lead to well-being instead of sickness are to be encouraged. It is a very important idea that each person should believe that this creation is here for his or her personal pleasure, avoiding harm to oneself as to others. To abstain from licit pleasures is sinful. So we who teach the wise search for sexual pleasure are doing a *mitzvah,* a kind and good deed.

To religious people sex is connected with spirituality. It is a sacrament. So is eating; so are labor, rest, conviviality.

Human beings seem to me to be born with spiritual cravings but without spiritual knowledge, which has to be taught by parents and teachers. A little Christian does not learn to put hands together and kneel, or to do unto others as he would have them do unto him, without human teachers. These ways of connecting himself with God and with other people will not occur to the little person, who will grow up wild and apt to hurt himself and others. His ignorance will certainly show itself in his sexual conduct as untutored sexual urges grow stronger and stronger.

All human behavior requires human teaching, from going to the bathroom to the highest mathematical or philosophical pursuits, and in spite of what we so fondly believed in the past, sexual behavior is no exception to this rule. So, if I and my fellow sex educators seem to have gotten into other people's bedrooms, it is not to insert ourselves between lover and beloved, or between them and their spirituality.

SEX AND MORALITY

I am definitely a spiritual pluralist, and I don't pressure people to be spiritual in some manner pleasing to me. But there *is* an inescapable morality to be taught with good sex education. Be responsible. Be loving. Be considerate. Avoid harm to yourself and to others. And, never forget that the ultimate harm is to knowingly and willfully cause others to die. If you have any suspicion that you may have AIDS—or even a less dangerous disease—it is absolutely immoral to pass it on to an innocent victim. Similarly, you must protect your life and health by minimizing the possibilities that you may acquire AIDS or any other sexually transmitted disease.

THE BEAUTY PART

Now—the complaint that teaching sex makes it prosaic. This is so if teaching biology seems prosaic. That may be a question of personal esthetics. I know students who feel they see a beautiful part of the universe if they peer at a drop of pond water under a microscope, who see a section of a leaf as like a part of a cathedral.

There is a TV movie about conception and birth that is an hour of beauty and wonder as well as an instruction in human physiology. To me and to most people who have not been indoctrinated against "insides" and nakedness and those things that were not to be mentioned in the airless parlors of our great-grandparents, to us the plainest physical facts of sex are interesting first, very helpful information second, and anything but prosaic.

As for the 90 percent of human sexual experience that takes place in the mind, that is as poetic, as dramatic, as the inclination and enrichment of each human mind makes it. Many artists contribute to the coloration of the mental appreciation of sex. Poets, storytellers, musicians, painters, architects, interior decorators, wine makers, clothing designers, cooks, preachers, teachers, prophets, all contribute to the environment of the human sexual experience.

Art has long had a sacred part to play in the enhancement of sensuality. The Song of Songs is the prime proof of this in Hebrew literature.

So, many life-enhancing hands work to make sex more beautiful for us. But the sex therapist, in the main, is concerned with the basics of sexual functioning. That is, after all, what we are for.

The sex therapist is a specialist, and has a good deal of special information to impart in the course of any lecture, article, book or hour in the office with a client. Nobody comes to us to ask us to play an instrument or to read a poem. That is not what people want of us. That does not mean that our teachings block out all the erotic effect of a culture. In fact, they often enhance it!

I certainly have my ideas about the effect of esthetics on lovemaking. I think more music and less football on Sundays would improve the general picture of American marriage, and certainly more gentle images and softer words and sounds than the eleven o'clock news would be better both for our rest and for our sex lives. The softening and fantasy-enriching effects of the love scenes and of human beauty, clothed and naked, as painted by hundreds of artists who may be seen in museums and art books, is something wonderful, and I can only urge people to let more of our sensuality-enhancing culture get into the eyes, ears, minds and feelings. And bedrooms.

"People go to a marriage counselor with their private married business that they should deal with themselves. If they have a spat, they head for the marriage counselor like running to the bathroom for aspirin or a Band-Aid. And they can't even make love without lessons from a sex therapist."

I hear this kind of criticism regularly. How fair is it?

First, as to marriage counselors, I think the custom of going to these arbitrators is too new to be judged as to its effectiveness. But we do know that in the past people took marital difficulties to a parson or rabbi, or to an authority figure in the old-fashioned extended family. Or they worked them out. Or the let them grow into incurable enmities. Now they go to a professional guide, more specialized than the parson or the rabbi. It is a way to get a dialogue going again, or of seeking to end a dispute they can't end by themselves. No doubt some couples run to a counselor too quickly, but that is better than letting a quarrel go on for years. I think the feeling against the practice is unconsidered and often frivolous.

As for going to a sex therapist, it is never done without good cause in my experience. People *don't* know how to make love, and they have been taught all their lives that this is the supreme pleasure of our world. Often a sex therapist can lead them out of their secret ignorance and unhappiness in a very short period. So why not make the appointment?

Sex as a component of lasting relationships can be

improved by greater knowledge. Bumbling sex is quite good enough for impregnating uniformed girls—indeed, I have often heard from women who, having had no pleasure from an act of sex, are astonished to find themselves pregnant. In the past a certain percentage of couples bumbled into pleasurable modes of sexual intercourse and play. But many people in every generation found the sexual part of marriage very disappointing, and this could have been improved by professional teaching and guidance. I am glad to be of this age, with all its dubious aspects, in which I can teach and guide people who want greater marital pleasure.

I *know* that people are taking my teaching into their bedrooms. They go from my office primed with advice from me, and they phone the results to me the next day.

"Dr. Westheimer, this is Don."

"Hello, Don. How did it go?"

"Fine. Things went really fine."

"She helped you, she played with you, you got in and you ejaculated inside?"

"Yes."

"Bravo! Keep it up!"

"Will I see you next week?" Don asks.

"No. Just keep doing what you are doing and call me in three weeks and let me know how it's going."

"Okay. I'll do that."

That phone call makes me feel wonderful! The sun comes out after that. But Don won't be calling me much after this. He may miss making that three-week call. Soon he will not even be thinking of me in the bedroom, except once in a while. I may never have him in my office again. In sex therapy, that is success.

8

When Two Clouds of Fantasy Merge

*T*HAT'S what happens when two people meet and court and become, for a time or for life, a pair. It is two clouds of fantasy coming together—or, as described by movie script writers, Boy Meets Girl!

Sometimes one party to the merger doesn't accept that the other has a right to private or partly revealed fantasies about the coming together, especially about the coming together in bed.

(When I say "coming together" I mean the joining of the couple in intimacy. I *never* mean having simultaneous orgasms—which happens infrequently and is not needed for high-quality sex, not at all!)

Very often the man or the woman, who has no doubt of his or her own right to sex fantasies, is very much upset to discover that the other half of the couple also has a fantasy or two.

Bob, in bed with Ann and reaching the point of total communion either with her or with passion, hears her say, "Clyde! Oh, Clyde!"

I will concede that this is a rough thing to hear, and it is hard to persuade Bob that Clyde is only a fantasy and not someone she met at the Cape when she was seventeen. But many a Bob has survived a Clyde or even a Roger.

Ann, having reached a point in her union with Bob that seems to her very close to pure bliss, the dreamiest love-making combined with mutual understanding at all levels, is shyly asked by Bob to dress up a little in blue-movie boudoir stuff. In this era of pantyhose, he suggests that she don a black garter belt and stockings—just to put some ginger into the proceedings. She is horrified and comes down out of her own dream of understanding Bob with a thump.

Bob, who seemed to be so nice and normal—maybe *too* normal, but that at least was *safe*—has turned out to be a sex creep!

"He doesn't love *me*," Ann wails. "I thought my Real People clothes from L. L. Bean and my classic nudity were what he wanted, but it seems he's really thinking about some revolting whore when he sticks his thing in *me*! I'm just some supermarket meat he uses because he can't get what he really wants because he's afraid of getting AIDS!"

When I hear a client say something so negative about a partner, I think, "Something is wrong here besides poor sexual functioning, or not liking to dress up." When one partner lets go like that, there is often a basic relationship problem. Otherwise the request to wear fancy undies would be taken as just a little playfulness, right? But there *is* resentment directed just against the other person's unwelcome fantasies. And there is the idea that if the other person has to *pretend* in order to make sex exciting, then the real thing must be uninspiring. It all comes from not accepting that the other person goes back a long way, has been a developing human being going way back to the bassinet, and has a big load of daydreams just as you or I have.

PATCHING HER PICTURE OF HIM

So I probably will chat away with the client about this little make-believe Bob wants and why it bothers her so much, and I listen for hints of something really big going wrong between them. I ask her if it isn't obvious that Bob likes a very nicely brought-up natural young woman, or why would he go for her in the first place? Because she is very obviously all those things. The only thing is, there is something especially arousing about just such a girl dressed up in that way, all strapped and girded but with the most delicious and most secret parts left exposed. On her, to his mind, the old-fashioned woman's gear emphasizes her willingness and desire to be specifically sexy, to bring that private part of her nice-girl nature as a present to him. It is really a compliment to her and—

Now she thinks I am definitely giving her a snow job and that my line is *so* farfetched! But I have made a dent in her hostility to Bob's little daydream. In a little while we are talking about Bob's nice points, and her Bob picture is beginning to look healthy again.

You see, *she* has a fantasy she clothes her Bob in, and if the poor guy unwittingly offends against the daydream role she has cast him in, he is in hot water.

Actually, her picture of Bob as a nice guy is close to the truth. Her picture of him as one who likes an outdoorsy girl who reads romance novels is one he will gladly plead guilty to. She can accuse him of having a secret yen to wear white cotton socks and he won't squeal. But when he confesses to a sophomoric fantasy about garter belts, it upsets her somewhat rigid and stereotyped notion of him.

We have to realize that the garter belt idea is one common to the class of men Bob belongs to. It is adolescent, or even pubescent, rather than something unusual or freaky. It goes with his whole decent, upright, conforming and performing lifestyle. Just a little fantasy about seeing a girl in certain female underclothes that girls don't really wear anymore.

I have a little friendly schmooze with Ann about this normal aspect of normal old Bob, and Ann has her picture of him back in shape with just a little useful change.

THERE IS NO "JUST YOU"

"I want him to love just me," a woman says, and I tell her that there is no "just her."

"Maybe there is a physical organism in the physical world that might be considered to be you, in certain circumstances," I say. "But even that has a stomach, and feelings in the stomach. So even the basic physical being is affected by thoughts and images."

She looks at me questioningly.

"There is no you without feelings and ideas," I say. "If you take a knockout drug and lie unconscious, you may be breathing but that creature is not you. Your facial expression, your regular movements are missing. You are what you perceive yourself to be, what I perceive you to be, what your lover perceives you to be. What your lover sees in you is partly your appearance, partly what you are like to touch, very much what you project to him of your self-image, and all of that as perceived by him, with all his accumulated feelings and ideas about the world, people, women. He came to you with a world-dream all formed in his mind. You became part of it. You fitted into his fantasy. You changed it, you'll go on changing it, sure. But with no preconceived idea or picture of his world and his life, what use would he have had for you?"

"I don't want to be a figment of his male imagination."

"Look, you have your own life-idea or image, and you fitted him into it when you met him. Isn't that true? Hadn't you dreamed of such a meeting with a guy a hundred times, with a certain time of day and the promise of all kinds of dates and trips and lovely events lined up for the future? Considered other guys for the picture? Squinted a little at this guy to make him fit it a little better?"

"Well . . . ," she says, meaning I have her dead to rights.

Winning this little point does not make me clever. I have been through this conversation many times before. The idea of people meeting and being fitted into their two life-fantasies is not original with me. I am fond of it, though.

No Fantasies, Nothing Going On

I mentioned an Ann and a Bob. These are handy names I like to use describing various two-person situations without using the real names I am thinking of. Ann and Bob, any real Ann and Bob out there, thanks for the loan of your names, and remember, I am not talking about you. Even if you think I am.

I have two little jointed wooden dolls in my office—let's call them Ann and Bob. I use them to show different positions for sex to people who don't seem to know what I'm talking about. Wooden Ann and Bob are so helpful, they bend willingly to any sexual task I give them without complaint. They have no objections—they are only wooden dolls, you see. When they come together it is the only case I know of sex partners meeting who bring no fantasies to each other or to what they do together.

If they suddenly became real they would begin to display fantasies at work. They would dress up instead of going around nude (even though their wooden bodies are really sexless). Real people dress up for a number of reasons any schoolchild can tell you, but the most important reason people dress is to create themselves, to effect their own images.

Bob puts on his jogging togs and looks athletic, hip, loose, comfortable; he puts on his office suit and looks and *feels* quite another way. Ann dresses (a flesh-and-blood Ann) in different clothes for different hours and days and seasons—to look different ways and *feel* different ways. They are suiting up for different parts of their life-fantasies.

No real life goes on for people without their fantasies about life and themselves.

Yesterday, Today and Tomorrow

Ann's past, present and her ideas for the future exist in her mind and are very much colored to suit her desires there. Let us say she remembers someone holding her on a lap twenty years ago, and she has a definite idea how that person felt about holding dear little Ann. Herself, she may have held a child to be obliging, secretly thinking that the child was gummy and would soil her dress; also that she, Ann, had a little cramp, and had to catch a 4:15 bus back to town. But as she recalls herself being held she believes fully that the grown-up holding her was expressing love.

Ann has a story about her parents meeting and loving each other before she was born. This story, based on a few scraps of information and some old snapshots, is part of Ann's fantasy of her past. She also dreams of the future, a future so unrealistic it is hard to believe that a real young woman can believe in it, but it is Ann's future. Someday she will wonder with wide eyes where it ever went! I am not saying that she won't be pretty happy. But at any point in her life she will need a picture, a fantasy, of the future.

Bob has his own past and future fantasies. They are not the same as Ann's. Bob and Ann know parts of each other's life-fantasies, and perhaps when they first lived together they had a quarrel or two about conflicting fantasies, but they realized that this was silly and boring.

Right now is the present. Ann and Bob are eating leftover beef and bean curd with Chinese vegetables in their apartment where they pay too much rent. Ann is pretending his father has died and left them the lake place in Wisconsin and she is doing the house over the way she would like it. Bob is thinking forward two hours, when he has persuaded Ann to make love in the living room and they are doing it dog-fashion with the lights out and the picture window uncurtained. Across the street they can see the young couple feeding their tropical fish.

They are fantasizing night and day, and each seldom knows what the other has in mind. Once in a while the truth leaks out and causes dismay! But they are not stupid, and if questioned seriously they each would say that human beings live largely in their imaginations.

AND WHILE THEY'RE DOING IT

Later on they are making love. Bob has worked it out so that they are doing it dog-fashion in the living room, in the dark with the picture window uncovered. As he wanted to. The young couple across the steet seem to have gone out for the evening, but in his mind they are there. He has no idea what this does for the sex, but it does something. He is also excited by knowing that Chinese people live downstairs. Why tell Ann? Look how upset she got about the garter belt! Ann is pretending they are copulating dog-fashion on a new redwood deck at her late father-in-law's summer place in Wisconsin. What terrific orgasms they both have! Bob first, Ann after.

They fall asleep touching each other, pleasantly drained. They both know that they love each other very much.

9

Love in the Morning

*A*S a pubescent boy he was full of sharp new feelings. These were set aside from other, established ones, such as the feelings of *love* he felt for his mother and grandmother and his collie. Also set apart from the devotion he felt for certain motion-picture actresses and fictional women in books about the frontier. At that age he began to construct sexual fantasies about women undressing and letting him look, touch and enjoy to his little heart's— and genitals'—content. He would put one of these fantasies together while he was wide awake, and they would take place, in his imagination, at all different times of the day. Sometimes at night, but mostly in the daylight.

"The advantage of daylight was that I could see every forbidden area of the female body," he says.

He played with nymphs in the woods, mermaids by the sea, dark-skinned women from *National Geographic*, etc. One fantasy involved a rather coarse blonde of mature years who lived on a leafy street in Queens. He met her, in his fantasy, by special arrangement to work out a dishonest reduction in her utilities bill, in return for which she was to let him enjoy her any way he liked upstairs in her bedroom from nine-fifteen A.M. until an hour before her husband returned from work.

The special thrill of this fantasy was its explicitly illicit nature and its complete separation from any affection between them. And part of the enjoyable immorality was that it all took place by daylight, during the working day.

Fifty years later he remembered these fantasies with some amazement because his entire feeling about Doing It by daylight had changed. By this time having sex any time he was in the mood was perfectly allowable. *If* his wife was agreeable—and she was, because she thought he ought to be a little more active sexually than he was. But he had a grudge against Doing It by daylight now because that was the time he *could* do it. It was like driving for him, best in the morning with good daylight and his energy and alertness at their peak. He could perform in the morning primarily because his testosterone level was at its height then, at the hour of seven A.M. When he woke up.

LET'S GET THIS STRAIGHT

"Let's get this straight," he said to me in my office. "Are you telling me that in a young fellow his testosterone level is higher at night, and in an old guy it's higher in the morning?"

"Not at all," I said. And I explained that the testosterone level is highest in any man, young or old, at the time he wakes up from a good night's sleep. But for a young man the level seems to be high enough for sex most of the time. For an older fellow the testosterone level is lower most of the time but rises enough in the morning so that he may even wake up with an erection.

IT'S NOT A FULL BLADDER THAT DOES IT

Naturally, most people have a full bladder on waking up. For this reason a lot of men came to believe that the morning erection, which seems especially strong and persistent, is caused by the full bladder. Believing this, men have been known to put off going to the toilet until after having a morning sexual encounter—which *can* be done. A man certainly will not urinate while he is erect—he can't. He can get an erection and go through the rest of the cycle to ejaculation and detumescence while his bladder is full—without urinating.

But it isn't always the full bladder that causes those fine morning erections. It is also as I mentioned a high level of the hormone testosterone, which is secreted by the testicles, and frequently the erotic dreams of sleep from moments before.

A NICE PATTERN TO SET

Many young couples set a pattern of having morning sex every so often, and I wish more of them did. But as time goes on, they may tend to fall into a routine and by the time they come to me the idea of morning sex seems strange.

I remember one middle-aged couple. She was the one who spoke up and answered questions frankly, while he was pretty glum and reserved. Her idea was that *he* was too depressed since retiring and that some sex life would perk him up a bit.

"What about *you*?" I asked.

"Oh, well, I sure could use some sex too," she said easily.

That made him sit up. "Well!" he said. "I never thought I'd hear you say something like that." He'd had this idea that he was a randy old devil by nature but that she was pretty prudish.

I asked them a whole lot of my fresh sex therapy questions about their most private business, and she spoke right up as if she were talking about cookie recipes at a church social. Well, I have found mostly women to be like that, rather shameless. Maybe you get that way having babies in front of male doctors and putting your feet in stirrups and having them peer into you. And so forth.

They hadn't had sex in a year or so, but she said, "Oh, he has lovely erections in the mornings," and that brought me around to suggesting that they try morning sex as one of the low-cost morale builders of their sunset years. This is not one of the great original ideas, as it happens. Suggesting that older people have sex in the morning is fairly standard, and very helpful.

SOME STUMBLING BLOCKS

Now, the first attempts at utilizing the husband's lovely morning erections were not the perfect bliss some of you hopeful readers might think, and the chief stumbling block seems to have been the old erector set himself. He said he felt like some kind of a freak, doing it "at the wrong time of day." Also that in the morning what he needed was breakfast, because his guts were growling and these sound effects seemed unromantic. And his breath stank. And his mouth felt like a chicken coop. And while his penis might be wide awake, *he* needed coffee.

I said that these were familiar complaints from people who had spent a lifetime conventionally having sex at night, and the thing to do was to get up, shave, brush teeth and hair, have a little juice and coffee and a roll; pull down the shades and create a nighttime mood with music from some twenty-four-hour music station, etc.

She said that if he were going to reach for her first thing, she didn't mind too much how she looked, but if they were going to bed *after* breakfast, she would have to perk up her looks. She got a new kind of hairdo that brushed up easily, and some new nightclothes for returning to the room in, for him to take off!

These did not become daily sessions. They continued to "sleep in" most mornings. But every ten days they had an assignation in their own bedroom, and there was no doubt that he cheered up wonderfully—so much so that he had the car tuned up and they went on a slow trip to Oregon from Mamaroneck to visit their children.

THE SPECIAL CHARMS OF MORNING SEX

Sex therapy means endless tailoring of advice to the very individual needs and tastes of the clients. I would like to say that it is not every couple that must re-create something of a night atmosphere in the morning in order to function sexually. There are special charms at that early hour for many lovers. The early bird voices and the sounds of other people stirring and going about their business while lucky you two are dallying in your bedroom. It enlarges the sense of being permanently on vacation, escaping from the burdens of the workaday life.

There is a great bonus of pleasure for people who learn to have morning sex either regularly or occasionally in early life. It encourages innovations in the marital pleasures. Morning sex encourages noon and afternoon and twilight sex, and makes the transition to mostly morning sex much easier as age creeps up.

10

Talking about Sex

I GUESS I don't like sex jokes very much. That doesn't
mean I never heard one that was funny, but too many
have a cruel element I dislike. The butt of the joke is
often the woman, or a minority person, or someone who has
sexual difficulty, and I am too softhearted to like that. Even
if it is a bit funny I find the cruelty spoils it for me. And a
lot of sex jokes are basically antisex and antifeeling, even if
they are told by people who think they are very worldly.
The classic traveling salesman or "tough" woman is so
often really puritanical. This comes out in the way they can
make sex only funny or cruel in their talk. If the talk goes
near kindness or tenderness or seriousness about sex, they
are really embarrassed.

I don't like talking about sex in a restaurant—not because
it spoils my appetite, but because I see no reason why
people at nearby tables should be offended. I think there is a
time and a place. Or, better, there are times and places—
you have to use your judgment, not live by an ironclad rule.

For instance, you might make a rule never to talk about
sex in a place like a synagogue. But I have been invited to
address groups in synagogues, with the ark and the scrolls

right behind me. And Christian groups have had me talk in chapels and parish houses, and so forth. They consider the new kind of serious and helpful sex talk beneficial to their congregations, something God's people should encourage.

I laugh a lot, but it isn't at sex jokes. I mean when I am on my radio programs in New York or California, or my TV show. Sometimes a caller-in asks me what to tell her boyfriend, or how to do something in bed, and I find myself giggling conspiratorially, like a schoolgirl planning a date or something. That is friendly laughing and giggling. But I don't laugh that much at jokes.

Well, there is something else—I don't always *get* sex jokes! They are in an entirely different mind-frame from mine. Sometimes I don't understand the English idiom that well, but mostly I just don't have the necessary antisexual attitude you need to think the joke is funny.

This is a confession—I'm not bragging about being Mrs. Wonderful. It's more to say that *nobody*, not even the ten-P.M. Sunday sexpert, is really up for all kinds of sex talk.

Partly, maybe even mostly, my resistance to sex jokes is professional. I hear one and I think, "Oh, oh, that would increase a lot of people's sexual anxiety." I am really in the business of lowering sexual anxiety, you see. It gets to be a full-time preoccupation!

A TIME FOR TALKING AND A TIME FOR KEEPING QUIET

I say, let's all honor other people's right to be not in the mood. Not in the mood for sex, sometimes. Not in the mood for sex talk at other times. Perhaps not to join the laughter at some joke. When I hear a cruel joke, what I do is involuntary. I smile at the intention of the joker to amuse me, then I say, "I don't really like that—it's too much against women and oral sex." Not coming down like a ton of bricks, just evaluating the joke as a joke among jokes.

Sometime you may be with someone and feel like saying,

"I don't want to talk about sex now." If the friend or lover is sensitive to your moods, that will be all right. You don't have to make him or her feel that something wrong has been done.

BUT DEFINITELY A TIME FOR TALKING

But in a marriage or long relationship there must be a time for talking about sex—it can't always be that one partner shuts off the discussion, because serious things between partners have to be talked about *sometime*.

The instinct to move toward a woman or man sexually *is* an instinct. But the actual performance of sexual acts, from the most preliminary, like hand holding or kissing, to bringing someone to orgasm, has to be learned. Kissing, for instance, is a custom among certain people. Like Santa Claus, it has spread through the world, so nowadays Japanese kiss, and all kinds of formerly faraway people do it. They see it in Western-style movies. What a couple do sexually they learn to do, and for the best mutual enjoyment they need practice and also a way to tell each other what they like and what they don't care for at present.

There is nearly always some stiffness in starting the talk about sex, the serious talk about what I want and what you want. What really comes close to our own personal desires and vulnerabilities. In getting that ongoing dialogue going. So I do suggest that couples listen to my radio discussions together! Also, for deeper learning about sex, to read books aloud to each other. Sex manuals, pamphlets about different kinds of contraception, poetry, love stories, fiction with sexual symbolism and feeling, like certain science fiction, and so forth. Reading to each other sexual literature that may be factual or exciting and feelings enriching. This gives the couple material to discuss, a common frame of reference and practice in talking about sex.

TALKING ABOUT IT IN BED

Certainly a couple can make use of words during sex. Why should our beautiful ability to use language be excluded from this? Words may not be necessary; they may not be the swiftest way to inform your partner at times. For instance, the one being caressed with intent to arouse or please can guide the other one's hand, or penis, or head without using words. But why should our great human ability to talk be wrong?

One young couple would get by in bed with as few words as possible, and when words were necessary, they talked to each other in their high-school French. That is touching; it is part of a period that may be almost gone. But as the embarrassment left them they began to tell each other what they wanted in English. That was good because they really knew more words in their own language!

In bed you have to consider the other's sensitive feelings. It is not the time to criticize performance; that should probably be saved for another time, and not in the bedroom—the temple of love. But the couple should allow and accept *some* awkwardness. Lovers bump heads sometimes! Or her breast gets pinched under his weight, or someone's funny bone gets a poke. A word of protest, as good-natured as possible, may be given and may be accepted without feeling hurt.

In some of the sexual exercises in sex therapy, which are really sexual pleasures and can become part of a couple's repertoire, words are used. In the start-stop exercises I'll talk about later the man *tells* (perhaps I should say *asks*) her to start, to stop, to go slower or faster. And once the silence is broken a couple tends to use words for communication whenever they are needed—without spoiling the mood. Words are no longer undesirable at that time.

I don't suggest turning lovemaking into a boring discussion! Words can be functional, plain, or they can be playful, encouraging, loving.

I suspect that words during sex, at least occasionally, are part of every great loving couple's repertoire. But a line of patter annoys some people while they are having sex, and in a good relationship a partner may be asked to refrain from too much commentary.

A certain guy had the habit of talking baby talk during sex, and trying to show that he was appreciative. Also of saying how excruciatingly pleasureful the feelings at the base of his penis were. I say terrific, if the woman likes it or doesn't mind. But it drove this fellow's wife up the wall and she asked him to do it *less*.

That hurt his feelings but he got over it.

Very often a sex partner feels the need to say right out that a certain thing during sex is no good for him or her, but won't because the other's ego may be wounded. I say, compromise! Do tell the other person, but softly, not hurting. Say the sex is so wonderful, you don't want this or that distraction just then! Is that lying? I don't think so.

I hear much more often from women that they are afraid of wounding the man's ego. The male ego has been depicted as made of flimsy stuff. To treat a man as if he can't survive a little direction about *your* feelings is to treat him like an idiot. Don't worry so much about the male ego. Like his erection, it will make a comeback.

A WEEKLY SEX TALK

Some people (thousands, thank heaven!) make a custom of listening to my Sunday night talk programs. They are not all earnestly tuning in to get expert advice or sex education! The program is entertaining for them. It is even—look, I know it—good for some laughs. It is harmlessly voyeuristic; it affords the human pleasure of hearing about other people's intimate joys and difficulties. But it does disseminate a lot of information in an easy-to-take way. My good old radio program!

Now, I think a couple might well institute a weekly sex discussion. At each one, let each partner bring up a topic close to home in the spirit of helpfulness. This doesn't have to be the soberest business in the world; there is room for a little frivolity, playfulness, and much more time for digression than on my talk show. But once a week let the couple talk about factual sex between them. Establish the easy habit of bringing out special pleasures and, if any, grievances. This would go a long way toward preventing a great silence developing.

JUST TO ME YOU DON'T TALK!

It is a shame how many husbands and wives and lovers there are who can't discuss issues of great importance concerning them both.

It is a wonderful fact that in this enlightened age a man can talk sex to his secretary or his female office manager without being thought vulgar, that his wife can bandy sex humor with bus drivers and maybe even the minister. But when it comes to issues arising in their own bedroom, this free-talking pair become tongue-tied. Superficially they are uninhibited about sex, but when it comes to revealing their real feelings they are back in the era of high button shoes. And as the issues become more and more serious, the silence between the pair deepens, so that in public they talk like Brave New World people, sexual flippancies plentiful as candy corn at Halloween, and in private sex becomes the unmentioned topic.

There used to be a joke about buses in Israel. All over the world, the joke went, the buses carry a sign that reads, PLEASE DON'T TALK TO DRIVER WHILE VEHICLE IS IN MOTION. But in Tel Aviv the sign reads, JUST TO HIM YOU HAVE TO TALK?

In certain marriages a spouse might do well to wear a sign saying, JUST TO ME YOU DON'T TALK SEX?

Even more absurdly, husband and wife may carry on conventional sexual chitchat and wisecracks *together*, but never, on any account, mention the serious subject that they have buried between them.

THE LOUSY LOVER AND THE UNLOVED WIFE

Agnes and Bert find less and less going on in the bedroom but neither will bring it up because each is so much ashamed and hurt. He is convinced that he is a lousy lover. She has not told him so, but he guesses that's because there is really no reason to. He figures that between kindness and contempt for his last few performances, she has decided to maintain silence. First from night to night, then from week to week, finally from month to month, sex and any serious mention of it have been avoided.

Agnes, meanwhile, is sure that he finds her undesirable. The novelty has worn off, and his eyes have opened to the fact that she is neither a lily nor a rose, nor a cupcake, nor anything like that, but perhaps more like a leftover boiled potato. He doesn't want to touch her and he is keeping up a cruel silence about it. As for those low-grade sexual performances the last three times, they only prove what she suspects. He isn't attracted to her.

If they had ever had the habit of talking about sex in any but a totally superficial, joking way, they might have discussed this away before it ever got started.

THE JEALOUS WIFE AND THE WORN-OUT HUSBAND

She is convinced that he is the most desirable fellow in the world. She made that plain from the first. He was so flattered he married her. You don't get that kind of admiration very often! But she is sure that women in the office, in stores, coffee shops, on commuter trains are all spinning webs for her hero. She *knows* that the way to keep him on the leash is to drain his semen daily. And any time he hasn't got an erection, she'll start questioning him about where he has spent every minute for the last twenty-four hours.

At last he balks at having sex every night at eleven-thirty like clockwork, and she screams at him that he is giving at the office. He becomes silent, and after a day or two she gives up trying to pry out of him the names of his three other women.

He doesn't want her to know that he is simply exhausted sexually. After all, why does she love him? Because of her inflated notions about his magnetism and sexual prowess. He can't tell her he's just a regular commuter who would like a night off now and then. He is beginning to wish he had married a certain co-worker, because she looks as if she hates sex.

Because of her delusions about his movie-star quality and his resentment at not being able to live up to them, they can't talk to each other about the important sexual issue between them. In the present painful circumstances it is very hard to begin such a conversation, and the truth is they have never had a frank sex talk in the past to use as a precedent.

THE POTATO MASHER AND THE FRAGILE FLOWER

From somewhere or other he got the idea that the way to act was fiery and forceful, though in truth he is a very mild-looking man who suggests Anthony Quinn to nobody but himself. Whenever he kisses his wife he mashes his mouth against hers; she's afraid for the enamel inlay on her chipped tooth. She protests a little, pushing him away with little shows of ill temper and saying, "Eugh, Bancroft!" This makes him laugh and he makes growling sounds and mashes her mouth again. She thinks of him as mostly stubble, buck teeth and the smell of bar-car booze on his breath. All these effects might actually be masculine and attractive if he ever had a heart and kissed her cheek lightly. He drives into her mouth the same way during sex, which she might otherwise enjoy.

Why doesn't she just say she'd like to be kissed in a gentler style? She does, but not in a way he hears. The fact is that the kisses have turned her off to him and she is past wanting to correct this misguided pretense of passion. She'd rather just turn her face away and say, "Eugh, Bancroft." And *that* he thinks is funny.

At an earlier point, before she decided she really didn't want him very badly sexually at all, a frank discussion of his kissing style might have turned their love life onto a pleasanter path.

SO YOU WON'T TALK, EH?

A certain wife wanted to talk about some things that weren't happening in bed, but her husband wouldn't talk about it. He resisted. She wanted to start a dialogue, not a war, so she just went out and bought a sex manual and began reading it to herself.

"Why are you reading that crap?" he asked.

"It's interesting."

"What's interesting about it?"

"It's about something real. I like to know about everything. After sex I'm going to read about investments, then the Middle East."

"That stuff is just a lot of crap."

"Okay, honey, you read about sports, I'll read about sex. Each to his own."

Later on he picked up the book and read it. His whole manner said, "I'm just curious what kind of crap you want to read." As she made no comment, he was free to read on out of real interest.

When he wanted to talk to her about it she let him. They began talking about sex seriously, and she saw to it that the dialogue continued.

It isn't always that easy. This husband was reasonable compared to some; he suspected she got the book to start a dialogue, but he went along in a face-saving way. Some partners, male and female, will do things like throwing the book into the garbage, or even out the window!

In the end many a partner who wants a discussion has to go, on his or her own at first, to a marriage counselor or sex therapist. The problem is serious enough to justify that.

CLINICAL CRITIQUES AFTER SEX

I do not suggest that people hold clinical critiques of each sexual encounter at breakfast. If that is what you *want*, okay. But it isn't what I suggest.

THE SEXUAL VOCABULARY

Since sex talks between lovers are not only for discussing clinical matters, the language to be used is not always clinical language. When a couple sit close and whisper naughty arousing things to each other, they may not want the medical-sounding Latin words but rather the plainer folk-language words like "cock" or "pussy," or words they make up just for private use. Couples know how they feel about the words.

I always use the Latin for a reason. It is respectable and gives the least offense to the greatest number of people in any audience. It suggests that we are talking about a dignified subject. And the Latin terms like *vagina, penis, clitoris, vulva, ejaculation, orgasm, erection* are clear as to meaning. If I say "penis" the whole audience knows what I mean. If I say "dick" it may mean the student you came to the lecture with. For being able to speak clearly, everyone should know as many of the scientific words for sexual things as possible.

11

An Indian
Love Manual

I WANT to talk a little bit about the great Sanskrit love
manual, the *Kama Sutra*. A few short decades ago
college students of the mildly daring sort would leave
Brooklyn College or Columbia, or other outlying points,
and take the subway to Greenwich Village and buy a copy
of the *Kama Sutra* in a Village bookshop. What a thrill!
Advice on exotic lovemaking from the land of tigers and
elephants.

Reading it was exciting, and for some young people even
arousing. That was before you could buy a magazine, in
your own neighborhood, with photos of pretty girls smiling
as they played with themselves. You had to look at the
National Geographic for photos of bosoms and read classics
for a sexy bit here and there. In those deprived times the
Kama Sutra was hot stuff.

The *Kama Sutra* was written by one Vatsyayana, who
himself said he wrote it while a student of religion and
higher wisdom, with the highest intentions. And he could
say that without being laughed at too much, because in the
Indian tradition *kama*, or the way of love and earthly

affection and sensual enjoyment, is compatible with a life of wisdom and grace.

A modern sexologist can have very kind feelings toward Vatsyayana and his book. We may be tempted to pat it on the head, this book written seventeen hundred to twenty-three hundred years ago, and say, "Good boy—how did you know so much without help from us?"

I myself love Vatsyayana for his recognition of women's feelings and women's right to sexuality. But it seems that this in itself was a common thing, though Vatsyayana's time was not an era of female liberation. It was rather a time when wise men preferred to use understanding instead of harshness in managing women. Brutal suppression was not harmonious. It was what you might fall back on if you were a failure at living.

The *Kama Sutra* of Vatsyayana was in an Indian tradition. There were earlier *Kama Sutra*s, or books of love admonitions. Vatsyayana would not have written a new kind of book. It would not have been respectable to do so!

I am especially pleased with Vatsyayana's advice on making love to a virgin bride. It embodies so much we teach today about not rushing or pressuring the young person, but slowly and gracefully building up confidence and intimacy. Let me quote parts of this charming passage from the *Kama Sutra*:

"For the first three days after marriage, the girl and her husband should sleep on the floor, abstain from sexual pleasures, and eat their food without seasoning. For the next seven days they should bathe amidst the sounds of auspicious musical instruments, should decorate themselves, dine together and pay attention to their relations as well as to those who have come to witness their marriage. On the night of the tenth day the man should begin in a lonely place with soft words, and thus create confidence in the girl.

"Women, being of a tender nature, want tender beginnings, and when they are forcibly approached by men with whom they are but slightly acquainted, they sometimes suddenly become haters of sexual connection, and sometimes even haters of the male sex. The man should therefore approach the girl according to her liking. He should embrace her first of all in the way she likes most, because it does not last for a long time. He should embrace her with the upper part of his body because that is easier and simpler. If the girl is grown up or if the man has known her for some time, he may embrace her by the light of a lamp, but if he is not well acquainted with her or if she is a young girl, he should then embrace her in darkness. When the girl accepts the embrace the man should put a betel nut and betel leaves in her mouth and if she will not take it he should induce her to do so by conciliatory words, entreaties, oaths and kneeling at her feet. . . . At the time of giving the nut he should kiss her mouth softly without making any sound. . . . When she is gained over in this respect he should then make her talk, and ask her about things of which he knows or pretends to know nothing.''

Later Vatsyayana says he should touch her young breasts, and if she resists he should say he won't do that again if she will embrace him, and by and by he should place her on his lap. . . . On the second and third nights he should feel the whole of her body and kiss her all over, then progress to slightly heavier petting, but he should not begin actual congress. After this he should teach her the sixty-four arts of love, should tell her how much he loves her and promise to be faithful. And at last he should begin to enjoy her in a way so as not to frighten her. All to create confidence in the girl.

This was how a young man who had been taught the sixty-four arts should behave with a girl who supposedly did not know them. Let me say that today it is nearly universal that the man is much less instructed, and it is not unusual that the girl is as much in need of having her confidence built up as any Indian maiden of two thousand years ago. And there is such bumbling and nervousness today as you might not believe!

How helpful this leisurely ritual would be to a young couple! He would know what he was supposed to do, and could proceed so slowly. No need to try to play the hero, like some movie actor who in reality has had to do the scene over and over to get a good take. Just the table of contents of the *Kama Sutra* is instructive. There is a section on the embrace, just hugging . . . on kissing . . . on pressing or marking with the nails . . . on biting, or making hickeys . . . on the various kinds of lying down and different kinds of congress . . . on courtship, with more about employing go-betweens . . . on how a woman should act in the absence of her husband . . . on the examination of the state of a woman's mind (what we call sensitivity) . . . on how a girl can talk to her lover when she is too shy . . . Much of which any woman might use.

Sometimes in the excitement of lovemaking people become a little violent. Even this is ritualized in the *Kama Sutra*, recognizing that it has a place but should not become harmful. There are different ways of hitting each other to express orgasmic abandon, with different appropriate vocal effects. About this the *Kama Sutra* says that such passionate actions may become uncontrolled; therefore, the man who knows his own strength and the tenderness, impetuosity and strength of the young woman should act accordingly. And the final words about this are that the various modes of enjoyment are not for all times and for all persons but should be used only at the proper time.

The *Kama Sutra* observes that men judge women's amorous propensities by the women's physical appearance. Now, we know this ancient idea lives today. Certain kinds of hips or breasts, certain kinds of lips or eyes indicate passion of certain kinds. But Vatsyayana cautions against this system of appraisal and suggests learning the woman's true nature and responding to this more slowly acquired knowledge.

India today is a country where women's rights hardly exist. *Suttee* may be outlawed. Women don't burn themselves alive on their husband's funeral pyres, but they are still inclined to devote themselves entirely to their men. But from honored Indian love teachings we could learn much.

12

You Say You Love Me but You Don't Even Come

*I*GET lots of letters from people who listen to my radio show. These letters usually have questions about the writers' sex lives, but they often begin by saying something nice about my show, so I call this my fan mail. I like to think I'm in show business! Sex educators have their fantasies too.

One fellow writes and says that his girlfriend always wants him to ejaculate. She is not satisfied with less than that. If he does not ejaculate, she thinks he doesn't love her. Maybe, she fears, he is ejaculating for someone else. Or maybe he just doesn't want her so much now. If he really loves her, the sure sign is ejaculation.

IT'S DIFFERENT EVERY TIME

I write back saying for him to try, very gently and lovingly, to persuade her to give this idea up. Wise lovers, couples who have sex together regularly, do not expect every lovemaking to be like all the other times—because each time is bound to be a little or a lot different from all the other times. Sometimes one partner wants to have an orgasm and the other just wants to be loving and to give pleasure without having an orgasm himself or herself. The other partner should accept this.

HOW DOES SHE KNOW?

But this letter raises a number of questions. For one thing, how does she *know* that he ejaculates or doesn't? Of course she can tell if she is stimulating him to orgasm with her hand or mouth, and *some* women can feel the seminal fluid in their vaginas. Probably most women cannot feel this. Past the area of lips and clitoris the vagina is largely insensitive. But is that what the letter writer's girlfriend means—that she is one of those who can feel the ejaculation? Probably not. Probably she means that she likes to have him moan and whimper and growl and thrust harder and faster and generally carry on, enacting the drama of sexual release.

No one will deny that a woman who likes that kind of flattery and fun and excitement has a right to ask for it, but not each and every time.

Why not? Isn't it easy for a man to ejaculate? Much easier than for most women to have orgasms? So isn't it mean of a fellow to deny a girl what he can so easily give her?

EVEN MEN HAVE THEIR MOODS

It *is* much easier for most men to have orgasms than for most women. The nerve endings that give the man sexual pleasure—sometimes called the pain that feels so good—are nearer to the surface. A boy's best-known sexual part hangs out and draws his attention and so he masturbates more, and in general more boys teach themselves to have sexual pleasure this way than girls do. But there are times when a man just doesn't feel like having an orgasm and ejaculating—

two things that nearly every male does simultaneously. A man sometimes doesn't want to have sex at all, and he shouldn't be pushed about that. Sometimes he can claim the right to beg off the same as she can. And it is wise to let him give pleasure sometimes purely in the spirit of giving, touching her as skillfully as he can, or tonguing, or letting her rub against his thigh, or holding her while she pleasures herself. Or whatever is in the couple's repertoire.

But why doesn't he want to have an orgasm? Isn't it fun, even if he's tired?

Not if he's too tired. And it isn't always a matter of being tired—at least not in the sense of being physically tired. One may speculate on other reasons, but the best idea is just to accept that a man who loves you may not want to take you fully every time you offer yourself. It doesn't mean that he doesn't love you. It may mean that he *does* love you.

A PART OF MALE PLEASURE

It is definitely a part of male sexual pleasure to be giving pleasure to the woman, especially with the more experienced male, and very often a man wants to indulge in this part of lovemaking without taking pleasure himself in any other way. He wants to be her love servant. That a man wants to do that can give the woman a very special pleasure too. He is saying, "This time is just for you." Now, that is very nice of him, and a man should be encouraged to be nice!

Sometimes a man is filled with intense reverence for Woman, for her body and her soul, and he wants to express this by acts of service and adoration—kissing her feet, kissing and tasting and smelling her. He wants to express his poetic feelings for Woman and for this particular woman. I say, let him! Encourage it! Let him love you that way now and play the conquering hero another time—in ten minutes, or next Wednesday!

Accept his making love to you in a variety of moods and ways. Encourage him to show variously his many loving feelings.

ORGASM AND EJACULATION

A little way back I said that men nearly always achieve orgasm and ejaculate at the same time. Just for general information, which may come in handy sometime—perhaps while making love to a man, perhaps while showing how much you know on a sex quiz—here are some interesting facts about that. Well, *I* think they are interesting, so they must be. It is not my fault if they make you yawn.

Men have orgasms and ejaculations at the same time, or very nearly the same time. When they reach the plateau phase they thrust and pump away, knowing the great release is very near. There comes a feeling that after this there will be no turning back, and then begin a series of muscle spasms at the base of the penis and in the surrounding area, and these produce pleasure. Jets of milky fluid shoot from the penis. A sight to see!

Perhaps you saw the movie *Personal Best*, in which the girl persuaded the boy to let her hold his penis while he urinated. He felt silly about it but she persuaded him by saying she wanted to because she had always wanted to pee standing up. She stood behind him and aimed it at the toilet. The audience only saw her back as she stood behind him and turned on the faucet to encourage him and then held his penis with both hands but out of sight. It was an amusing scene and of course she was satisfying a girlish curiosity. There is another thing many a young woman has found absolutely fascinating, and that is to watch for the first time ever, a penis ejaculate. This usually happens because she is ready to do for him what he has usually done for himself but is not ready to go the whole way. But sometimes it is after she has gone the whole way but is very curious about his apparatus. To see the semen shooting out of the penis and think, "I did that!" is both informative and thrilling.

Generally the penis is hard when it ejaculates, but not always. Sometimes by milking a soft penis like a cow's teat the semen can be induced out. The man's pleasure then is much less. It is much better, whether he is doing it or she is doing it for him, to go slowly and teasingly until the penis is very hard. (This is part of the charm of the stop-start exercises used for training a man to control the timing of his orgasm. And I do want people to think of those exercises as pleasure.)

Some woman is asking, "If a penis is soft, why would anyone be masturbating it? Isn't an erection the signal of wanting?"

A CASE OF POOR CONCENTRATION

Sometimes a man has other things on his mind when he should be thinking about enjoying himself sexually. He may have the habit of always thinking about his business affairs. He can drive through the Rockies and not see a mountain, go to the movies and not see Brooke Shields, read twenty pages of a book and take none of it in. He can go fishing and have a fish on his hook ten minutes without noticing. He never hears anything his wife tells him. A man like that may think, "I feel tense. If I masturbate it will help me relax." But his mind is not on it; he can't hold a fantasy. He is masturbating, believe it or not, out of a sense of duty! His penis only becomes half-erect, then droops; he is impatient and he pulls on it roughly or rubs the base of it, underneath, until he has a very minor orgasm and some semen is released.

This kind of low-grade sexual pleasure can become a habit. The man can be depressed about the very fact that it gives him so little pleasure and so wants to get it over with and stop thinking about that. He may be unhappy masturbating because he perceives self-pleasuring as shameful. It isn't something he can brag about to anybody. He wishes he were a hero and had a movie star to have sex with, or that he had enough money to hire a classy call girl, or any combination of unhelpful ideas about himself and what he is doing.

I would like to point out that this is not a contemptible man. He may be a very nice fellow, with good instincts, but at a bad point in his life where this practice is becoming habitual. Pure sexual guilt will not do this; it is more likely to be connected with all kinds of failure feelings about everything he tries to do. From worrying about everything he can concentrate on nothing and do nothing right, not even masturbate. One good experience may put him on a happier path of behavior. For instance, performing some calming, constructive task like digging a flower bed in his garden or splitting some logs for his stove or fireplace may give him a sense of having done a good thing, had some exercise, become pleasantly tired.

Of course it would be helpful to see a therapist, who will listen to him and give him some advice—maybe about having sex in a better way, maybe even telling him to do something like digging a flower bed, or making up a schedule of things to do daily and trying to concentrate on doing whatever he is doing at any given time.

EJACULATING ON DEMAND

There is a certain occasion when masturbating may become difficult for almost any man. Suppose he is at a clinic where sperm counts are made. He is in for a sperm count. The nurse gives him a little cup and says, "In there, Mr. Jones." Next he is in a strange room by himself, a very clinical-looking closet, with a strange woman outside timing him. He finds it hard to fantasize. By just massaging himself industriously he can get some semen out. It doesn't look like much, knowing that someone will be seeing it! Regular sperm donors get better at it, of course. But it is not a situation that is conducive to sexual pleasure.

And that brings us back to the beginning of this chapter, about the fellow whose lady always demands that he ejaculate. That is much like having the nurse send you into that strange, clinical little room to ejaculate. In neither case does the man really want to do it, and demanding is not the way to get the best out of him. Maybe it is the most businesslike way to get a sperm sample, but it is demeaning to the man. A sperm clinic can't keep a stimulating woman in the little room to collect sperm samples. But a loving woman is unwise to demand an orgasm every time. That is too businesslike too. She should let him off when he is not with it. Either let the sexual moment pass gracefully, or let the man pleasure her without having to "produce" this time.

13

Clitoral and Vaginal

*I*T has been said that the average American knows more about cars than about the clitoris. This is deplorable from my point of view! I would like in my lifetime to raise the level of sexual literacy, especially in this country where I have such a good time. Especially in Colorado, where the skiing is magnificent!

A sexually literate person should know about the clitoral-vaginal controversy. This will make him a very interesting person to sit next to at a big dinner party. It is easier to master the basics of vaginal-clitoral than the monetary problem or Central America or the Middle East. *Much* easier.

A MAP OF THE TERRITORY

One should have in one's mind a picture of the territory of the female genitalia. One student studied a few drawings and made a practice of diagraming female genitalia on the endpapers of textbooks, on desk tops, men's room walls, etc. Well, if we must have graffiti, at least let it be literate and instructive.

A child asked me once, "Where is the lady's vagina?" Only he pronounced it "bagina." We were in an art museum and looking at a statue. This afforded me what we call a teaching opportunity. There was the question, and there was the nude stone lady. Very quickly I pointed and said, "In there. Vagina." I did not hold forth at length, only because there was a museum guard nearby and I had not, after all, been invited to give a lecture. On my radio show I will describe things in detail, but there I am *supposed* to. You'd be surprised how proper I am in public places, or with people who have not invited me to enlighten them.

Once an actress, in a movie I saw on a plane, said, "You showed those children a picture of a woman's bare vagina." That was funny, because you can stare at a naked woman all day and never see her vagina. It is inside, you see. If she lies with her legs spread enticingly you do not see her vagina. What you see are her external genital parts. These *conceal* her vagina. They also conceal her clitoris and her urethral opening, where the urine comes out.

Her external, or visible, genitals are grouped together under the term *vulva*. This means the visible lips, inner and outer, and the slit between them.

To understand the clitoral-vaginal controversy, you must know where the clitoris is and where the vaginal opening is in relation to the clitoris.

Imagine one of those pretty young women who show their vulvas in the magazines. Just for us she is lying back, legs spread, knees raised and holding the lips of her vulva apart so we can look in. Thank you, my dear.

Near the top of this vertical mouth, as it has been styled, is a little protuberance. It is a little redder than the surrounding pink mucous membrane. Our obliging model points to it delicately with a forefinger, still holding the lips apart. When she masturbates her practice is to stroke the area *near* the clitoris rather than the clitoris itself. There! She is showing us how she does it—more or less, since she doesn't usually hold the lips apart when she is pleasuring herself.

When she has aroused the clitoris to a certain pitch of excitement, it gets erect, the hood of tissue around it swells and covers it. This is the clitoral hood that you have heard about. With that in place she rubs much harder and the protected clitoris produces stronger and stronger throbs of pleasure until she reaches orgasm, making pretty sounds in her throat. Soprano sighs and cries.

That was the clitoris. Now, traveling downward for three inches, we come to the opening of the vagina, so called because that is the Latin word for *sheath*, and this orifice makes a sheath for the penis.

Inside that opening *is* a limp elastic sheath, to be sure, that stretches to accommodate quite a large penis or, if the invading penis is of more modest size, envelops it closely.

At the outer end of the vagina, near the opening, there are some nerve endings. The lady can feel touches there. Farther in she can feel nothing.

Let me point out that when she masturbates, her finger is *nowhere near the vaginal opening*. If you pictured her working her finger in and out of the vagina to produce pleasure, or imitating the pistonlike action of a penis with a candle or a dildo, you were wrong. She does the whole trick, from start to finish, without going near the vagina. It is the clitoris, the rudimentary penis, that she stimulates. This is how most girls and women masturbate, by stimulating the clitoris and not going near the vagina.

Please keep two points in mind.

The clitoris is not in the mouth of the vagina, but a distance above it.

Female masturbation is possible by playing with or around the clitoris, going nowhere near the vaginal opening.

I think that is enough for today. Next time we'll consider a penis going into the vagina.

THE CASE OF THE MISSING ORGASM

Good morning. The last time we considered the fact that the clitoris and the vagina are really not together. The clitoris is at some distance above the vaginal opening. Miss X obliged by masturbating and having a good time for our benefit as well as her own. All without touching her vagina, mind you.

Today Miss X is with us again. As she prefers to be called Angie, let us do that. Angie was going to have sex with a fellow we shall call Bingo, who is to be seen in his bathrobe. Angie and Bingo, any time you are ready!

Well, I think you will all agree that it was very nice of Angie and Bingo to have sex for us like that, and I think we should give them a nice round of applause.

What I want to point out to you is that while Angie had a good orgasm yesterday by masturbating for a matter of three minutes, seven minutes of sexual intercourse with Bingo produced no pleasure at all. The secret of this failure is purely physiological. Bingo's penis, of more than respectable size, thrust and thrust inside the vagina but was nowhere near the clitoris. But now as you see, Angie is masturbating for us again, in the same way as yesterday, and she is beginning to become aroused, very much aroused, and in a minute or so will again have a terrific orgasm all by herself, without Bingo and without, as I want to make plain, without touching her vagina. While she is finishing let us make use of the time by considering this phenomenon.

Angie has shown that a woman can have a terrific orgasm by stimulating her clitoris and then have no orgasm at all from having sex with a great big hunk like Bingo, with such a penis! And then after becoming excited by the episode with Bingo she decides to have a good orgasm again. This is typical of millions of women in this world, who have clitoral but not vaginal orgasms—to use a very much discredited terminology.

There is nothing Angie can do about not having orgasms just from intercourse, real or simulated. That is just the way she is. It is possible that in the future she may change in this respect. Ah, there she goes—another terrific orgasm!

Well, yes—we have already given Angie a hand for having sex, but there is no harm in applauding her again if you want to. Thank you, Angie, so much!

I see our time has run out. At the next session we shall consider further ramifications of the clitoral-vaginal controversy.

JUVENILE AND MATURE, HE SAID

Angie—I hope everyone understands that her demonstration was purely fictitious, and that I do not run classes like that, not even for sex-therapy trainees—has orgasms only by directly stimulating her clitoris. This is not true of all women. A vast number, though certainly not the majority, have orgasms through sexual intercourse, while a penis moves gratifyingly inside the vagina.

Sigmund Freud, the father of psychoanalysis, theorized that women who had orgasms only from direct stimulation of the clitoris were sexually immature, while the women who could have orgasms from intercourse were mature sexually. He characterized the first type of orgasm as clitoral, the second type as vaginal. The implication of his theory is that the clitoral orgasm is a little-girl-masturbating thing, and that the vaginal orgasm is a sign of being a grown woman, like fully developed breasts.

This characterization of the so-called clitoral-orgasm women as immature made them feel inferior, and also guilty since they supposed that somehow they had damaged themselves as children by playing with their clitorises.

Now, I don't want to blame Freud too much, because his theory seemed to make sense. After all, the supposition was that intercourse was the real sexual act, the central one, and that sexual pleasure should be derived from it. But his theory was in fact only a theory, never proved. And in modern sex therapy we do not go on the supposition that there is any truth in it. We have a theory of our own.

ALL FEMALE ORGASMS ARE CLITORAL

There are not two kinds of orgasms. All female sexual pleasure is connected physiologically with the clitoris. But different women have considerably different ways of having orgasms.

Angie, the woman in the imaginary demonstration of masturbation to orgasm without vaginal stimulation, represents an extreme of the type of orgasmic female who never achieves orgasm by vaginal penetration. She strokes the clitoral area (not the clitoris directly!) and never goes near the vaginal entrance—a possibility since the two points are far enough apart to allow this.

Let me point out some phony or theatrical aspects of Angie's performance, useful though it is for a certain purpose. First there was her never going near the vaginal entrance, whereas some touching of the entire genital area is almost universal in the arousal stage of masturbation. Women touch their inner thighs, run fingers through their pubic hair and massage their mounds, pet their outer lips and touch their vaginal entrances, all this providing a good deal of mental stimulation and a certain amount of low-level nerve-end reaction. Touching the vaginal entrance also provides some wetness, some lubrication, for the adventuring finger or fingers. This will be needed for rubbing along the clitoral shaft without irritating this dry area.

The alternative would be to have Angie put her finger in her mouth in an appealingly infantile way; that would lubricate the finger. Or she could anoint the finger(s) with hand cream or something of the sort.

Another stagy aspect of her performance is the presentation of her orgasmic ecstasy, so visible and audible and convincing—and so fakable! We took it all for real. You have my assurance that she really was having an orgasm, but in fact only Angie can know this. Neither her lover nor any other member of one of Angie's audiences can be sure of her sincerity. A close examination of her clitoris at different stages of excitation would show changes that are associated with different levels of stimulation, but in the end we have only her assurance that she was really having a good time. Which is really *my* assurance—the final one, since she is my creature, based on a vast amount of observation of female sexual behavior.

Just for a moment let's talk about the husband who is interested in whether or not his wife has real orgasms. He has to take her assurance of this, given in movements and vocal effects during the sexual act, and afterward in words. But it is *her* orgasm after all, and only she knows how good it was or whether it was faked or real. So the husband has to trust her in this, as in so much else. It is a marvelous example of the absolute necessity to have faith in a wife! The wise man has faith in her; the fool drives himself nuts with doubts.

Nowadays we warn women against faking orgasm to please men. This leads them up a blind alley, because when they really want to ask the man for help in having real orgasms, they have to admit having posed as "sexually competent" women for so long. Which is pretty embarrassing, though not impossible to get through.

However, we do in a sense urge women to fake orgasm by being exaggeratedly demonstrative—bucking, squealing, breathing hard, crying out, speaking wild words. We urge this breaking of a dread sexual silence because these sounds and actions are so encouraging both to her man and to herself. They have an aphrodisiac effect. So we are not asking for total honesty in the sexual act, which could have the effect of turning the thermostat down and chilling the room, and at the same time we are warning against a specified kind of dishonesty. And let me tell you, sex therapy goes on like that from one end to the other, because sexual experience is not to be managed in a rigid way—it is altogether too personal, subjective and individual an experience to be produced by cut-and-dried procedures and regulations.

The person seeking sexual pleasure must, like the woman learning to pleasure herself, feel her or his way. Books and therapists may give good guidance, but you have to *feel* it for yourself.

OTHER WOMEN, OTHER WAYS

Returning to the female orgasm and the ways in which women reach it. Angie reached it purely by manipulating her clitoris. But hers is not the only way.

A woman I know can rub over the outside of her mound and external genitals, which moves the flesh around the clitoris in a stimulating way. And with certain men in certain positions this same mechanism produces orgasms for her during coitus. Think of that! She gets pleasure from having sex in the conventionally prescribed way. But it is still clitoral stimulation, you will note, and she has had orgasms by letting men, who have spent their seed early in the encounter, rub their pubic bones over her mound and the top of her genital opening. On one occasion a woman has brought her to orgasm in this way.

Adele has orgasms during intercourse by the induced action of her inner lips, which are moved over the clitoris as the shaft of the penis moves in and out of her vagina. This too, you will note, is orgasm by stimulation of the clitoris. But I fear that Freud and his followers would have classified it as vaginal orgasm.

For a great many women the presence of a penis in the vagina (or a penis substitute) intensifies orgasmic pleasure. They may have the trick of stimulating the clitoris with their fingers during intercourse, or having the man do it. Or they may hold a dildo of some sort in the vagina while masturbating. The effect of having the penis or penis substitute in place is probably both psychological and physical. This enhancement of orgasm by filling the vagina is especially keen among women who have strong pubococcygeal muscles with which to grip and release the contained phallus. An exercise to strengthen the pubococcygeal muscle (the Kegel exercise) is described in Chapter 30.

LET IT COME AS IT WILL

For couples who seek greater orgasmic release for the woman, we urge taking advantage of every avenue to this goal. Don't insist rigidly on achieving orgasm in a certain limited way. For one thing, certain couples may never reach that narrowly defined objective. For another, that kind of narrow goal defining can be a harmful inhibition and may prevent exactly what the couples are looking for—orgasm through intercourse without other clitoral stimulation. It seems to be the case that the more ways a woman learns and uses to come to orgasm, the wider her orgasmic possibilities are. The nerve ends down there seem to learn from each other and to cooperate better as the woman expands her orgasmic experience.

A NEW WAY OF SEEING THINGS

I think it is undignified and impious to pillory Freud as a male chauvinist monster for having promulgated the clitoral-vaginal distinction. He deserves perpetual honor for having opened the search for human self-understanding, particularly with regard to the role of sexual experience and the interplay of physical and fantasy in this area. You might say that his clitoral-vaginal distinction is simply a way of looking at, and organizing, the previously unconsidered evidence about female orgasms.

Now we have another way of looking at and organizing the material, and a great deal more direct observation of sexual behavior to use. Our new way gives a break to the majority of women who do not have orgasms by unaided intercourse. It says they are okay, and their ways are okay. This is kind and sensible and it seems a great relief to everyone to accept it. Not the least relieved being men who have felt inadequate because they could not "satisfy" their wives in the prescribed way.

There is a powerful lesson here. Why should all those women, and their men, have felt inadequate because of a misconception? Why did they not feel instinctively that their sexual lives were their own, and disregard the interfering disapproval of the tiny minority that laid down the Rules? It was, of course, because they were social creatures, law-seeking and law-loving, wanting to be whole and right in the eyes of the world, of God, and of themselves. Respect for expert opinion is not a bad thing—but new information is discovered in each generation.

14

Masturbation

*T*HIS little experimentation is for the woman who believes she has never had an orgasm. Can't remember ever having one. Never played with her own genitals, or has forgotten doing so, or something like that. The idea is to discover at some advanced age, such as seventeen or twenty-seven or thirty-seven or seventy-seven, those feelings that quite a number of girls discover when very young. These discoveries can be made at any age.

It often happens that a girl or a woman exploring this way may well hit on a very pleasant spot to touch, or a good way of touching, and she will repeat and repeat this action until something wonderful happens and she has an orgasm. I don't mean something high on the Richter scale, or anything like that. I mean something small but very pleasing. Once she has done this she will find time to do it again, in most cases. And with practice she can make that little orgasm grow bigger and bigger and bigger. And make it come quite reliably.

Here's a little exercise to start.

Casting aside all shame, the thing to do is to lie down naked on your back and abandon yourself to your own

112

fingers and your own most pleasing private thoughts. With your nice clean gentle fingers, explore yourself down there. The softest movements of your fingers are most likely to bring on the first tiny feelings. You may find one of these feelings almost at once—something like being just barely tickled, or like that feeling inside your nose when you say, "I think I'm going to sneeze."

Go in with your finger at the top parting of your genital lips and find that tiny penis, that nub, that "boy in the boat," and feel gently around it. For most women, stimulation in the area of the clitoris is more pleasant than on the clitoris proper. But this is for you to discover for yourself. Circling and rubbing movements should be tried.

Find the opening to the vagina, somewhat below the clitoris. There are nerve endings there and for a little distance inside the vagina. Stroking in this area may produce gentle reactions.

WORTH A SMILE

When you find a feeling, however tiny, stay with it awhile, just touching, rubbing back and forth, or in a circle, pressing lightly and stopping, finding which does best to bring that hint of a feeling. Suddenly you may cause a nice exciting sensation—on a tiny scale. This is worth a smile! I have often said that women don't smile during an orgasm because it's too overwhelming, but this little feeling is a small but sought-after thrill and certainly deserves a little smile or a silent "Hurrah!" A suborgasmic triumph.

Knowing how to get that feeling when you want it, you can learn to move. in a way that brings it on while making love with your man. Or you can show him how to give you that pleasure.

That's the basic idea, so now you can throw away the book and go have a happy sex life! On second thought, keep the book. Reading informative material is a nice pastime too—and you may learn something of good use to a friend who has a little more trouble with sex than you.

HARD WORK OR FUN?

Some women have a difficult time learning to find their own sexual responses. Yet they can learn to be orgasmic, and in the end they will be glad that they took the trouble. I would always prefer that the learning period *not* be grim but pleasant. I'm inclined to believe that the ability to feel good about "trying to masturbate" comes before the ability to have an orgasm. When the prospect of masturbating seems like a very depressing duty—well, it's too bad. I won't say that if a woman just keeps trying to find her "love nerve," as a certain poet called it, even though she hates the whole business, her efforts are doomed to disappointment. It can be done, even in the spirit of grim determination. But learning to masturbate and to have an orgasm through self-indulgence seems more sensible, of course. Why make learning such a chore?

I don't tell women to examine themselves with a mirror or to set aside a long period every day to explore their genitals. This sets up a resistance to the task, it seems to me. Let them look at their own reflection someday if curiosity overcomes them, but not think of this as a barrier to get through before beginning the little pleasure of touching down there.

There is no reason for them to rearrange their lives to make time for long sessions of this activity. I would rather they thought of this homework as easy, something that can be done almost anytime. There is something to having the security of a time and place where there will be no interruption. To drawing blinds, turning on soft lights and soft music, perhaps. On the other hand, some experimenting can be done in the shower or the bath as well as on the bed. It is nice to have this homework as something for which a woman might set aside some considerably more boring tasks around the place.

It is a good idea to buy some arousing books to read, and to read them in comfort, naked or loosely clad to give your hand access to your genitals and other parts. *Lady Chatterley's Lover* is really nicer reading if you can caress your breasts and thighs absently while reading of Mellors and Connie in the woods and glades.

The old picture of an idle woman reading French novels and eating bonbons can be replaced by one of her reading and idly stroking around her own pleasure zone.

DOING IT YOUR WAY

Women who learn to masturbate from a book or from a therapist are likely to begin by using their fingers Down There. Women who have other ways generally happened onto them while being "naughty little girls." Or just being little girls if they grew up in homes where a relaxed attitude prevailed. Whether you were a naughty girl or a nice girl depends almost entirely on how some grown-up made you feel.

There are lots of ways to masturbate, and here are a few I have gathered, given in the words of the girls and women who generously confided in me.

These women are safe in being quoted here. No names are used, and none of their methods is unique. No patent could be taken out on any method you find here.

A couple of these contributors may think they deserve a bigger credit! Well, darlings, I'm sorry. I'm grateful for what you have told me. But if I say in print that you are the Alexandra Graham Bell who invented one of these time-honored methods of self-pleasuring, people will only laugh. All these ways of doing it are old as the hills.

So, here is a modest—or *immodest*, if you insist—sampling of ways to get off by yourself on a modest budget.

THE JOY OF BICYCLING

"I learned on my bike when I was thirteen. It was a Schwinn, but I have had beautiful relationships with several imported ten-speeds since. What can I tell you? When you pass one of these girls in your car you see her buttocks working up and down and that hard leather seat right in her crotch and you think, 'How can she not be getting off?' In my case I do get off. Not off the bike, I mean. I get horny and have a grand old time. I feel sure that a lot of girls get nothing but a hot, sore crotch from cycling, and I swear I'll never understand how men can ride bikes at all. But me, I ride a bike and I am clitorally stimulated and I come. I also get to ride around on a bike, which I love for itself. I work in advertising and keep a bike exercise machine in my bedroom. My boyfriend knows why.''

ME AND MY PILLOW

"I knew this boy, he was about fifteen. I loved him out of my mind. I wanted him in the worst way. I was only eleven or twelve but I thought about him day and night. I knew it was wrong but I wanted him between my legs. I don't know how I knew about that. At night I lay and thought about him doing it to me. Then I got this idea of putting the pillow between my legs. At first I lay on my back, but then I turned over on my knees and really humped on the pillow and I came. After that I did it that way until I was fifteen, then I stopped until after I was married. It wasn't because my husband was no good in bed. He was okay. But sometimes I would lie in bed after he left in the morning for work and I would want to do it again, so I would hump the pillow. When I was about fifteen my mother asked how I got my pillow so messed up. I said, 'I don't know.' But we both knew.''

HOW I LIKE IT BEST

"I have done it a lot of different ways, but this is the way I like it best. I figured it out when I was in puberty. I close my four fingers and hold them down over my privates and move them in an upward and downward movement; up toward my mound and back toward my anus. I do this gently until I feel something and then faster and faster. My fingers are outside, over my lips. I can do this lying on my back, side or stomach. Also standing up or in the bathtub. I pretend I'm having sex with all kinds of men—some very nice, some horrible. When the orgasm is over I drift off to sleep. Sometimes for all night, sometimes just for a minute or two if it's in the daytime.''

REMOTE CONTROL

"I just think dirty thoughts and after a while I come. I don't know how it works but it always does. No, a few times I got bored or sleepy or something and just stopped. I have done this nearly all my life. I have never had any trouble having an orgasm anytime I wanted it, especially having sex with a man. Don't tell me that my thoughts aren't dirty! I like to have dirty thoughts.''

WHAT'S IN A NAME?

"I never did have an orgasm the way you're supposed to have it. My husband and I would just have sex, and he would have an orgasm and I started doing this thing. We never discussed it, but he never seemed to mind. I would roll over on top and kiss him and rub. Pretty soon I would get my vagina against his thigh—my thighs straddling it—and I'd rub up and down until I had an orgasm. That's the way we did it. Was that masturbating or what?''

A hard question to answer. Some people would definitely file that under masturbation.

NO PRELIMINARIES

"I discovered how to do it to myself when I was about nine or ten. Maybe I had done it earlier and forgotten for a while. It wasn't very subtle. I just put two or three fingers against my clitoris and rubbed. I learned this long before I ever saw my clitoris. When I was thirteen I balanced a little mirror on the arm of a chair and looked at myself, straddling the chair arm. I was pretty surprised but I survived. I always rubbed hard and fast, so I learned to put something slick on my fingers. I have used hand cream, olive oil, butter, Crisco, soap, spit, baby oil, mineral oil and who knows what. The point is, I would be dry until I started to rub hard and then after rubbing hard I would lubricate. I have also thought sexy thoughts and made myself lubricate that way, but sometimes I'm not in the mood. I'm like one of those men who can't waste time on foreplay.''

What this woman did was harmless for her, but an awful lot of women have to be gentle with the clitoris, especially before they are excited and the clitoris is covered with its protective hood.

USING A VIBRATOR

"I tried so hard for months after my therapist told me to masturbate. I had never masturbated and had never had an orgasm. I wanted to do both after talking with my therapist. I got discouraged and quit several times. I mean I quit masturbating and quit seeing the therapist. Then one day I got hold of a vibrator. It wasn't the kind that's shaped like a penis and runs on batteries. It ran on household current. The first time I used it I had my first orgasm. After that I was hooked on it. I would think about it at the office. I couldn't wait to get home. Sometime after that I met a man I liked and we had a good relationship even though I never had an orgasm without the vibrator. Who cares? I never had one before I got it. Why don't therapists tell their clients to go straight to the vibrator?''

Therapists shy away from having clients use the vibrator first as a means to achieving the first orgasm. We want them to learn to have orgasms from gentler stimulation—and, if possible, from coition. But one can get hooked on the vibrator and then learn other ways to have orgasms. Not that one need give it up entirely, just learn to have orgasms without that relentless vibration.

WHY NOT?

"My sister does it with a dildo and says it is very nice. She pushes it into her vagina and rubs her clitoris with her fingers. Is this normal?"

This is like a certain way of having sex with a man. With him inside and either him or the woman stimulating the clitoris manually. The feeling of the dildo or penis distending the vagina helps, and the direct stimulation of the clitoris does the rest. This is a normal means to orgasm.

SAFE, BUT USE CAUTION

"As a child, I learned to pleasure myself by sliding way down into the bathtub with my behind up against the end and the water from the faucet plunging right onto my clitoris. Now I have my own place with a flexible tube in the tub that sends a strong water jet wherever you want it. It's terrific for tired muscles too. Is this dangerous? I heard somewhere that it might be."

If you have used it without harm so far, it should be harmless. Naturally I can't guarantee the harmlessness of every mechanical device. You have to try them a little cautiously at first. I've never heard of a woman hurting herself with water from a household pipe. Water at higher pressure could be dangerous, and so could air from an air compressor—*never* use that.

Examine any kind of device or dildo and try it on your skin to be sure it has no abrasive places or sharp points. A mature cucumber has prickles sometimes—these should be rubbed off before you insert the cuke. Which makes a fine dildo, incidentally. I would use a lubricant on any foreign object to be inserted in the vagina. And I would clean any foreign object before I used the lubricant!

FINE FOR ITS OWN SAKE

Masturbation is a way to learn to have orgasms that can be continued for its own sake as a variation of sexual experience. The woman who knows how to pleasure herself can teach the art to a lover for a variant, for foreplay or afterplay, for an accompaniment to intercourse. To repeat, many women require direct stimulation of the clitoris to reach orgasm, and many others have never had an orgasm but probably can learn to have one. Women who have orgasms from intercourse alone are in the minority. No one should reproach herself or her life for not providing a minority pleasure—not when shared pleasure with a loving partner is an available blessing.

SOMETHING FOR THE MAN

As an appendage to this chapter, much as the unaroused penis is an appendage to the male body, I want to say a little about male masturbation. I really want to, I don't mind talking about it at all, and something should be said about it.

The reason it gets less space than female masturbation is that men nearly all know how to do it. It is not as it is with women, who come to a sex therapist with tragic eyes, wondering how to do it. With a man it is mainly whether he should do it or not do it.

A man may decide to do it because he has to kill some time by himself. Or he sees an old movie with a certain actress and recalls that he always wanted to masturbate while thinking of her but never got around to it. Or he goes to a party and finds some lady very exciting sexually but she goes off with a guy who had hired a limousine, or *something* stood between our hero and making it with her.

A man may decide not to masturbate because he has some feelings against it, and the sexual urge is not so strong right now that he can overcome those feelings. And then sometimes it happens that he starts masturbating but gets bored and quits. That really happens. It's a little like the woman who is having sex with her man and can't stop thinking about the shopping list or the twelve dozen napkins for the organizational lunch. Outside matters crowd her mind, or his mind, and destroy concentration on having sex. Making the fantasy fade out.

Sometimes I teach a man how to masturbate a certain way so that he can make a learning experience of it. I teach him the start-stop way of doing it so that he can learn to control his ejaculation—can overcome what is termed premature ejaculation. After that he will tend to masturbate that way because it continues to be a good exercise in controlling ejaculation and, as a matter of fact, it offers much greater pleasure sensations than just rubbing away until ejaculation occurs.

Women masturbating men really should know how to do that, because it is so pleasing to the fellow. I urge them to read the chapter on premature ejaculation.

WAKING A SLEEPER

Some tips on arousing a penis. This is very nice work and it is interesting to see the limp fellow begin to come to life. It may be done while the man is dozing, or when he seems to need some pleasuring but doesn't realize it himself, or is too pooped out to bring his attention to it. Try!

Feathery stroking with the fingertips.

Feathery stroking with long fingernails! Some of this on the scrotum, or testicle sac, may start things up.

Slide a finger just under the head and lift it slightly and let it drop. Repeatedly.

Brush your soft woman's hair over it.

Brush your breasts over it.

Hold it in your fist and squeeze just gently and rhythmically.

Kiss it and blow on it softly.

Press and rub penis and testicles through a satin sheet or pajamas.

Get the idea?

15

From the Sex Shop

*T*HERE was a very pretty woman who knew how to live her life, dealing briskly with problems and enjoying all kinds of things that chance put in her path, but also ordering things to please herself in every way she could. She was fond of good-luck pieces and cheering-up devices, "little things" that helped a great deal. There was her special perfume, used very sparingly, and her special shade of lipstick. And there was a certain little vase in which she always kept a cut flower on her desk. Her life wasn't entirely made up of things like this; she made a good salary and had lots of male suitors. But she used these little things to flavor life. She subscribed to a foreign newspaper because the news from that country always made her smile. She wore red shoes because "they make me walk faster." She *knew* that was an illusion, but a pleasing one.

A PRETTY WAY WITH A VIBRATOR

Another imaginative woman had a special way with certain sex toys she used. She kept her vibrator in a special blue satin-quilted box. That was its home. When she took it out or put it away she was doing something pretty and showing affection for this private possession. She wasn't fond of the buzz that it made when switched on—it sounded too "gadgety." But she had earphones she put on to listen to a tape of crickets and katydids. These sounds had important meanings for her; they were full of sweet late-summer sadness. The heavy pulsing sound of that chorus of insect mating calls filled her with the sensuality of life. They carried her back to childhood nights when she lay in bed in the last week of summer vacation, reveling in the tag end of a lovely idleness. And the sound was connected with tender partings from vacation sweethearts who would be leaving, going back to college. She could lie on her bed with her two appliances plugged in and her remembered feelings turned on and take herself into a private world of prolonged erotic sensations and, when she was ready, orgasm. She was even pleased with her thoughts about the electric current she was tapping. She thought of it as part of cosmic energy. This was not her only sexual outlet, either—she had a man she liked and had been sharing sex with for years.

The vibrator was a sex toy or sex gadget, if you like. What about the cassette player, the blue satin box and her memories? Without those the vibrator might have been, for her, just a little store-bought electrical appliance. But she used her human mind to invest this sexual experience with pleasant meanings.

Of the sex aids on the market today, the vibrator is the only truly modern one, and probably the most valuable to thousands of people. It has put many women in touch with long-buried sexuality. I am sure that lots of these women would have been too discouraged to persist in slower methods of reawakening sexual feeling. Once it has provided the key to orgasm, the vibrator often moves by degrees to the back of the drawer, but there is no reason why it can't be kept as one of a variety of enrichments in a full sensual life.

Not all the sex aids are found in the mail-order ads in sexy magazines. Wine, music, soft lights, food, soft snow falling in the twilight, atmosphere—those are sex aids too.

And the storekeepers, restaurateurs, musicians, innkeepers, travel agents and all the others in the pleasure industry know it. Look at all the lovers pictured in their advertising.

All these commercial products are there for lovers to use. I don't say they are required on every occasion for sex. A pair of healthy Appalachian Trail hikers, dressed in jeans and sensible shoes, carrying packs or rucksacks, tangy with fresh sweat from their exertions, find themselves on a fir-scented ledge with a glorious view—and make love on fir needles or an outcropping of rock. Sometimes in the rain or even on a bank of snow! As unimaginable as some people may find this, it is done all the time. As a sex therapist and avid alpine hiker, I have observed all this at first hand. Let me say that a blanket or groundsheet is good for keeping fir needles out of the crotch, and quilted winter gear can be adjusted for an inspired quickie amid snow and ice!

For sex in a warm summer rain no equipment is really needed. Doing it wet is part of the fun. Don't lie on needles, sharp stones or poison ivy, that's all.

One hiking enthusiast tells me that the smell of insect repellent has become quite an aphrodisiac for him!

You might say that for these people a plane ticket to hiking country is a sex aid. Other sex aids: cabin cruisers that take lovers away from the shore; vans; cars; cruise ships; airline package vacations...

Many women find the sound of breakers on a long beach arousing. The mighty ocean is a sort of sex toy for them....

An actor had to rehearse a scene with a very sexy actress. They showed up in rehearsal clothes—drab things totally unlike the bright Gypsy costumes they would wear in performance. She laughed and lifted her long skirt to show tennis shoes and short black socks she had borrowed from her husband. "Sexy, huh?" she asked. As a matter of fact, the actor thought they *were*. You never know what odd effect will seem sexy.

But that's as far afield as I am going to go. I only wanted to make the point that sex toys don't all come from sex shops. As for those that do, make sure you clean them before each use, no matter how you plan to use them.

THE EDIBLE GREEN DILDO

Let's talk about cucumbers. One night on my radio show, *Sexually Speaking*, a sprightly woman in her seventies phoned in and said she was looking for a man of a certain age—her own. Though younger lovers presented themselves, she preferred a man of her own generation who would know what she was talking about. But men of that age were apt to shy away from a relationship. I told her, the next time she met a nice man of her age, to talk to him about this. To tell him that she wouldn't expect a lover to have erections every night. Meanwhile, to masturbate, perhaps to use a cucumber. She thanked me and a year later she phoned back and said she had found a nice man her age and was going to marry him. A very heartening story!

But the cucumber; why tell her to get on a bus and go to a nearby city and visit the sex shops to find a dildo, or to look in *Playgirl*, find a mail-order dildo supplier and wait a week or two until her purchase came in a plain brown wrapper, when you can buy a cucumber or zucchini or banana at any supermarket?

(I wonder if anything really comes in a plain brown wrapper. That would be such a giveaway! A plain brown wrapper shouts, "Hey, mailman! Hey, neighbors! Something in a plain brown wrapper!" All you erotic book and sex-toy mailers, use a little imagination, okay?)

But a cucumber, a nice, natural cucumber. Nothing nasty or sleazy about a cucumber. A nice, natural green penis. Any seventy-year-old lady can keep it openly. A nosy visitor picks it up and asks, "Hmm—a cucumber?" All the owner has to say is, "I thought I'd have it for lunch."

"Seems to me you eat a lot of cucumbers."

"They're good for my system. They're full of vitamin S and tungsten. Besides, I like that sort of thing."

"What sort of thing?"

"Oh, cucumbers, bananas, zucchini, kielbasy . . ."

Artificial cucumbers (or penises) are a very ancient sex toy. And a very modern one. Dildos can be bought that look very much like erect penises, covered with soft latex to simulate skin. The phallus-shaped battery-powered vibrator is a kind of dildo. You can use it even if the battery has died. Douche nozzles used to be made large enough to serve as dildos; I haven't heard much about those of late. There are dildos men can slip over their penisis to make up for supposedly inadequate size. There are dildos attached to harnesses for women to wear and play the male role with other women. (It is wise to lubricate these substitute penises, incidentally.)

A sculptor made one of fine-grained hardwood to leave with his lady when he was away from home. Something like this is better than the end of a broomstick because broomsticks are made of splintery wood. And this sculptor's *object d'art* was carved of ebony or lignum vitae and polished, and had a little curve in it so she could simulate different positions.

They tell of a warrior prince who, on leaving his wife to go off to war, left her a silver dildo fashioned to look just like his own penis. It was hollow and could be filled with warm fluid. He also left her a greyhound puppy that got hold of the dildo and chewed it and ruined it.

If a puppy chews up a cucumber, who cares?

There are double dildos like Siamese penises, joined at the base. Theoretically two women can use these at the same time, simulating coitus. Reports on the practicality of these items vary, but not much. Lesbians generally say that there are better things to do!

There are several ways to use a dildo of the ordinary sort. A man can hold it in his hand and move it in his lady's vagina while she perhaps stimulates her own clitoris. Or she can work it back and forth while he manipulates her clitoris. Or she can simply insert the dildo and squeeze it rhythmically with her pubococcygeal muscle while using fingers of one or both hands on her clitoris. This is a very popular way to use the dildo.

WHY A FAKE PENIS?

There are plenty of situations in which a good fake, not necessarily a costly one, is better than a real penis. You may be shocked by the idea of the man using a dildo on his wife, but at a certain stage in their sex life that might be a good idea. To get her to have an orgasm in his presence, for instance, when she has great trouble reaching orgasm. This need not be their entire sexual repertoire, but it could be a valuable part of it. A dildo might be useful when he cannot have an erection every time they want to have sex together. They can use the dildo alternately with intercourse, oral sex, manual stimulation.

For the woman who finds herself on her own after a long sexual relationship has ended, the dildo may be a solace. Release from sexual tension, with pleasant fantasies, can give her leisure to consider her situation. She need not take up with the first man who comes around, however unsuitable he may be for her, just to try to assuage sexual longings. She can take charge of her own sex life.

And the dildo can be just one of a number of sexual variations a woman uses to keep alive her interest in sex.

A NIFTY ATTACHMENT

For many women coitus is unsatisfying because the clitoris is so far away from the action. If only it were in the entrance to the vagina instead of an inconvenient distance from it! To rub the clitoris with the same movement that strokes the vaginal nerve endings, some men attach to the base of the penis a device that massages the clitoris. Their feeling is that they have improved on anatomy to make sex better. This tiny ''finger'' parts the clitoral hood and touches the sensitive organ itself.

It works well for lots of people; others say not. But there is little harm in trying it. I only warn against wearing such a device if it is too tight around the erect penis. Never put a tourniquet around your neck or your penis—nor around anyone else's!

AND AS FOR PENIS RINGS!

By penis rings I mean, in my correct sex therapist's language, those things they write about and advertise in sex magazines as cock rings. You slip them down over a penis to the base and they strangle it and make it erect and keep it erect. They don't work for everyone, but they have that effect on many men—and they also bruise the penis and damage tissue and blood vessels, so find some other way to get an erection.

If these devices were faultless and harmless I suppose 40 to 50 percent of my clientele would disappear. If men could wear rings to give them lasting erections and women had hair ribbons that made them have orgasms easily, maybe sex therapy would disappear like quill pen making. But cock rings are dangerous. If you must wear one, better wear it in your nose.

FRENCH TICKLERS AND OTHER FANCY CONDOMS

Condoms with feathery rubber petals, ribbing or corn-kernel textures are supposed to drive women mad with pleasure, and perhaps these may do a little something extra if the texturing is near the open end, where the condom rubs against the entrance to the vagina, but the inner two-thirds of the vagina is insensitive. Any kind of fancy hat or neckpiece around the head of the penis is merely costume-party stuff. It may add to the gaiety of the occasion while the lady is putting the condom on her friend the penis. Ordinary condoms are so plain! I say a giggle during foreplay is fun, but I do favor serious standard-brand condoms because the makers take pride in reliability more than comic effect. I suggest using a diaphragm with condoms that are made for laughs.

CEILING MIRRORS

A large number of sex-aid users like to pass for very sedate pillars of the community most of the time. Call this hypocrisy if you are very young. If you are older, just call it having a change of pace, or the joys of being furtive. But with a looking glass on the ceiling you invite every guest who ever piles a coat on your bed during a party to label you a swinger, a show-off, a sheep in wolf's clothing or something like that.

If you are the one underneath in certain positions, the ceiling mirror lets you have sex while watching a live porn act—an orgiastic effect well worth paying to have the mirror installed, some people say. If you're doing it dog-fashion and keep looking over your shoulder, you may need to visit a chiropractor—it could put your neck out.

Mirrors all around, ceiling and walls, create the effect of all these other naked people going at it hammer and tongs, visible out of the corner of your eye. A scene from a porn flick. Or the best kind of swinging party—because they all go home when you turn out the lights! But this does mean having a whorehouse bedroom all the time, even when you feel like flannel pajamas and a good detective story to read in bed.

There are times when a couple feel like being *The Little House on the Prairie* people instead of the wildest scamps on Buena Vista Drive.

WATERBEDS

People don't always like to admit that they don't really like these once-trendy items, even now that the novelty is past. The fact is that the movement under you is worrisome unless a good deal of instability is what you like. I can think of a number of couples who need all the help they can get when copulating. Trying to do it on a bicycle or a tightrope or a waterbed is the last thing they need. These people are better off on the floor.

Any couple might try it a few times for the challenge, if they have no bad insecurity about doing sex acts at all. It is a stunt that can be learned with perseverance. But if just completing a sex act at all is a challenge, don't try it on a waterbed.

VELVET ROPES

There is nothing kinky about playing with bondage. Haha! If you believe that, you can believe anything. The whole *point* is kinkiness. But a great many people just like to play at being kinky. Take my clients Bob and Ann. Bob says that there is a way to tell whether your spouse is really a rope freak or just likes to play at it on certain nights or afternoons. Of course he's joking.

"Tie her up securely with half hitches and clove hitches or whatever knots you can devise—use only soft ropes that won't hurt too much. Actually, Ann made hemmed strips of some blue velvet curtains her aunt in Middletown passed on to us. Well, to see if she's really weird or just playing at it, tie her up and leave her there a couple of days. If she's still with it after forty-eight hours, she's from Strange City. If she's really normal, you have a divorce action coming your way. Just kidding, of course."

In the mail-order ads of the erotic journals there are fairly pricey sets of chains, straps and snaps for bondage games, but these are not for the once-in-a-while bondage people like Bob and Ann.

Bob has tied Ann to several beds since they first tried bondage. Often they don't even *do* bondage in places like a motel, but he just likes to show his ingenuity with ropes. The easiest bed is, of course, one with posts or legs, so he can spread-eagle Ann, tying her wrists and ankles to the four corners. Additional crisscrossing and half hitching binds her down by thighs, midsection and diagonally between her breasts. Then Bob very teasingly begins to draw a velvet rope end across her erogenous zones until she is excruciatingly aroused, whereupon he begins to pleasure her genitals so slowly and repeatedly and for so long that by the time she is close to orgasm she is straining strenuously against her bonds. That's the idea—to create the ultimate tension. Bob loves to see her body straining and writhing.

When it's his turn to be restrained he prefers instead to tie the velvet strips across the bed at head and foot and then to slip his feet under the lower strip and to grip the upper one with his hands. He obeys his own rules—no letting go of the "bonds." But in fact he can release himself at any time. "The reason for this is, well, we pretend it's because Ann can't tie so well. But really, frankly, I don't trust her. I never really gave her the two-day test, and for all I know she might go too far if she had me tied up and helpless. The act she puts on when she's tied—well, it's something. My trouble is I'm not sure it's an act."

This pretense of Bob's that Ann is potentially dangerous is something that he finds extremely arousing. I am not perfectly sure that he is *pretending* to be afraid of her.

Ann says nobody can ever be sure the other one isn't going round the bend, but that's the thrill, and that's why she insists on being tied up so that she's helpless.

"Of course, I wouldn't let anybody do that but Bob," she says. "After all—well, you know, *Bob*."

FUR, FEATHERS, SATIN, ETC.

When Bob draws the end of the velvet strip across her thighs and breasts and other sensitive skin, he is doing what is also done with bits of fur, feathers, satin and the like. Sometimes these materials are used teasingly in a more relaxed kind of behavior, much like the gentle pleasuring of the sensate focus exercises I discuss later—but they are wonderfully enjoyable as part of the bondage charade.

Satin sheets and pillowcases are delicious to slither about on as you kiss and caress, touch and tease in the arousal and slow stimulation ceremonies of foreplay. People joke about sliding right out of bed, or having a partner slip out from under. But even if these things happen, they are part of the fun.

Men are so seldom in slithery clothes that to dress them in totally friction-free nylon pajamas or gowns is a great pleasure to them and to their wives. Ann particularly likes to run her hands and herself up and down Bob's legs and body over a satin garment! Then to caress his genitals through the cloth—a preliminary to a sexual encounter of high intensity.

LOCAL ANESTHETICS AND STIMULANTS

Anesthetic ointments are sold in various forms—sometimes in tubes and sometimes as a coating inside condoms—that are supposed to delay ejaculation by making sexual contact less stimulating. In short, to prevent premature ejaculation by doping the penis. This is part of the strategy to make sex both longer lasting and more boring, like a treasurer's annual report. Hardly an aid to sexual enjoyment.

Spanish fly. This is a dangerous drug. Never use it—it can cause great pain, and injury. In fact, never use any aphrodisiac drug except, for relaxing or perking up, a little wine or a cup of coffee.

16

Accepting Pleasure

*P*LEASURE was put on earth for us to enjoy. A deep thought! But people do not accept pleasure automatically. It grows on them.

I am not going to talk about vice, or self-destructive habits that exclude all other milder and more beneficial habits. That is to be avoided. Pleasure is to be cultivated.

Young people seeking each other sexually act on an urge that is nearly universal in human beings, but perhaps it is not pleasure they seek but something young, green, overwhelming, passing. When Romeo and Juliet as young teenagers go to bed, that is as romantic and heartbreaking as can be—but cannot be called pleasure, something that will be returned to many times and will undergo many changes as life goes on. Romeo and Juliet died shortly after they met.

A man who has been married and had a good sex life, when asked, at age seventy-five, when was the happiest time of his life, said, "Now." He smiled and added, "It has always been the present, at every stage of my married life." No one would suppose that his whole married life had been one long record of unchanging sameness.

WHERE THE BROOK AND RIVER MEET

Longfellow pictured the budding young female as "standing with reluctant feet, / Where the brook and river meet." That is, where the gentle little stream of girlish feelings flows into the powerful current of womanly love and passion.

That is a picture of a girl maturing that is fairly lifelike for *some* girls. Here is an account of one woman's changing feelings. "When I was that age, midteens, I fell in love with boys at a little distance. I loved a certain kind of boy— handsome, rather serious, athletic, not rough but tough enough. He was not sexually aggressive. The boys who tried to rush to push the clock ahead and kiss me and put their hands up seemed piggy to me. I liked a boy who was a little indifferent on the surface. I dreamed of his kissing me in a white ruffled dress like the ones on romantic paperback covers. Then I imagined his Taking Me blissfully in a great house with grounds sloping down to the broad river. Okay? The details of penetration were vague, but the general idea gave me a feeling I liked. A week later it was the same fantasy with a different boy.

"When I began to date, the guys seemed to play up to my dreams. I had to make adjustments for their being able to talk, unlike the guys in my daydreams. And they talked in funny gravelly voices, and they'd do unromantic but nice things like giving me bubble gum. They would kiss me with increasing power but they would call it off just where I wanted them to. I was good at picking fellows who would not get rough.

"I never went in for heavy petting or oral sex in my daydreams. But the first boy I got sexually involved with, we did nothing else. That was for 100 percent sure contraception. We carried on like that for three years. All that time I was having the old daydream of unspecific crinoline love and fitting my real boyfriend into it. But in real life we'd masturbate each other sweetly, and by degrees we got into going down on each other. I was technically a virgin until my senior year in high school and then we thought we ought to really do it. I was so nice, and he was so well behaved, our parents let us have a lot of freedom. So we went on a group bike trip for a week and we did it on top of a sleeping bag. It was a little disappointing but I could still fit it into my fantasy.

"When I got married it was to another guy and right away my fantasy fell apart. I thought that now, married, I would begin to have good straight sex. I mean intercourse with big orgasms and big breakfasts the next morning and so forth. The sex wasn't any good and we had some fights about it, each accusing the other of being a sexual dud. The breakfasts were Wheaties. My sister wised me up and gave me some books and told me to study them and learn how to make love to a real man that I was married to. He and I dutifully read the books and began to go through the whole drill but it didn't fit into my old fantasy. I saw myself as a dumb thing living in a grad-student apartment and wearing grubby running shoes and doing sex like homework. That went on two whole years! Then what do you know! We got a job house-sitting for the parents of some friends, a big lake house up in Ontario. It was the best free time we had had, and the really lavish house made of logs with grounds sloping down to the lake—it fit into my fantasy. My husband got brown in the sun and lean from canoeing and seemed like a new, romantic person. So one night I felt really romantic and lured him into bed and I had an orgasm from intercourse! In that environment I could really let myself get into it."

In that environment she could give herself permission to have an orgasm. She could accept the pleasure.

A TOTALLY DIFFERENT STORY

Benita never stood with reluctant feet. When she was thirteen, by her own account, she was "about as reluctant as a rutting bull rhino."

"Look, I gave my parents a rotten time. I was the neighborhood bad girl—Little Roundheels, Dad used to call me. When they saw me coming, mothers would lock up their sons. I did sex, booze, pot, hash. I ran away, got pregnant, gave it away for adoption, the works. Until I was twenty-four I made it with a different guy at least once a month or I thought I was underprivileged. Then I met Harry and we got married and I got pregnant and turned into a domesticated, faithful wife. I mean, I have this house, a garden, children, I sell pottery, nobody but Harry lays a hand on me. Sending guys on their way who try me is so easy! I wonder if it would be that easy if I had been a quote 'nice' unquote girl before I got hitched? The sex is fine, though Harry is not such a hell of a stud as one other guy I used to shack up with. But what I like is the whole thing.''

Until she met Harry and got into the combined pleasures of her life with him, she couldn't accept the pleasure of being with any one man. Something kept putting off that happy surrender to another person.

ACCEPTING PLEASURE

Holding back from certain pleasures is a *normal* kind of behavior. Some requirement of the soul has to be met before it will allow the deal to be signed, the celebration to be held. It used to be that the only approach to the inability to enjoy sex, in any one or all of its aspects, was to relieve the soul, or the psyche if you prefer that language, of its major burdens. Psychoanalysis for years. Now sex therapy offers relief from sexual dysfunction within weeks or months instead of years. This allows people to have a good sex life, which may be all they wanted, feeling that the deeper peace of the psyche is a very dubious goal to pursue through a narrow route. Or, as many people in reality know, that they simply cannot afford long-term psychoanalysis.

The ability to accept orgasm, or to accept a love for another person, is something a person probably seeks selfishly for herself or himself. In a long relationship there are pleasures that one would like to be able to give for the pleasure of the other. These are odd little side issues, varieties of sex, enhancements. A partner—more often the woman—may not accept oral sex, or the sharing of certain fantasies. The man may not willingly give in to being pleasured. Which, incidentally, could be the best solution to living with a woman whose natural appetite is lower than his. In a mature marriage, these issues can often be resolved by discussion and by the partners' sensitive accommodations to each other's needs.

APE MAGIC

Abbey didn't want any ape magic with her sex, but this filled Bill with boyish sadness. Ape magic was sometimes called ape medicine. They imitated the actions of gorillas and chimps in the bedroom; it was one of those releases from dignified grown-up behavior that lovers may seek together.

"Don't get the idea that ape medicine was all mine," Bill told me. "She really got into it. She was good at it. But now it has become an issue, for Pete's sake. I think she thinks I want it as a sign that she really is apish and not a dignified and lovely woman; that I'm trying to drag her back and down. I never thought it was ugly; it was a special language just for us, something private. I take it as saying that she rejects something we used to have between us. That she won't give me our secret sign anymore."

I asked Abbey if she wouldn't try something. Think up another pair of roles to play—Romeo and Juliet, or Sleeping Beauty and the Prince, or Abbey and Bill as real-life grown-ups approaching each other in a very dignified way. Say that she just didn't want ape magic *all the time*. She was not always in the mood to be apelike. But to promise Bill that they could go back to it sometime, as a sign that something from the beginning of their love was not dead but still theirs to bring back. In my presence, believe it or not, these grown-ups worked out a deal. She was to be the one to initiate ape magic for a while.

Each of them phoned me later on and said happiness had

come back to their lovemaking. The dear old ape magic was a part of their repertoire.

REPERTOIRES

A couple's repertoire. We sex therapists borrow the word from the world of musicians and performers. A pianist's repertoire is the list of pieces he has studied and practiced and brought to concert level, that near-perfection, or personal harmony between performer and piece, that can be shown. An actor may have a collection of roles in plays that he has made his own. In the lovemaking of a couple it is all the signals, fond actions, arousing actions, bits of technique they accept mutually and use as the spirit takes them. Not always in the same order, not making a boring routine. Rubbing noses, kissing toes, nibbling all over, missionary position, dog-fashion, manual stimulation of genitals, going down, using spit as a lubricant or always using K-Y, etc.

We sex therapists are always saying "Variety!" to the point where *that* is sometimes boring, but it does freshen and nurture a mutual sex life. And there are the practical reasons for it. To be able to use spit when the K-Y container is misplaced, or to be able to masturbate or go down on the other in the case of a bad back that forbids intercourse. Or just to suit a period of lower energy, or a passing mood. Sex can be used to soothe and comfort a partner who is tense or sad. It isn't always passionate.

There is one part of the repertoire that is most often a bone of contention. She doesn't want to fellate him, to give him pleasure orally. This is extremely common.

First, it doesn't *have* to be part of the repertoire. If he has a nice woman and she is loving in many other ways, he can make this concession to her preference. Let him feel generous about it. It will feel good to feel generous.

But it can be more complicated than her simply refusing to do it and not wanting him to suggest it. Many women feel they are being prudish, meanspirited refusing something that is widely accepted as playful and certainly normal. But they don't want to do it, for whatever reason. They want to *try*, but feel sure they will do it badly because it goes against the grain.

In this case I say to avoid those particular things about fellatio that put them off. It is not necessary to swallow the ejaculate, or even to take it into the mouth. The penis can be licked and teased with lips and tongue and finished with her dainty fingers. She can ask him to say when he is about to come and catch the ejaculate in a tissue. If gagging on the penis that is pushed way back in the throat, if that is the thing feared, then let her be in control of the whole act. He is to lie back and let her do it. Not to thrust farther than she allows. It can be done most delightfully this way.

Then there is the problem of wishing she could do this, but not wanting to do it at all. I say don't make an issue of it. Say to him, "*Sometime*. Sometime when it's Christmas in August or when the swallows come back to Winnetka, I will surprise you, my precious one, but don't push it, okay?" And to yourself just imagine that it will at some moment be a thing you will do on impulse. Some night after a party. You have had a good time, he was the life of the party, everyone laughed at his stories, tomorrow is Sunday and nobody has to get up to go to work. In the midst of lovemaking it will seem like something to do. That's all! Just give yourself permission to think that, and let the moment come when it will.

Nowhere is it written that a good sex life has in it everything you have read about in a paperback novel. But allow yourself anything you would like to do to show love or receive pleasure—short of very obviously dangerous things. I say *never* do it on a chandelier; if you want to swing that way, train and look for a circus job! But every lover can have a wide repertoire of loving things to sing, say, act out, do to the other, allow to be done.

17

Genitals— Yours, Mine and Ours

I DON'T believe much in what is called penis envy. In my heart I am not and never have been convinced that I want to have a penis down there instead of "nothing." I never thought I had nothing down there. I always thought it was quite a contraption. What I think and feel, other females think and feel. In fact, nowadays many literate people share my skepticism.

A little girl gets an idea that men have something that hangs down. One way or another that suspicion comes to her; then she sees a picture, or perhaps she sees Daddy in an incautious trip from bathroom or bedroom. She saw, but is not sure she saw. Like the lady who thinks she heard the minister say, "Oh, shit!" But isn't sure. She'd like to play back the tape but there is no tape.

Then one day it is all right to look at a penis. A little brother or cousin is being bathed and she may watch. *Then* it is all right to gaze at a penis. Why? No one tells her, but the big ladies smile and say, "Isn't he darling? Doesn't he like his bath?" For some reason it is all right to be there watching.

This penis she is allowed to look at is pink and little, with a little fat pink balloon of flesh behind it. The whole thing is unnecessary. It doesn't make sense the way a hand does. She feels pleased and a little scared to be looking with big ladies.

A big set of male genitals, when she first sees it, may not be to her liking. It hangs down, moves, has a funny color, a vein. The big balls are covered with wrinkled skin. *Ick!*

It isn't like the baby boy's little pink thing; it isn't familiarly rubbery looking like a Walt Disney drawing. It is part of the real world that is sometimes not comforting—like those big words and silly and boring things grown-ups say and do. She will not think about it.

She may feel that way for a while, then accept the look of the penis as the knowledge of grown-up things comes to her. Perhaps she goes on through life not really liking the look. But at times the very "ugliness" of it is exciting! That is part of the on-and-off feeling about sex. Or she may become totally used to the way real men look nude and take an interest in the different ways penises look, like all the different ways hands and faces look.

Men go through similar feelings about female genitalia. That part of a woman is of a different order from her made-up face, her neat dress, all her public parts and accessories. In extreme cases, it is said, some men fear that Down There mouth, fear that it has teeth and will bite off their penises! But I feel sure that to many men this is truly not a problem. They may in fact develop an unhelpful attraction to the vagina or clitoris to the exclusion of other female features. Or such feelings may fluctuate from one to the other extreme.

A REASONABLE REVULSION

I think it is reasonable, in a child or young person who is not ready for sex, to have fears of the genitalia of other people. We are a slowly maturing kind of creature, and we come to readiness each in his or her own time. But in a long-standing relationship like marriage the genitals of the other partner become in a sense one's own possession, giving a feeling of pride, contentment, security, continuity. Pleasure in looking forward to the future. In looking backward into the past.

A man comes home late from overtime work, thinking of his home and bed and that home of homes, that secret place between her legs that sleeps and waits for him. After showering and slipping into bed, he begins the exploration and presently slips a hand over that place that is his in all the world. His wife moves and says, *"Mmm."* That means, *"Mmmm."* Or she may say, *"Nnnh!"* Too bad, that means, "Not now." That is his special vagina, but just now it is hers alone and must be left alone. He cuddles up to her and composes himself for sleep, accepting a different kind of closeness and homecoming.

In their love play either of this couple will at times concentrate only on the genitals of the other. It becomes more important than getting the orgasm in one's own. She titillates his penis and teases it and in the fullness of time makes it ejaculate, an action that says, "This is all for you." And he can do that for her sometimes.

Crossing a room, they meet. One fearlessly uses the privilege of putting a hand over the other's genitals, which are shared property, like the house and its contents.

But not always. Sometimes a person is separate, needs that feeling of separateness. At those times one's crotch is one's own exclusively! All understood, causing no anger or fear in a happy marriage.

18

Bodies

ONE night a man and his wife were making love face-to-face and she said, "We're fat!" That next day she told him they were going on a diet-and-exercise program. They worked at it together and in a short time they had lost ten pounds apiece and looked very trim. That was very satisfactory. But, he told his wife, he had sort of liked making love with fat bellies!

"Yes," she agreed, "but we had to give *something* up, and that was it."

If the bellies are not too fat, it is pleasant to push them together. The feeling of two lean naked bodies interlocked is not the only good feeling.

I like the story because it shows that there are different ways to enjoy your body sensually, and also that you can alter your body to suit your self-image—within reason. And that sometimes you have to make a decision and stick to it. Which shall I enjoy—being fat or being thin? It isn't that being fat is sheer misery. Oh, the pleasure of pushing those two fat bare bellies together! But that way lay getting fatter as they got older and still fatter and pretty soon having to change the way they make love because the bellies would be in the way. Not the worst thing in the world, but perhaps the alternative really is better.

THERE'S MORE THAN ONE WAY TO LOOK

Erotic art is fascinating less because of the sexual actions it represents—after all, one picks up the idea of a great variety of sexual techniques quickly—but because of the way the artist represents the people taking part in sex. The Oriental artists are not interested in showing people with Olympic bodies playing with each other. It is often a soft, self-indulgent-looking man, somewhat effeminate by our standards. This is true of Indian and Japanese erotic drawings. It introduces the idea that the pleasures of sex are not only for long-limbed people who do conditioning and body building *every* day.

Your mate's body is your property, if you grant a similar equity in the flesh that you inhabit. It is nice to think about it, building positive feelings for that bone structure and that special flesh and skin; a body with its own kind of attractiveness, to be liked for itself. And susceptible to good treatment, especially if encouraged by someone who loves it.

Pat the arms, run a hand over that flank, know it; it is yours. And when you eat together develop reasonable habits that can be maintained—not crash-and-fail dieting but pleasant, often self-indulgent eating combined with walks, health-club swimming or some sport for every season. When caring for your mate's body, encourage it by caring for your own, and both of you will benefit physically.

"Sensible people take care of their bodies." And paying attention to your body and caring for it develops good sense too.

If you want to love your spouse's body, love your spouse—and help him or her with the care of that body.

Thinking Lovely Thoughts

A MOTHER came into her little boy's room and he was awake. By the kind of swift understanding that makes mothers seem to be mind readers, she knew that he was sexually aroused. Quickly she felt under the blanket and touched his hard little penis. Now this was before mothers were taught to regard sexuality in young children as natural and not to be taken notice of, to be permitted within harmless limits. But she was sensible and not one to make a big fuss or make the boy feel terribly guilty. She told him, therefore, that he should be asleep and to fill his head with "nice" thoughts. So the boy felt guilty but understood he was not to be guilty forever but could guide his course through life, leaving behind his errors! So, believe it or not, he filled his head with thoughts that were not arousing and drifted off to sleep.

I would like to point to this as an example of how a parent could be wise within the limits of what she had been taught. When a parent asks me what to do in a case like that I say to ignore it, but I know perfectly well that long before I was born women were raising children and doing a pretty nice job, and such mistakes as they might have made did not destroy their children. The encyclopedia is full of men and women of high achievement who grew up before modern ideas of sex education were dreamed of.

But even more interesting is that the boy *knew* he could choose what thoughts to think, and to change his mood at will. He could summon up images that would make his penis hard, and he could change his thoughts and get into another mood entirely.

This is useful to the man who has an erection on a bus or at the dinner table and wants to get rid of it. He doesn't have to be a student of psychology or sexology to know this.

MORE THAN ONE KIND OF LOVELY

A person can summon up mental images and even sounds that, inside the head, are hard to distinguish from real sounds made by physical causes. One can hear whispered words, lyrics, bands playing, the wind in leaves. One can sense sunlight on the closed eyelids when the room is pitch dark. And one can call up images that bring high sexual arousal. Or others that soothe, lower the pulse rate and let slumber come.

Oddly enough, the same letting-go images that can let a person relax into sleep can also help with sexual functioning. With holding an erection, keeping at the *plateau* of arousal, going into orgasm.

The mental images used by women as an aid to sexual functioning have always been assumed to be images only of a generalized sensual pleasure. But I am not convinced of this. For one thing, we have reason to believe that women do have sharp, vivid mental images of men's bodies and violent sexual action, more than they were believed to have. Maybe the reporting has been exaggerated, and maybe some women are trying to be in style, claiming to like those male centerfolds showing the penises of famous fellows. I am inclined to think that everybody is doing everything, and the old strict male and female lines regarding fantasies and visual stimulation were in error.

Still, more women than men have reported to me personally a type of fantasy, which has little specific sexuality, that they use to help intensify sexual functioning. That helps them concentrate on enjoying a sexual encounter.

Because many times women have trouble *getting down* to it. They have so much on their minds! Women still seem to take care of a greater variety of things during the course of a day than men do. Household and child-raising work involves so many activities. The housewife is the top management and all the work force, with checklists a mile long in her head! And even when she is in her husband's arms in bed, that everlasting shopping list may be what she is thinking about. Or her calendar for the day past (have I done everything I should?) and the week coming (have I written down everything I will have to do by the weekend?) is tyrannizing her mind. And she just isn't concentrating on the feeling in her loins.

I TRY BUT IT KEEPS FALLING OUT

That's what a woman told me. She didn't mean that her husband's penis kept falling out. She meant the sexy image she was using kept falling out.

She would think of something that seemed exciting—that her husband was ravishing her with heavy boots or shoes on. She got that from some raunchy Western movie, or reading a book about how the miners in the brothels on payday weren't allowed time to take off their coal-dusty shoes. Or something. That would be momentarily exciting, but the shoes would make her think of totally inappropriate things. The mailman's shoes. Had she remembered to mail the check to the phone company? The mason who was coming to look at the basement floor. Would she be in when and if he should come tomorrow, probably earlier or later than he said he would, like all these damn repairmen? Or would she be picking up the kids at school?

She needed some kind of lovely thoughts or images that would be pleasing, relaxing, and would block out all those busy-busy, worry-worry, useless and intruding thoughts.

A USEFUL COLLECTION

Over the years I have collected some lovely atmospheric thoughts for blocking out the shopping list and letting sensuality come in. I suggest these to women, with the idea that they use these same reveries or find some like them from their own memories and imaginations.

What about the slow and rhythmic sound of the ocean on a beach? Lying spread-eagled on the sand in the sun, in the moonlight, in a bedroom within the sound, giving oneself up to it?

Lying back in a powerful car, the most expensive make you can think of, speeding through the night, the moon racing along with you?

Endlessly skiing down the expert's slope in the moon-light, with that sense of speed, commitment to the force of gravity, control of one's downward plunge, the hissing of the skis over the powder?

In a motor ship cleaving the sea, some great body of water somewhere in the wonderful watery world, through moonlight, or the wonderfully obliterating effect of a snow-fall at sea?

And so forth, and so on. Try it, if you can't get rid of that shopping list.

20

Music to Masturbate By

WHEN you hear of a radio station using that slogan, do write me a letter. I feel sure that it's coming and I want to be the first sex therapist on my block to know! Music taped or on the radio can make a sensuous background, a soothing sound for jangled nerves, a baffle to check all those interruptive thoughts that keep the leisurely, exploratory, learning masturbator from the tranquil pursuit of self-knowledge through self-pleasuring.

Music to enhance sex is ages old; singing, clapping, dancing to music are preludes to sexual encounters now as they have been since the beginning of time. Arousal music. The practice of playing selected music in the bedroom, for most people, is more of a recent thing. The phonograph and all the music-playing equipment that followed put sex-to-music within the reach of the citizen. Before that it was a matter of hiring musicians to play in the garden or behind the screen while the duke and his inamorata strove together passionately.

Music serves very much as certain generalized sensual reveries serve—daydreams of lying at the sea's edge, genitals lapped by the surf, ear full of its slow roll and crash; of

150

speeding, hearing wind in trees—to gently crowd out the shopping list from the mind of the copulator or masturbator.

KEEPING A COLLECTION OF EROTIC READING

It is best to keep it openly on the shelves. This will raise the level of sexual literacy all around you. Nine out of ten people will make little of the titles of classic erotica. Looking at the book backs, they will think you are very well read or else very pretentious.

I must say that when I tell a client to buy some erotic reading, I don't suppose he or she will be going the rounds of the interesting bookshops hunting for these quite seriously regarded works, but simply into a drugstore, airport bookshop, candy store or the like, where all the shiny masturbation magazines are sold. Often these shops have a few shelves of explicit porn paperbacks.

A very well read person tells me, "Sensuous and erotic writings are to be read for themselves, and perhaps to tone up the sexual readiness of the reader. But for sharp stimulation the best is sleazy porn. It wastes no time, and knowing that this writing has no other purpose but to get people's genitals engorged is part of its effectiveness." And she adds, "When you are idly caressing the shaft of your clitoris with one hand, you want something *light* to hold in the other. I mean light in ounces, not in quality. A magazine or thin paperback is ideal."

She goes up to any counter or any clerk in the world and makes her purchase without a moment's embarrassment. "But what if you met one of your friends who is old-fashioned? While you were buying a book like *Spanked Bottoms?*" I asked her. She said she would say it was for her mother in the old-folks' home. I think her attitude is fine. For myself, whatever I want to buy I walk in and buy. It is an attitude that comes of long years as a student, buying or checking out books of all kinds and learning to worry more about the coming exam than about what the clerk or librarian thinks of me. But if you feel funny, send your boyfriend to buy. This robs you of the firsthand privilege of leafing through the material beforehand, but there you are. If you have no male at present whom you can ask to buy your masturbation reading for you, or who will read these things aloud with you before you go to the mattress together, I say to get, by hook or by crook, a copy of one of the big-selling sexy magazines and comb the mail-order columns for dirty books.

There—I said "dirty books." That is for a friend who begs me to stop saying "sexually explicit reading," because it is only, he says, a form of prudery. Okay—I said it.

I do not like to call movies or books "dirty" or "porno" because these words make the viewing or reading of them something shameful or blameful, and nobody has to feel that way about it. You may keep the books and magazines out of sight, to avoid tiresome conversations with certain people who come into your home, but you need not feel ashamed of yourself.

"There you go," says this friend. "Taking the fun out of it. The shame, the furtiveness, is part of the fun. No shame, no erection."

Okay. You call it what you like to suit your own interests— to me it is sexually explicit material.

THE AMORALITY OF FANTASYLAND

I advise reading whatever it is that arouses you sexually, without worrying about the real-world morality of it. In the imagination that is linked with sexual responses there is no morality; things are permitted, are harmless, that have very definite drawbacks in the world of reality. Incest, sex with the very young, sex with crazy funky strangers you meet on the streets by the docks or the rail yards will in real life cause you and other people a lot of grief. You use your head and you avoid. But in the imagination . . .

About using arousal fantasies that involve illegal and frightening situations, you have to worry only if you use certain fantasies exclusively. If you think of falling from a high building every single time, maybe you need some counseling! But if you move from that to other images, getting bored and moving on, there is nothing unusual. What is forbidden is exciting—that is a very important element in sexual fantasies.

The hookup between the fantasy sex life and the real one is through a very mysterious country. The sexual imagery of fantasyland means things to our unconscious selves that our conscious minds can do no more than guess at. The sex-with-a-child fantasy has, at a guess, something to do with wanting to return to that stage of clear, untarnished, unencumbered emotions, to our real selves. Something in us also seeks the child in our real-life lovers.

The incest revery is often indulged in by people who in actuality dislike their relatives! Perhaps they are seeking a nicer kind of relatives with whom they would like to be closer.

WHERE I DRAW THE LINE

The use of children in sexually explicit films is of course criminal exploitation of people who can't defend themselves, and it is cruelty to the children and an offense against the parental feelings of anybody with the slightest amount of sympathetic imagination. I think the makers of such pictures must be tracked down and imprisoned. The making of arousal films using adult actors is something else, and can be allowed by any society tolerant enough to be called civilized.

Films overemphasizing cruelty, encouraging the growth of cruelty in the audience, perhaps involving real cruelty in shooting the torture scenes, are nothing I could recommend as stimulation or an enrichment of the sexual imagination.

AVOIDING DEPRESSING SLEAZE

"But that's what I'm after," moans my irrepressible acquaintance. Nevertheless, there are many people who would like to watch explicit films but don't because of the sleazy places where they are shown.

"Besides," a lady tells me, "I don't care for all those shadowy people who slip into the porno pits. Gray fat salesmen with their sample cases, masturbating in the orchestra all around me. I don't care what *they* think about *me*. *I* am a nice person who just wants to get her crotch hot. But they are *creeps!* So I am sticking to the late-night cable porn and saving up for a videotape attachment for my TV—so I can lie back with my pants off and play with myself while watching my porn in solitary comfort."

That probably is the best way for a large audience of would-be watchers of sex.

WEATHERING DISAPPOINTMENTS

Explicit films are often ineptly directed, acted by young people who wouldn't get into the scratchiest stock company as actors, and so poorly plotted and incredibly situationed that arousal is miles away as one watches. A porn flick connoisseur tells me that there are two classes of truly arousing movies. "One is high-class movie making with genuinely artistic erotic scenes related to human reality. The other is low-budget porn produced by off-duty wage earners in their home garages. No plot, no dialogue, nothing but certain repeated actions over a quite long period of time. A body of a woman moving up and down on a shaft of flesh begins to reach an uncomplicated liking in the watcher. Some voice inside says, 'Hey, this is a good thing going on here.' And the scene performs the true function of genuine porn—it provides an erection."

FANTASY ENRICHMENT

Going to sexually explicit movies is something I suggest to clients who seem not to carry with them to their sexual encounters a normal amount of fantasy-making equipment in the head. For good sexual functioning this ability to make images, fantasies, is as important as having genitals or being alive. I can't overemphasize that. We don't know what dogs think about when they Do It dog-fashion, but the supposition is that they have no mental appreciation of the experience, no memory of it, no desire for it when there is no direct physical stimulation. When that odor of a female in heat is not in their noses they have no interest in sex. So one is told.

In fact, I doubt that—only because all well-established idea are dubious. Why, when they are dreaming, do some dogs get those big red erections lying in the middle of the living room rug, with the minister smiling and pretending not to see? They would seem to be having dreams about sex.

But in any case, people do fantasize during sex, and can use fantasy to improve sex at certain times. To keep a needed erection, for instance. And, madam, when your lover thinks about you during and after sex, it is an enhanced you that he carries in his mind, that changes from encounter to encounter. There is no need to cry; he is in love with you. But not with you alone. You with all those other you's he has in his imagination.

Women often do not want to watch explicit movies. I say that no one should do anything that goes against the grain. But I also say that a person who does need to watch such movies at times is not perverted. He may need a few more pictures in his memory, or he may need to live awhile in sexy-mindedness, getting away from business and from all the sex-repressing company he has to keep so much of the time. He needs sexual cheering up. If the movies he watches are of low caliber, that isn't his fault. He probably wouldn't mind a very well made porn flick at all, if some high-minded filmmaker wanted to make it.

The most fortunate of lovers is one who has in mind pictures of what has passed between him and his real mate in playful and passionate moments in the past: blue movies from their shared memories. He has less need to spend time looking at actors simulating the acts of love.

WHY SO BIG, AND WHY OUTSIDE?

People ask me why the penises are all so large in the porn flicks and why the men always ejaculate outside the vaginas. And how they ejaculate so much seminal fluid, such cascades.

Usually the ejaculations are faked. It is a theatrical effect using a thin flour-and-water mixture.

The ejaculations into the air satisfy a curiosity about seeing an ejaculation take place, someone else's. And they show that the movie watcher is getting his or her money's worth. Sex is really happening—or *seems* to be.

Men with fairly large penises get the roles in the movies because the big-penis idea still holds sway in the popular imagination. And actors with less astounding penises are shy of getting on camera.

Moviemakers like huge tigers and huge penises to overwhelm the scene. It is picturesque. Think—the frightening big tiger is a tame one that lives on commercial animal food with lots of cereal in it. In the jungle, in a real-life encounter with a real wild tiger, a much smaller animal will be quite sufficient to your needs. If you live to tell the story, the tiger will get bigger every time you tell it. And in real sexual encounters the functioning penis is big enough, in the same way.

21

Daydreams and Fantasies

A MAN I shall call Barry sits in my office trying to recall sexual fantasies—at my invitation. I have the idea that he and his wife might share fantasies a little more. They keep each other locked out of their private worlds, although physically they become intimate. I think that perhaps if they share fantasies a little they may bring more zest to their lovemaking. Later I mean to ask *her* to tell me some of *her* fantasies. It may be useful to see how their fantasy worlds differ or are alike.

AN OCTOPUS LOVER

Barry says he sometimes imagines that he is a sort of octopus making love to a woman. A human female of the regular kind, not a female octopus.

This man imagines that he is a warm-blooded human octopus with a big penis in the middle and all those eight tentacles so that when he is making love to her (in his imagination) all those eight totally flexible arms are wrapped around her, touching her delicious flesh packaged in warm

157

smooth skin, everywhere and every which way, and his penis is way up inside her vagina.

He can be kissing her mouth or nibbling her ears with his penis inside her and those warm arms all at once squeezing, caressing, encircling, feeling her neck and waist and breasts and back and buttocks. Wrapping lovingly around her thighs and the insides of her knees, her calves, the arch and insides of her feet and playing with her toes. All at once.

At this point, as he is telling me this, I wonder, what would *she* be thinking about if she knew of his fantasy? The shopping list? Or how she could get out of this tangle if she suddenly wanted to? If she got panicky? After all, sex is fun but an octopus may be more than she bargained for!

I ask him if he has indulged in this fantasy while he was making love to his wife. He seems a little startled, then he says he believes he has. Sometime. He is no teenager. He is in his forties and has been married a total of fourteen years, adding up two marriages. So it isn't surprising if he has lost track a little, and forgotten whether or not he has used this fantasy while making real love to a real woman.

HAVING HER ENTIRELY

A number of Barry's fantasies or daydreams are about wanting to have the woman entirely, to envelop her. In one of these fantasies his body changes form and he becomes a big warm membrane, a blanket of human tissue, that wraps her intimately and completely and moves upon all her surfaces like a total massage until she murmurs with pleasure. Then she begins to moan imploringly, begging for the ultimate touch, and part of the great cloak that he has become forms, at his willing it, a penis that enters her and thrusts again and again, drawing the energy to do this from the entire blanket of flesh enfolding her. At last she cries out with joy and writhes and thrusts and struggles against the net of flesh she is trapped in, enjoying every pressure on her body, inside and out, from the all-touching membrane.

I want to remind anyone who has just tuned in that this is

a fantasy that a man is having about having sex with a woman. And this is not a science-fantasy book but a guide to married sex, meaning sex in a variety of long-term relationships. By Ruth Westheimer, Ed.D.—the Dr. Ruth of radio and TV. The lady sometimes known as Grandma Freud because with an accent I sound like a chicken-soup matriarch, and because anyone who talks about sex with an accent is supposed to be a follower of Freud, though few of us are nowadays.

There is more to this fantasy Barry indulges in of being a great blanket of flesh.

"What does this blanket do at other times, when he isn't making love?" I inquire. We are in my office facing each other on two chairs, no desk in between. I think sitting behind a desk is too businesslike for the kind of talk we have in here. That is just an idea of mine. Other sex therapists do differently, and do very well too.

Barry says that Blanket Man, the name for the comic-book form that he assumes in his imagination, is always making love. When he stops doing that he becomes Barry in his ordinary and quite pleasant human form.

"When he gets out of bed to go to the bathroom, he has to have legs," I suggest.

Barry says no, the Blanket Man can form a long, sinuous tube that reaches the bathroom door, turns the knob, opens the door, goes to the toilet, works the flush handle when through and shrinks back into the blanket on the bed. Very convenient.

Barry says Blanket Man can go to the roof of the condo, grasp the master TV antenna by two corners and float on the wind like a sheet drying in the sun. That feels lovely. And the sheet can stretch and stretch way out beyond the building, casting a huge shadow. Any woman walking in this shadow feels lovely warm sensations and thinks about having sex that night.

WHY NOT TELL HIS WIFE?

I confess that I am charmed by the story, but I suspect that Barry is being cute now and making up as he goes along. Nothing wrong with being cute! But while I enjoy my work, I am not paid by Barry so that he can entertain me.

The truth is, he should be entertaining his wife with stories like this. I feel pretty sure she would like them, from what I know of her, and his imagination could create more intimacy between them.

Out of the corner of my eye I see the photo of the pretty girl I keep on the wall. She is amused by the story. So are the two jointed wooden dolls on top of the bookshelves. They seem enchanted—

Enough! That is *my* imagination running a little wild. But I don't feel guilty because this little daydream of mine all happens in an *augenblick,* an eyeblink. I have not wasted Barry's time with it. And it shows how his imagination might stimulate his wife's sometime, if he shares it with her.

"Something else," Barry says. "The Blanket Man swims along the bottom of the sea, like a manta ray, ruffling the edges of his body—"

EARLY MASTURBATION FANTASIES

But I have to cut off Barry's flow of Blanket Man ideas and ask for any other sexual fantasies he can recall. Most of those he presents have to do with his interest in touching his dream women all over at the same time.

Earlier in life, when he was beginning puberty, he began to think about women taking their clothes off in fantastic circumstances. He definitely did not believe at that age that any woman would undress for a man because she wanted to. Not any real-life woman. Not in places like his hometown. Not in ordinary houses like those on his street. It always happened on islands, in tents in the middle of the Sahara, in castles on mountain peaks. In one fantasy a bold and beautiful woman came to his palace to find out what sex is like. She had heard about it and, darn it, she just thought she would give it a whirl. All alone with him in a great marble hall she took off her glittering evening gown and stood naked and watched curiously as Barry kissed her feet and worked his way up. This was a terrific fantasy, and his heart pounded and his penis got hard but he didn't masturbate. Later he had a similar fantasy in bed and he began to move around in the grip of an impulse he didn't recognize and then he had his first orgasm, ejaculating on the sheet. It scared him, but the next night he arranged to have another. He didn't know yet how to masturbate with his hand.

In due time he heard about that manual method and he tried it. It seemed less exciting than his own way, but he learned to do it quite effectively. He would imagine a movie star or a girl in an ad doing a striptease, and then he would possess her in the missionary position (his fist serving for her vagina). He imagined these women Doing It for some obscure reason quite aside from their taking pleasure in sex themselves in the way that he wanted to have it. Later he became very dutiful about wanting to bring women to orgasm as well.

LITTLE SCENARIOS

He recalls a number of fantasies that were really little scenarios.

He would be a naval lieutenant on duty in the Aegean Sea. For certain favors a prominent Greek family lets him have his way with their glorious daughter. Over a moonlit sea he would pilot a high-speed launch to a landing where steps ascended from the water's edge to a classically pillared villa. In his smart uniform he ascends the steps to a chamber where the beautiful girl waits and submits to his cold and insistent lovemaking, her purple nipples dark against snowy breasts in the moonlight...On another occasion he forces himself on the girl's mother.

He strips a captive virgin (blond, plump and, like all of them, speechless) and carries her naked over his shoulder along the sounding surf to a place under palm trees where she is not only naked but far from every familiar object, and possesses her utterly. . . .

A musketeer, he ties up a dangerous villainess in seventeenth-century costume and possesses her. (The word *rape* is foreign to his fantasies.) This fantasy is based on the bad woman Milady in *The Three Musketeers*, Barry informs me.

AUDIENCES

Barry had a number of audience fantasies. A mother watches him having sex with her daughter. The daughter watches him having sex with the mother. Then with a younger sister. . . .

In all these daydreams there is an element of forcing the woman, of unwillingness on her part. People are sometimes frightened of their own reveries, thinking that they reveal something evil in their basic nature. One must understand that aggression is not all bad. In real life the man does try to overwhelm—but not by brute force. By, for instance, charm, attentions, gifts, grooming, shows of power. To some extent a woman is a fortress to be overwhelmed.

Barry is a pleasant fellow and I have no reason to believe he would hurt a fly. Well, perhaps a fly, but not a human female. In real life it seems he is bold with women sometimes and shy at other times. He is most at ease with college-educated women. Less well educated women intimidate him; they seem more instinctual and mysterious. They seem to expect a more instinctual male, whereas college alumnae accept a tamer fellow like himself.

Women never know what he is thinking; he feels sure of that, and it is for the best because lewd thoughts are with him nearly all the time. And then he is almost constantly appraising women in a cold way, even his wife, whom he loves. He does not want her to know how critical he is beneath the surface. Or how he quite consciously puts these negative thoughts out of mind when he is throbbing with lust.

Barry's wife is named Arlene. Of course, these are not their real names. Arlene has her own fantasies, none of which she shares with Barry. Barry thinks she is very intelligent and rather haughty, so she feels that it would never do to tell him what silly things turn her on.

FANTASY BRAGGING IN THE DORM

Although she has not told Barry any of her fantasies, Arlene had told seven or eight girls in her dorm at college about them. You had to talk about your fantasies or they wouldn't take you in. One girl was a Methodist from way up north in Wisconsin and she wouldn't talk about sex, so nobody talked to her or sat with her in the cafeteria. She cried a lot and never came back after Christmas.

The girls like very tall fantasies and the raunchier the better! Black guys with mile-long penises were well thought of. Another thing was that you were supposed to be having real sex with a fellow on campus. And you had to give the girls all the details. Arlene chose a tall blond anthropology major who played the vibes in a band. If anyone suggested that he was creepy, she would say, "But he's so sweet." Sex with this fellow was more for status than for real pleasure. Her pals in the dorm had a vivid image of the vibraphonist's penis from Arlene's description.

The fantasies she told about in the dorm were all made up. She didn't feel like telling the ones she really indulged in because they were silly and very dear to her. She was afraid the girls would poke fun at them and spoil them forever.

The best one she told the girls was about being kidnapped by thugs and held in a gang hideout and forced to have intercourse with them and to go down on them and have anal sex until they were tired of her. Then they sold her into a whorehouse in Central America, where they intended to use her up and then kill her in a sadistic orgy, but she saved her life by giving such fine exhibitions that they kept her alive. So she became a sort of star. Arlene got all this out of a paperback novel.

What she told them about sex with the vibes player was factual because she figured one of the others might check him out sometime and report on her reporting.

SPARKY FANTASIES

Arlene's real fantasies fall mostly into two categories—Sparky fantasies and Funko ones. Sparky and Funko are opposites. Sparky is based on Leslie Howard as seen in golden oldie films on late TV, and Funko is the low, mean, criminal type. Funko is also known as Sludgebucket.

Sparky is pale and slender all the time, but he varies in age from episode to episode, being a grown man on a Wednesday night and a teenager on Thursday. Friday and Saturday are date nights, but Sparky is around again Sunday or Monday as a little boy. In Sparky fantasies Arlene is always in charge of things.

She might be Catherine the Great reviewing her troops. Sparky as a young lieutenant attracts her attention. She orders him into a private apartment and makes him stand at attention in both senses. While she talks to him teasingly he has to keep saying, "Yes, Majesty," and keep his blue eyes straight ahead while she strokes his genitals through the tight silk uniform breeches until his penis strains against the fabric. She uncovers it and teases it with her fingers until it comes. Or, always dressed in elaborate powdered coiffure and low-cut, wide-skirted gown, she loosens her breasts and softly moves them against his genitals, talking softly to him as if he were a baby. He is her sex slave and toy.

Sometimes Sparky is younger, anywhere from four to eleven years old, and she poses as various kinds of child-care people. A weekend baby-sitter, a Sunday school teacher taking him on a trip as a reward for perfect attendance, an elementary or junior-high teacher. Sometimes she is a rich lady who adopts him and makes him forget his real mama. She undresses him and does a striptease for him, talking cooingly to him. She puts her ear to his chest and hears his heart pounding against his thin young ribs. At this point Arlene is apt to go wild and bring herself to orgasm. With this young Sparky she has an extensive sexual repertoire. They do everything, but of course she is his nurse, his mama, exciting him dangerously with her majestic woman's body. The most exciting thing with Sparky is arousing his wild, inexperienced sexual excitement.

In one Sparky fantasy she is a great lady returning to her mansion from a great ball where powerful men have flocked after her to no avail. She sinks back in her furs on a chaise longue. What will Madame require? Sparky! A governess brings him in and undresses him and Sparky dives under Arlene's clothes, burrowing to her genitals. . . .

FUNKO, ON THE OTHER HAND...

. . . is a hairy ape, a Conan figure. He has a powerful odor all his own. Sweat glistens on his biceps and stubbly jowls and thick body hair. Usually he is a Viking.

She is a teacher in a prison and her classes are entirely male. She teaches them lovely aspects of the good and decent life, and the convicts adore her in her bright, cheerful, very sexy clothes that bring a breath of the free world into the penitentiary. She favors tight knit tops with no bra, to show her nipples. That's to motivate the poor devils!

But one prisoner does not respond to these pretty ways. Funko. He glares at her with hard eyes and makes plain his lust. Nothing she does will make him smile or take any interest in class discussions!

He dishes out split pea soup in the cafeteria. Always split pea . . . She smiles as he fills her bowl, but does he smile back, even an itty bitty? Zilch. She brushes her lovely breast against his hard arm in the corridor; no cigar.

Of course Funko is going to rape her—but when? Sometimes she rushes past the opening scenes to get to the rape. Or is it really rape? Funko appears in her living quarters on the prison grounds. She tries to ask him what is he doing there and what does he mean by it, but her throat is too tight with terror. Old Funk just stands staring at her insolently and her mouth trembles. And her breasts tremble, and the lips of her genitals. A hint of a super-mean smile is at the corners of his mouth.

Funko is never brutal or violent. It's just that he frightens her into doing these things. Without even being told. Trembling in the most humiliating way, she kneels and unzips his fly and out of the prison dungarees springs his huge engine, as she calls his penis. She can barely get the head into her mouth. Terrified, she is overcome with desire to bring him to orgasm. When he does, quarts of thick fluid gush into her mouth and spill down over her breasts.

On other occasions Funko will silently paw her with his criminal paws and force her into various positions in such a contemptuous way, sneering at her wanting what she is getting. How big he is; how ashamed and frightened she is—and how ecstatic!

Funko has her on Viking ships amid icebergs, in smoldering volcanic caverns, in the middle of the Colosseum with the slavering Roman crowd watching. And so forth.

Arlene is a pleasant woman to meet, both shy and businesslike in her demeanor. She teaches art in a private school. Barry is an investment analyst for a Wall Street firm. Neither has told the other of the fantasies described above. They know what fantasies are, and each assumes that the other uses fantasies to some extent. But they are not curious about each other's fantasies.

Arlene has never used a Sparky fantasy while having sex with Barry. But sometimes, with Barry on top of her, she endows him with the personality of Funko.

WHY THEY CAME TO A SEX THERAPIST

I no longer see Barry and Arlene. They came to me because the sex in their marriage seemed to be getting stale. The problem went away after a few sessions. I suggested only a few changes in their sexual routine—trying different positions, different times of day, changes of scene.

They were reluctant to share their habitual fantasies with each other, and there was no reason to force this idea on them. But I did suggest that they work up some new fantasies together. They began to create an adventure comic strip with erotic scenes, using her drawing and their combined ideas. This proved an arousing form of fun. I think that in time, having found a way to share fantasies, they will sometime get Sparky, Funko, Blanket Man and Octopus Man all into the strip.

Arlene was already using Funko fantasies during sex; I asked her, why not use some Sparky ones? Sparky the love slave would fit some of those all-touching and total-pleasuring octopus yearnings of Barry's.

I suggested to Barry that some of his domination fantasies might be used while making love with Arlene—and do you know what he said? He said he thought of her as too gentle and sensitive for anything like that.

A QUITE PRESENTABLE COUPLE

I hope nobody gets the idea that I am telling about two weirdos. They go through life passing for rather tame and unimaginative people. Even to each other!

The person you marry is a live creature made up of long-term dreams, yearnings, memories, fears. Fears mixed with poetry, lust mixed with tenderness, raunchiness mixed with shyness. In fact, your spouse is a creature like yourself, with a great store of secret feelings and images. You will never know all of them. But if you ever get some inkling of your loved one's fantasy life, be ready to accept it as part of the desirable mystery that is another human being.

22

Positions and Maneuvers

ONE or the other of the partners initiates—makes that first move, often having sensed something in the air. Or *thinking* there was a signal, or a prompting from inside. . . . I don't want to go too far back for the origin of this sexual encounter.

It may have been at breakfast, before they went their separate ways. A smile, a drooping of eyelids, a smile in return—an invitation given and accepted wordlessly. A promise of tonight, a thought for both of this couple to hold all day while they do all kinds of busy things.

But now one or the other, the man or the woman, reaches out to touch. Or crosses the room to sit on a chair arm, or catches a hand as the other passes.

THE RITUAL OF AROUSAL AND BEYOND

The ritual of arousal has begun, and one or the other takes the lead in pleasuring. But if she is going to be fully aroused, he will take over at some point, worshiping, nuzzling, kissing, stroking satiny skin, feather-touching erog-

168

enous zones—having in mind, at the right moment, when she touches him in a certain way, to move into one of their known and often-practiced positions for intercourse. To enter her smoothly, with an acquired skill. When she wants him to, and lets him know.

From the way he moves to her, or touches her, she knows the position he has in mind, and she collaborates. Or, being in another mood, she moves in a certain way, showing him another position.

As foreplay has continued, up to this point, they have very likely changed positions already. He has caressed her lying facedown and then faceup, pleasing her and enjoying this journey of exploration himself—for the hundredth time.

Now as they continue after intromission they may change positions once or more than once, as the impulse takes one or the other of them, moving in a way they both know.

When accomplished lovers use a position it is for their pleasure, and can be discarded as other ideas become more exciting, perhaps to be returned to in the end.

This continues until one and then the other has come to orgasm. (Seldom simultaneously, though that can happen.) Then they lie touching, still giving that loving reassurance, conveying affection, and completion. Drifting toward sleep, or toward a reawakening, depending on what sort of night this proves to be.

I mention all this ritual and movement from phase to phase because I don't want anybody to think the positions soon to be described are something static or mechanical or military. They are fluid, spontaneous, usable.

There are, I need hardly say, not just ninety-nine or a hundred positions for lovemaking; there are closer to a thousand—but these do not all fulfill the function of intercourse. There is lying apart, big toes only touching—suited to a passing mood but not to the purpose of impregnating, starting a baby, nor to the satisfying of that special man-woman need to join together and move to a climax with the penis contained in the vagina.

The positions for intercourse, for penis-in-the-vagina encounters, are only a few, basically. The first, the roast beef and potatoes of all this bill of fare, is the missionary position, or male superior.

MALE SUPERIOR

As European travelers ventured into exotic lands, bringing back strange cloths and skins and scents and spices, they also brought tales of how far-off people Did It in unaccountable ways. The one correct, God-fearing way, of course, being with the man on top. Now, in spite of anything you have heard of this being a very staid and unsophisticated attitude for intercourse, it is an excellent one. It is great for beginners, and experienced lovers often return to it. But, it isn't the *only* position.

The woman is on her back. Her legs are apart, knees bent outward a little. The man is facedown above her, between her legs, supporting himself somewhat on knees and elbows. They touch thigh to thigh, belly to belly, breast to breast. In this position he can guide his penis with his hand into her already lubricating vagina. Quite easily. She may like to help with this. He thrusts into her, withdraws partway, thrusts again; she meets him thrust for thrust, moving her pelvis. They can vary this, moving in a number of ways. They can grind in a round or figure-eight motion, or they can move together without his thrusting. She can use vagina muscles to grip him rhythmically.

They kiss and fondle faces, hair, upper bodies; she can grasp his buttocks and pull him closer, circle him tightly with her arms, fondle his testicles.

A variation on this: she lies with legs together; he encloses them with his. Sometimes this is good when she wants to lock his penis inside, to hold it for further enjoyment when it is spent and limp. And she can move her pelvis more freely.

She can lie on her back with knees raised toward her shoulders; she can lock her legs around his waist, or wrap them around his shoulders. All these variations make the vulva, the mouth of the vagina, more available. A pillow under her behind helps with this.

In the male-superior position the man has good control of his thrusting movements, which may help him to contain ejaculation until the moment he likes best—near her orgasm or after it.

FEMALE SUPERIOR

Many couples, not just the woman, like this position best because it gives her control of the action. The man lies on his back, his penis having been aroused and standing ready for her to straddle him and lower herself upon it.

Once he is inside, the woman can sink down on him, remaining upright from the waist up. Or, moving cautiously so that she accommodates his rigid penis, she can lie down on him as he would lie on her in the male-superior position. She can switch around so that her back is to him and she is facing toward his feet.

In this position the woman controls the depth of penetration and the pace of thrusting; she can push her clitoris down on his pubic pone for greater stimulation. For the man, whose hands and arms are now free, this position offers a variety of touching pleasures; he can grasp her anywhere—buttocks, breasts, clitoris. The position is highly stimulating to both partners.

As a variation, the woman can lie across the man at an angle, with one leg in between his. This gives a great deal of freedom to thrust to both partners.

ON THEIR SIDES

The couple should keep pillows at hand to use as they seem needed, for bolstering and padding, while trying this position. Lying on their sides, the couple try various leg combinations. First, both of his inside hers, her top leg over his, her other leg taking the entire burden. That can be too heavy for her, so presently they switch. Now he is embracing her legs with his, his lower thigh supporting. Then they can try it with his lower leg supporting hers, and his higher leg between her legs, rubbing against her clitoris to enhance her sensations.

REAR ENTRY

This is entry into the vagina, not into the anus. A very exciting position in its many variations. I advise the couple to try this when in a playful and experimental mood.

In one variation the woman lies facedown, then raises her hips so that she is supported on her knees and her chest, with her head turned to one side on the mattress. Kneeling behind her, the man inserts his penis into her vagina.

Or they lie on their sides spoon-fashion and she slips his penis between her thighs into her vagina.

Or he sits on the edge of the bed, and she, straddling his thighs, lowers herself onto his penis.

Standing, she leans over, supporting herself by grasping a low piece of furniture.

Rear-entry positions give both partners much freedom to touch and fondle each other—especially for him to stimulate her clitoris with his fingers during intercourse. These are very exciting positions to use once in a while. The character of this excitement I leave to you to discover or define for yourselves.

SITTING, FACE TO FACE

He sits on a straight chair or the edge of the bed; straddling his thighs, she lowers herself onto his penis.

STANDING

She stands against a wall for support, legs apart. He enters her, knees bent slightly, supposing that he is her height or taller. This has often been used outdoors in wet weather. But don't try it under a tree in a thunderstorm.

When the man is quite strong or the woman very light it can be fun, once she is penetrated, to have him clasp her strongly to him and let her twine her legs around his waist.

These latter positions offer psychological stimulation much outweighing in importance any physical advantage. The idea that the man is actually holding her off the earth, having her all to himself during intercourse, is very pleasing to both man and woman.

Pleasuring

Often good lovers will masturbate each other, either to arouse or to continue to orgasm; as part of foreplay or as a separate pleasure in its own right. They can do it simultaneously or take turns. Probably the latter can be done more attentively and skillfully. As most people know how to pleasure themselves manually, it is best for partners to instruct each other in this art.

When she wants to arouse him orally, or to bring him to orgasm in that way, the woman can kneel between his legs on the bed, or on the floor alongside the bed, or find some other way to get her head comfortably close to his groin. Probably she will start by fingering the penis: gently lifting and dropping the head, caressing the shaft and the testicles, possibly ever so gently with sharp clawlike fingernails! She kisses the head, nibbles and licks the shaft, takes the testicles into her mouth partly, and continues as her whim moves her to excite that organ to rigidity. At last she takes head and shaft into her mouth, being careful not to harm it with those teeth, and simulates the thrusting, in-and-out movement of intercourse. Some women, relaxing throat muscles to avoid gagging, can take the penis quite deeply into the mouth—but this can be kept as a goal. You need not be able to do that the first or second or third time. If you want to swallow the semen, it has little taste and is quite digestible. If not, tell the man to warn you when it is coming so that you can catch it in a tissue or any other way that suits you. For the woman the pleasure is in her mastery of arousal and pleasure giving—especially in stop-and-start teasing leading to a terrific ejaculation.

Sometimes the woman who becomes adept at this changes her mind one night or afternoon and decides to swallow that semen after all. But don't push the idea, either one of you.

The man who wants to give pleasure or arousal to his lady by mouth usually starts with lovely kisses to her abdomen, mound of Venus, inner thighs, then moves to the outer genitalia, nibbling and sucking the lips and licking around the clitoris. It may be that she will like that tongue right on her tiny penis, but approach is cautiously. It is a center of pleasurable sensations that can suddenly become highly irritated.

Find what she likes, letting her guide you by words or gently by hand.

The man's willingness to do this is essential. If he is reluctant there is no pleasure in it for either partner. Again, this is not essential to fine lovemaking, and need not be part of your repertoire.

I have not tried to describe every known love act, but only the basic ones to indicate the world of love to be explored. As lovers proceed they will find all kinds of clever variations that give them pleasure. Lovers can feel free to try anything if common sense is used. Don't try swinging from that chandelier.

23

When Baby Comes

WHEN baby comes, at first the new person is there but hidden away, making its presence known increasingly as Mom gets bigger and feels stronger and stronger kicks inside. During the first trimester of pregnancy (the first three months) parents tend to be nervous and cautious about having sex, especially in the first pregnancy. Even if told that it is all right to have sex they may avoid it, because it is *their* baby, and better to be safe than sorry. In the second trimester the expectant parents relax, less fearful of miscarriage, and make love more easily. In the last months she is probably very large, and as the birth approaches both become apprehensive and tend to shun sex.

After the baby is born there is a period when sex is very correctly avoided; beyond that point it may be a sign of trouble if one or the other parent avoids sexual encounters.

I would like to put before you some very common questions about this period when a new person is part of the family.

But before the questions begin, I would like to mention a folk belief about sex during pregnancy—that it is the way to feed the baby. Or that it is a marvelous diet supplement for the child in the womb. This could be used by either parent to encourage the other to join in sexual intercourse, and it is a very cute idea, but of course there is nothing to it. What do I mean "of course"? I mean if you believe this story you are just too quaint, and really need to learn how the unborn baby is fed!

Dr. Ruth, my husband and I get pretty wild when we're Doing It. It is definitely our style. Now I am pregnant and we are very shy of making love. I am and he is. I think we should, though, because I don't want to be the one making the most fuss about pregnancy. But how do I know we won't get carried away and do something to bring on a miscarriage?

Well, you definitely have to make love like the porcupine couple. Very, very carefully! You can do it. Have you ever tiptoed in after a date without waking up your parents? Walked a line? Carried something across the room balanced on the far end of a ruler? Played jackstraws? Threaded a needle? There are a lot of things we have to do quietly and cautiously. When it comes to making love, wild and rough is not the only way. In fact, the slow, teasing, putting-off-orgasm ways are regarded as exquisite by sexual connoisseurs.

Anytime you are very nervous about making love with the penis in the vagina is a time to use an alternative—mutual pleasure with hand, or tongue, or toes or nose. Rubbing, between the breasts, under the armpit, anything.

But you can do it vaginally unless the obstetrician has forbidden it. This is a good time to take a vacation from male-superior, or missionary, position, and of course this is the position most people are afraid to use. The man's weight on top of that water-filled womb with the baby inside is a poor idea, especially if he does become too vigorous. Female-superior (woman-on-top) is good because then Mom can be entirely in control. Lying on the side is good. Rear entry, into the vagina, with both lying on their sides is quiet and strain-free. With her on her back, feet on the floor, genitals at the edge of the bed, he can kneel and enter her without putting any weight on her at all.

Aren't the contractions and excitement of an orgasm dangerous to the baby?

Generally no. They have nothing to do with the baby. They have no effect except to give the mother pleasure! For all that an orgasm is such a fine experience, it really is a small reaction in a limited area, involving some minor muscles and nerve endings. It is not Mount St. Helens going off. Now some people do some acting with an orgasm—arching the back, hollering and thrashing around. *For your own peace of mind* you might give up the dramatics for the duration of pregnancy. Also, in certain women, the contractions of orgasm might induce premature labor—this is something to discuss with your doctor. But generally speaking, a nice orgasm presents no danger to the baby.

Have you ever heard that the invasion of his realm by the penis seems like a threat to the baby, and provides a psychic trauma?

That kind of idea goes back a long way, to when Freudmania was in flower. When people took off in all directions with Freud's theories and proposed ideas that Freud would have scorned. The penis can go into the vagina without bothering the baby in the uterus. There is room for both of them. The baby is quite unconscious of anything like that. A sudden loud noise and the baby tenses, and the mother can feel that, but quiet lovemaking is all right.

How long after birth is it safe to start having intercourse?

Six weeks. Ask your doctor, but six weeks is time enough for the episiotomy, the little cut in the vagina that the doctor makes, to heal. If the birth was Caesarian the time is about the same; again, check with your doctor. Six weeks is a good round definite number and that is why doctors give it. The cuts are usually *well* healed by then.

Why does avoidance of sex set in during and after pregnancy?

There are many reasons, but the main thing to remember is that this avoidance is not something every couple goes through. Enough couples have a little problem with this that nobody has to feel really set apart by it, but there is no law that says it must happen. If something like that seems to be happening, be patient and loving and remind the other partner gently that there is such a thing as physical love, and you love doing it with him or her. The avoidance may be on the part of either partner, either the man or the woman. There may be fear of harming, fear that the vagina is going to feel pain and be fragile.

After the baby is born there may be fear of another pregnancy. The mother may feel run-down, panicked by her motherly responsibility, unable to relax and think about sexual pleasure or giving love to her husband. She may temporarily resent sex as the cause of so much worry, pain and work. If the baby is waking up a lot at night, she may be worn out. She may be undergoing temporary hormonal changes—there are any number of reasons.

And then there are people who had become unhappy in their sexual performance and were glad to have pregnancy as an excuse to give it up and don't want to recommence it now. That calls for counseling.

Is it all right to have sex in the room with the baby, when the baby shares the parents' bedroom?

I would rather have the baby in a nearby room, where it can be heard, so that your needed privacy is maintained. That frees the parents from inhibitions during sex. The sex won't bother the young baby. The baby will bother the parents' sex. And if the baby starts in a room by itself, there won't be the period of getting it used to being on its own (with or without a nightlight—there is no reason for leaving it in total darkness).

When it is accustomed to sleeping in the room with the parents, there comes a time when it should have its own bedroom if at all possible. It is not always possible, and then people have to live with that; they find ways to have sex in private when they can. But it is best for the parents to have their own room for rest and love.

The first night the child is by itself it will cry out for attention often; go to it and reassure it and in a short time it will be giving in to sleep in that room by itself—instead of forcing itself to stay awake.

What if the child walks in on you when you are making love?

What if? What if? What is this what if? It *will* do that. Suddenly a little figure is gliding into the room while you are going at it hammer and tongs! This is nothing. If the child asks what you are doing just say you are making love and let it go at that. Don't begin making up stupid lies, and don't act as if you have been caught by the corporal of the guard.

Very often the child walks in and gets in bed saying nothing, having noticed nothing, only interested in getting to a sleeping place closer to Mom and Dad for this particular night. And if the child has seen something, it will usually take it for some kind of play.

I suggest putting a hook on the parents' side of the door. Then if the child comes to the door there is time to break off the lovemaking. The hook is easier to disengage in case of an emergency in the night than is a lock. Or you can put a chair against the door.

If the child is old enough to ask questions like "What was Daddy doing to you?" and "Why were you crying?" just say that he was loving you; it's a grown-up thing that mommies like. And you weren't crying; those are sounds you make when something feels good.

24

Married Contraception

MARRIED people (and all those live-in lóvers) really have to know everything about contraception. Maybe the news of a little stranger in their midst, or anyway in her midst, is not such a social disaster as it is for the unwed teenage couple, but an unplanned pregnancy changes life radically. It can mean putting off professional advancement for one or both of them. Abortion—well, there are religious couples who can't turn to abortion. And for the others, abortion is a bitter experience when the couple know that they could have avoided it.

I am strongly in favor of two simple, long-established birth-control devices—the condom and the diaphragm. These are the methods I recommend on my TV show and in my lectures, and I am going to tell you again in this chapter why I prefer them to other methods. But as responsible people you should know the other methods available, how they are good and what's wrong with them. And decide for yourselves what kinds of chances you want to take. Because no method is one hundred percent satisfactory for everybody.

Back before World War II there was a couple, legend has it, who sent out a super-cute birth announcement: "We are announcing a blessed event; nothing's effective one hundred percent.'' Today there are methods that are absolute protection against conception but they have very serious drawbacks. You may nevertheless want one of those methods for your special reasons—but you should be informed before you make your adult choice for yourselves. (A woman's gynecologist may refuse her certain methods because of some physical condition; as a doctor he or she may well refuse to be responsible for his patient's health unless she follows his or her guidance.)

There is another reason why married people should be well informed. People look up to them as responsible sources of advice. A friend, sister or brother may turn to you for information, and you will feel much better if you can give it, or hand over a reliable book on the subject.

I want every one of you to know what to say to younger people on this subject. Hundreds of times I have hammered the point that sex without contraception, unless you want a baby and are ready to raise a child, is criminally foolish behavior. I am too modest (yes, I am) to say that I am famous for this, but perfect strangers hail me, hold up a finger and say, ''With contraception!'' They smile and try to say it the way I say it. Some of them, to tell the truth, impersonate me very well.

Terrific! Every time they say that, it burns the message further into their memories. I really like that.

CONDOMS

You may think of condoms as the juvenile method. I do wish every sexually active young fellow would take the responsibility for preventing conception by using a condom every time he puts his penis into a vagina, but it is also a good idea for the established partners to keep a supply of condoms in a bedroom drawer. They are a wonderful stand-by measure. Suppose the lady has forgotten to take her pill a few times? Suppose the foam dispenser is empty? Or the diaphragm has been left at the Holiday Inn in Charleston, West Virginia?

Here is a scene from real life. Toby, a darling husband, wakes up next to his beloved wife and he is full of the quiet happiness that follows a good sexual encounter the night before. He rolls over and nestles up to her spoon-fashion. Somehow his penis becomes erect. Somehow he knows his wife is awake. Presently she arises and goes into the bathroom and returns. Such a quick, deft creature! She had her nightdress on a moment ago; now she is naked. But she says, "Better put a ghost suit on the little fellow, dear boy."

"Really?"

"Much the best thing to do."

"Diaphragm still in, angel mine?"

"Yes, but it is too soon to remove it and very chancy to insert cream merely. The foam dispenser is finished."

"Ah, well, then." He fishes a little packet from the drawer of the table on his side and opens it. He holds the rubber in his hand and stares dreamily at the ceiling.

"Put it on, my love," urges his wife. "Time passes."

"Thing is not as it was," he says.

"Then I shall restore it right away," she says cheerfully, "but first I shall turn off the alarm in this rotten little clock." The alarm attended to, she throws back the cover and taps the sleeping penis gently with her finger. "Up, up, sleepy head," she says. "Rise and shine! Join the frolic."

"Is everyone truly awake and eager?" Toby inquires.

"Oh, indeed," she says, meaning she is wet down there already. She purrs and pets the penis and presently it is quite firm and erect. Taking the condom from Toby, she rolls it skillfully down the sturdy shaft and, gently clawing his scrotum with her sharp nails to be sure none of that fine erection is lost, she straddles him and prepares to intromit.

This shows how a couple can be careful and enthusiastic at the same time. There is no need to spoil the spontaneity. Not when you know how to make putting the condom on the penis part of the (in this case brief) foreplay.

Spontaneity doesn't mean saying, "Let's do it! Not next week, not tomorrow, not in an hour, but now!"—and he drops his pants and she throws herself on her back. It can mean saying that and running for the drawer where those condoms are kept. Only, if you make a dramatic gesture of tearing open the package, be sure you don't rip the delicate sheath.

When I lecture a class about using the condom, I put one on my finger and let them all touch. This is to show how very, very little loss of touch there is with a condom on. And when a couple are together and on good terms, they can make a game of practicing with the condom. I am certain of one thing—if the lady wants him to keep an erection, she can do it. Let her put the condom on him, and if the erection goes down a little, let her pet it back into life. Talk to it cooingly, stroke the penis, brush her breasts across it, caress the testicles . . .

The condom is a seamless rubber device that can be blown up like a balloon—but if you do that with it, don't use it for contraception afterward because inflating it weakens the thin rubber and may cause a leak. It usually comes rolled except for a little of the end. You slip the end over the head of the erect penis, hold it so that there is a half inch to spare to hold the semen when it spurts out of the penis, and unroll the rest down the shaft of the penis. Some condoms are made wih a little bubble at the end to catch the semen. If there is no room for the semen at the end, the fluid will be forced down the sides of the penis, making it slippery, and the condom, which normally clings to the penis, may come off and semen may get into the vagina.

The condom-covered penis slips easily into a well-lubricated vagina, but sometimes there is need for a little lubrication spread over the condom. When you need that, use K-Y jelly. Or use, in an emergency, saliva—but don't use petroleum jelly, otherwise known as petrolatum. Petroleum jelly may weaken rubber.

Don't use a condom twice. No matter how careful or clever you are, you will probably get some semen from the first ejaculation on the outside of the condom.

When you withdraw your penis from the vagina, hold the rim of the condom against the base of your penis and then pull out. That prevents the condom from slipping off. And it is best to withdraw while the penis is still partly erect, or the softening member may pull right out of the condom. Then remove the condom and dispose of it right away. Use a fresh condom for your next act of intercourse, whether in a few minutes or the following night or whenever.

The married couple's way of keeping the condom supply in a drawer is better than the high-school boy's way of keeping it in a wallet in his hip pocket for months or years. Body heat, rubbing and time will cause the rubber to deteriorate. Even kept in a drawer a condom is probably not reliable after twenty-four months of storage.

Trust the condom of a reliable maker. Use it as it comes from the envelope. Don't test it by blowing it up or filling it with water to see if it leaks. This overscientific approach may weaken the rubber without showing any leak before use.

Condoms come in two basic designs—with reservoirs for semen at the end and without. The plain kind is fine if room is left for the semen when you put the condom on the penis. Fancy or novelty condoms—French ticklers or ribbed condoms—supposedly made to enhance the lady's sensations, are just a gag. The special features are usually so far up the condom towards the closed end that no sensitive area of the vagina will be in contact with them.

For a little extra money you can buy the lubricated condoms that are said to enhance male sensations rather than lesson them. They are also said to slip off more easily.

Some men and women are allergic to rubber and are likely to get rashes in and on the genitalia from rubber condoms. It is a rare problem. For these consumers there are "skin" condoms, made from lamb membrane, that are non-allergenic. Aside from this rare and temporary itch, condoms cause no harm to men or women. They are extremely effective in preventing conception. But you must be careful using "skin" condoms because they do not work in preventing the AIDS virus from passing through even when they are not broken. Ask your pharmacist for the best condoms available to prevent sexually transmitted diseases as well as for contraception.

For history buffs, the condom used to be known to army doctors, and others concerned with venereal disease, as the prophylactic. That is because it is a very good barrier against gonorrhea infection during intercourse because the gonococci, or gonorrhea germs, attack the body through the mucous membrane.

THE DIAPHRAGM

Up at the top end of the vagina is the cervix, or neck of the uterus. It protrudes into the vagina like a round little mound. The diaphragm is a rubber cup with no handle that fits nicely over the cervix—because a gynecologist examined the lady and saw that she got the right size and taught her to put it in there nice and snug. This is not instinctive behavior. You have to learn how to put the device up into your own vagina and then check to be sure it is snugly on the cervix.

Before you put the diaphragm in, you put the spermicidal jelly or cream inside the cup and around the rim. Then you press the rim of the device together and insert the entire thing into the vagina. This is done standing with one foot on a stool, or squatting, or lying back with knees drawn up. When the cup is inside you push the tips of your fingers behind the rim and push the device way up behind your pubic bone, which will locate it pretty well over the cervix. Then you feel around to be sure the diaphragm is snugly over the cervix.

When you get your diaphragm, the doctor will show you how to put it in and you will practice doing this in his or her presence. Then you take it home and practice for a week, after which you return to demonstrate your new skill to the doctor so that you can be sure you are doing it right. During that practice week you can't really count on the diaphragm to keep you from getting pregnant. Have your lover use a condom during the learning period.

Sex can begin right after insertion and frequently does. Just as the lady can learn to put a condom on her lover, so a male can become a good diaphragm installer, and having him do this can become part of foreplay. Together, the diaphragm and jelly or cream protect you for four hours after insertion; after that you should put fresh jelly or cream in with the applicator—without removing the diaphragm. That must stay in place for eight hours after intercourse to be sure the spermicide has killed all the sperm. After eight hours you can remove the diaphragm without fear.

When it is put in right, the woman can't feel the diaphragm, nor should it offer any discomfort to the thrusting penis. A woman can walk around town or hike out into the woods quite comfortably with her diaphragm inside. In fact, the doctor will ask you to wear yours to the office when you go to have its placement checked.

Periodically you should have the diaphragm checked for wear or damage, and you may be ready for another size after childbirth, abortion or miscarriage, or pelvic surgery, or if you have lost or gained more than ten pounds of body weight. Sometimes a doctor will suggest another form of birth control if you have poor vaginal muscle tone or if you are allergic to rubber or the jelly or cream.

The diaphragm is also extremely effective against conception, when the user is meticulous about insertion every time she has intercourse. Both the man and the woman can love the diaphragm because it is so safe for the woman.

After you remove the diaphragm, wash it with soap and water, rinse it, pat it dry and dust it with cornstarch—never with talc. Store it in the container it comes in. Check it regularly for wear or tiny holes.

If you do a lot of woman-on-top coitus, put an extra application of spermicide in the vagina, or some foam, or have the fellow wear a condom, because the diaphragm can be dislodged occasionally. Many people are using spermicidal creams and jellies alone as contraceptives. While this is better than nothing, it is relatively ineffective and I do not recommend it. Use them in conjunction with the diaphragm as they were intended.

INTRAUTERINE DEVICES

These are more usually called IUDs. You have to go to a gynecologist to have the right kind prescribed. The doctor inserts it and you leave it in; if you want it out again you go back.

There are a number of designs, but all IUDs are small plastic devices that go up into the uterus through the cervix. Once in the uterus its little arm or arms open out so that it won't slip back into the vagina. It has a threadlike tail that hangs down through the cervix into the vagina. When this tail is quite new, it is apt to be a little annoying to the penis, but it softens after it has been in place awhile and has absorbed fluid. The wearer should feel in her vagina fairly often (every two or three days) to see if the tail is there, because sometimes IUDs work up into the uterus or slip out completely.

The IUD is not a barrier device like a condom or diaphragm. It doesn't block the sperm from going up into the uterus and on up through the Fallopian tube to fertilize an egg cell. But when the fertilized egg cell moves down into the uterus it does not become attached to the uterine wall. The IUD affects the wall of the uterus in some way not really understood, so that it rejects the fertilized egg, which exits the body with the menstrual flow. One theory is that the IUD causes a mild inflammation of the uterine wall.

You can see why this device appeals to many couples—they never have to think about protection against conception when the mood hits them to have intercourse. And it is extremely effective. There are, however, serious drawbacks which must be explored by you with your gynecologist.

THE PILL

Birth-control pills taken as directed are almost 100 percent effective contraception. You get a package of twenty-eight pills and take the first on on your first day of menstruation if that is a Sunday—otherwise you start on the

Sunday after the first day of menstruation. Sunday has no religious significance here. It just helps you to keep track of your four-week pill-taking routine. If you forget one or two pills pregnancy may occur.

If want to get pregnant after some time on the pill, stop taking the pill and use another contraceptive method for three months. This allows your body to readjust to its normal fertile functioning. *Then begin* having intercourse without contraception.

Some clients are so afraid of pregnancy that they can't function sexually or socially while using less absolute protection. To them I say, See a doctor. If he or she recommends the pill, so be it. But personally I am against tinkering with the body's natural hormonal balance unless there is strong reason for it. I am not a physician. This is an informed lay person's feeling.

Also the pill is not carefree contraception. You can forget to take it. There are lots of people who are not good at remembering to take pills and not good at remembering if they have taken them.

Again, consult your doctor for the medical side, and consult your own sense of responsibility about taking the pill as directed.

THE SPONGE

The contraceptive sponge is another method available to you. It is a soft sponge permeated with spermicide. It is easy to put in, no training or skill required. If you can find your vagina, that's all you need. No going to a gynecologist to be fitted—it's an over-the-counter product. Some doctors have warned against its usage because there is not enough data on it, and because of a potential danger of Toxic Shock Syndrome. I am not a medical doctor. But I must say I hope this proves safe, because obviously lots and lots of people would use it who need contraception badly. It *should* be very popular with teenagers, since it can be purchased and used with hardly any contact with older people such as doctors.

But I suspect that some youngsters will not want to spend their soda-and-burger money on these dollar-apiece items.

SURGICAL CONTRACEPTION

A woman can have her Fallopian tubes tied (tubal ligation). A man can have his vas deferens severed (vasectomy). The first will prevent her ever getting pregnant, and the second, if done properly, will prevent his ever impregnating anybody, unless a better method of reversal is found.

A woman hardly ever has her tubes tied until she has had a certain number of children. Often it is done because having more children would be dangerous to her life. I think a woman can decide pretty well whether or not she wants to risk pregnancy after a certain point in her life.

A man can make such a decision too—but he is much more in danger of being sorry that he did. I have known cases. One fellow did it to get a woman to marry him. She didn't want children because she didn't want them, that was all. That was her right, but unfortunately for the guy, she ditched him and there he was, thirty years old and nothing to offer a woman who did want children. And men have remarried after disasters in which they lost wife and child, and they have wanted to start all over.

Still, a grown man can make this decision—especially after a certain age, when he is sure he is too old for the hurly-burly of children in the house.

REALLY DUMB WAYS TO GET PREGNANT

A smart way to get pregnant is to do it deliberately, when you know you want to have children. A dumb way is to get pregnant when you think you are using contraception.

The most foolish way is coitus interruptus—having the man pull his penis out of the vagina before he comes. Many a sixteen-year-old male claims to be expert at this. The trouble is that no male on earth can feel the first semen that seeps out before the big deal of orgasm and ejaculation. He just doesn't know when to pull out.

Having intercourse standing up is no preventive for conception. Having it the first time ever can get you pregnant as well as any other time. Douching afterward is about as effective as clenching your fists, closing your eyes and wishing hard. That includes douching with vinegar-water or Coca-Cola. Rolling over on your stomach hard after Doing It in the missionary position is useless. More of this would be silly. The best rule is not to trust any old wives' or young rascals' method that you haven't read about in a reputable sex manual or learned from a sex educator or your physician.

RESTRICTING SEX TO INFERTILE DAYS

Every woman is infertile on certain days. If she has intercourse on those days only, and if there are no live sperm cells in her vagina, cervix or uterus when fertility returns, she won't get pregnant. Acquiring the knowledge of each woman's fertile periods and using it correctly to avoid impregnation, without other forms of birth control, requires study and daily awareness. The several methods of doing this are rated reasonably effective against conception.

The woman must know when her ovulation is likely to occur during her (roughly) twenty-eight-day cycle. She marks her personal calendar and consults it daily. She takes her vaginal temperature daily and checks the consistency of her vaginal mucus.

I can't conscientiously give more information than this because any woman who wants to use the method should get instruction in person from a physician or teacher who is well versed in it and can check the student's understanding.

No religious group objects to this method of birth control. Contrary to what you may have heard, it can be made to work—but you must understand what you are doing and live dutifully by the method. It has no bad effects on the woman's health, of course.

25

The Limitations of Sex Therapy

O N the radio I often suggest going to see a sex therapist. I don't give my telephone number! I only point out that there is a professional counselor, called a sex therapist, who will help people sort out sexual problems. I am a sex therapist; I believe in sex therapy. I suggest that if a sexual problem comes up in a marriage, the couple should consider seeing a sex therapist the way they would consider calling a painter or a dentist or any other professional. But I don't think they should have a monthly bill from a sex therapist all their married life, or become sexual hypochondriacs and call the therapist every time something different happens in their lovemaking. Getting people addicted to sex therapy is the very opposite of what sex therapy is for.

Sex therapy sets limits on what it will do for people. I think it will be helpful to give an idea of those limits.

FOR MARRYING PEOPLE

This is a book for marrying people—a group of very respectable size, if that impresses you. I myself take marrying people very seriously—for nonstatistical reasons. I am one of the marriers myself. I come from marrying people. I seem to be surrounded by friends, relatives, neighbors and clients who are marrying people.

These people tend to join into pairs. If they don't stay married or joined until death do them part, they tend to pair up again soon after splitting. Whatever courses their lives may take, they end up in pairs. For good in some cases, not so good in many others—but for these people the picture isn't complete unless they are part of a pair.

There is another way of putting this. Great numbers of people want, and search for, and try to form, meaningful sexual relationships. For these people the picture isn't complete unless there is a sustained relationship. They may not have the picture framed—they hang it on the wall for a while to see if it really goes with the room. Maybe they frame it later, maybe it comes down—or falls down.

People who search for and form relationships without the formalities of marriage can't really claim that they are not the marrying kind of people, as far as I am concerned. They have the same needs urging them into what they hope will be meaningful matings. Their relationships contain many of the elements of marriage. Similar pleasures, similar problems.

SEX WITHIN RELATIONSHIPS

What I do know for a fact is that in all kinds of marriages the physical mating can bring joy or disappointment. In recent years couples have come more and more to people like me, hoping for help in finding sexual pleasure in their marriages.

What they can get from me and other modern sex therapists is not magic. Informed advice, and a good deal of detective skill in finding out what is wrong and what may be done about it, is what we have to offer.

EDUCATORS AND THERAPISTS

Happily, since we sex therapists know a good deal more about what has happened in hundreds of bedrooms than the average couple knows, we very, very often can remove pain and fear that come from simple misunderstanding and lack of information. In doing this the therapist acts as little more than an educator. One or two meetings with the therapist are all that is needed.

In the more complex problems that develop between the members of a couple we offer real therapy. The couple may visit the therapist weekly, biweekly or at longer intervals, for six months or a year. Seldom for as long as a year, and often for no more than a few sessions. Sex therapy is short-term. It doesn't go on for years or forever. It was not designed that way.

SO WHAT GOES ON IN THAT OFFICE?

What is sex therapy? I know that people have some wild pictures of it in their heads! Partly this comes from the word *sex*. That word produces pictures of things going on. But *therapy* is to blame too, because people do think of it as touching. The most familiar kind of therapy is physiotherapy, in which the therapist often gives the patient passive exercise.

Now if *that* therapist takes hold of you and moves your arms and legs and massages you, what does the sex therapist do? Hah? Naturally, people think that way.

Let me tell you—in my office there is nothing going on but talk! Sometimes I show the client or clients some pictures to show what I'm talking about, or I use a pair of dolls to demonstrate sexual positions. See? These dolls are wooden, without fingers, toes, faces, penises or vaginas. But they are jointed much as real people are, so the positions one can put them into are practicable for real people.

They are the kind of dolls artists have used more or less

forever, for reference, when they don't have a live model at hand. They are called, don't ask me why, but they have been called for generations, long before sex therapy came along, lay figures. That is purely a coincidence.

They are not very sexy.

First people come to my office and we talk and try to find out what is really wrong. If it seems to call for certain physical treatments—what we call exercises—the clients go home and do that part by themselves. Not in my office nor with me watching. That would be very embarrassing for them, even if not for me, and it would interfere with the homework the clients are supposed to concentrate on doing.

There isn't even a couch in my office. Unlike Sigmund Freud, who was a psychoanalyst and who died before sex therapy was born, I have no use for a couch in my practice. I sit on a chair; the clients sit on chairs. That's the way to carry on a conversation.

There is a couch in my outer office. No one sits there. It's for dropping things on—my sling bag, shopping bag, coat, mail, things like that. Or sometimes I take a little nap on it between clients, or after the last client and before going out to have dinner or to give a lecture. I wouldn't have a couch in my office because it would make new clients nervous. "What's going to happen on *that?*"

There is nothing to make anybody nervous. Nothing medical looking, because I am not a physician. I won't even prick your thumb or ask for a specimen or stick things back into your throat to make you gag.

I won't hurt you, and nothing in sex therapy will hurt you. It isn't that kind of thing. I have said elsewhere in this book that learning to have an orgasm won't change a person's life in a major way, beyond bringing a little joy into it. Nothing so overwhelming as to justify fear. And nothing else in sex therapy will do that, either. You can stay, essentially, what you are and want to be.

THERAPY AND THERAPY

I'd like to disassociate psychosexual therapy, to use the full on-our-dignity term, from some other experiences you may have heard about.

Therapy is a broad term meaning "treatment." Some therapy calls for swallowing medicine, absorbing heat or rays, exercise, training. Speech therapy, for example, is for people who have trouble forming sounds or words or speaking clearly and smoothly. Eliza Doolittle had speech therapy from Professor Higgins in *My Fair Lady*.

But sex therapy is something else. So far I have not tried to improve anyone's way of talking, except to tell a guy not to bark at his wife while having sex, perhaps.

Sex therapy may be no more than giving some special information to the client. I have had to explain to married people where the vagina is to be found, and, in more complicated cases, to explain what is meant by *dog-fashion* and *sexual fantasy*. Or how to arouse a partner by foreplay to make intercourse more enjoyable.

When sex therapy does involve exercises, it is the clients who do the therapy. There is no physical touching between you and the therapist beyond a handshake.

FINDING A RELIABLE THERAPIST

You may have read about sex therapy or psychotherapy involving sex between client and therapist. I cannot deny what is so well known—but this kind of unprofessional behavior is easy to avoid. You go only to a sex therapist who has been recommended by a competent medical authority, or by a trustworthy social or religious agency. Ask your doctor to give you the name of a sex therapist, or ask your clergyman or a hospital or clinic. If talking to someone you know embarrasses you, look up a human-sexuality clinic in the phone book. They will steer you in the right direction.

No member in good standing of the American Association of Sex Educators, Counselors and Therapists will attempt to touch you or to take part in any activity violating your conscience.

And when you go to see that therapist, state right away that you want to know what the treatment is likely to be. There is no need to be embarrassed about that. After all, you are going to be talking about your very private problems, about your vagina or penis and such very personal things, so there is no reason not to be open about possible misgivings. The therapist understands, has heard about misgivings before. Long before taking any client, a therapist is taught about misgivings as part of therapy training.

If you have fears of going to a sex therapist the first time, let me assure you that these fears are very sensible. No one will regard you as strange for having them. And you are very unlikely to run into a sex therapist who is anything less than professional. As long as you go through respectable channels to find your therapist.

In the recent past a number of centers for sexual enrichment—I suppose you might call them that—have been given play in the media. These places offered mass nudity and treatment that seemed to be little more than sex orgies. You are not likely to get into a thing like that *unless you want to very much*.

These comments on often stated misgivings are meant to guide and reassure timid readers, and not to start a panic. I think this reassurance needs public statement, and if any colleagues think I should never have mentioned the possibility of fear, or of unethical behavior, I can only say as civilly as possible that I disagree.

A NEW DISCIPLINE

One reason people need to be reassured is that reputable, respectable, ethical sex therapy, connected to respected universities and hospitals, is a new thing, no more than twenty years old. Masters and Johnson began their pioneer work in St. Louis in 1954. Before that, treatment of sexual problems was by physicians or surgeons for organic disabilities, or by long-term psychotherapy.

The new kind of treatment worked wonders in thousands of cases, and to the many people who came to it, this new treatment seemed the greatest thing since sliced bread. Which I do not like much myself, being a bakery-bread person.

Well, sex therapy is not miraculous. It is practical, down-to-earth, helpful, a blessing—and limited. It will not accomplish many of the things that people come to it hoping for. We don't treat people who have false expectations of us—not if we can help it. We steer people to other, more appropriate forms of treatment.

WHAT SEX THERAPY CAN'T DO

Sex therapy works to improve the sexual functioning of men and women. That is a worthy goal; but improving your sex life will not cure your neurosis, if you have one; it will not release a Mount St. Helens of creative ability and make you the new Michelangelo; it will not cure the bald patch on your front lawn; it won't even make the earth move every time you have an orgasm.

I will always speak well of the orgasm. It is a wonderful experience. But people who have never had one, who have read about them, seen them simulated in the movies, heard their friends brag about them, fallen for the false idea that orgasms will cure them of every shortcoming from always losing their glasses to a weak serve in tennis, are disappointed sometimes in the real thing. It may be like the first taste of caviar. You must cultivate the taste.

And having a good sex life is a wonderful thing in a marriage that has other things going for it, but without good companionship and mutual support in endeavors like careers and making a home in the world, marriage will not work. The divorce courts are full of couples who do very well in bed together. Sometimes the bad feeling between two people is too long established to be overcome.

People have to *want* to find sexual pleasure to be helped.

Where the mind is set against trying for a better sex life, no therapist can help.

A FEW PHONE CALLS

There is no harm calling up a human-sexuality clinic or a reputable sex therapist. One of the good things about sex therapy is that, while it cannot always solve every problem or cure every ill, it can't do you any harm.

My phone rings as I sit in my office dictating this. It is a man who says that he has a sore penis. I tell him to call a urologist right away. I give him a phone number. I explain that I am not a physician. There—I've cleared up a confusion in his mind and pointed him on his way.

A woman phones and says she supports three daughters who seem to be getting into all kinds of trouble. I recommend a social service agency run by her church. I am not equipped to help groups of teenage girls who keep dropping out, hanging out, going with wayward boys, shoplifting, drinking, driving without licenses while under the influence, smoking dope and so forth. My sympathies are stirred, but there are other people who are better at dealing with things like that.

A woman makes an appointment to talk about her vaginismus (I'll discuss this later), which began after the death of her husband. This is well within the scope of sex therapy, so I make an appointment with her. I talk to her for half an hour and send her on her way, recommending a psychiatric clinic. She may have vaginismus, but the first thing to deal with are her delusions. Among other things, she is certain that Washington is controlling her brain by electronics. I am not a psychiatrist.

A woman phones and says she has never had an orgasm. I chat with her a little longer than I usually do because the brain-controlled lady has made me suspicious, but my new caller seems rational so I make an appointment with her very happily. I tell her what the first hour costs and say that subsequent hours are negotiable. I am cheered up because I have a very good prospect of helping this woman to get what she wants.

Not a Cadillac. Not a whole new life. Not a new lover who looks like John Travolta. Just an orgasm, just the ability to have orgasms. That I can manage.

26

Erectile Difficulty

THERE is a story about a certain famous man, and since I am not absolutely sure it is true I won't name him. But as a sex therapist I know the story *could* be true, and it makes a very important point—and an encouraging one.

One day after a good part of his life had gone by, much of it enlivened by memorable love affairs and sexual frolicking, he noticed that his famous erections had left him. So he thought, "Well, I'm old. That's it." Some years later he woke up one morning, and to his amazement, amusement and great pleasure, he had a big erection. It came back several times. He had been living a hermit's life, but now he set about finding a nice woman to live with him. He found her and they got along very pleasantly. How would I explain that?

DEPRESSION AND ERECTIONS

A man who is going through a bad time, who feels depressed, can lose his ability to have erections for a while.

That can increase his depression and make him even less likely to become erect. Then his life can change for the better, he cheers up, suddenly he notes that his sexual potency has come back to him. This can happen to him even at an advanced age.

I am not saying, "Don't worry, my dear man, just wait around and your erections will come back like the swallows— if not this spring, perhaps when your beard has turned white." But if your erections have become undependable, you should know that they can make a comeback. And there are ways to help them. The least you can do is try.

WHEN A FELLOW NEEDS A FRIEND

Of course there are males who have never had any trouble with their erections, except sometimes finding someone to share them with.

The class of males who have the least trouble having erections are males under twenty. Erections plague them! At all hours and often in public places. But later, when they begin to replace fantasy girls with real women, they often come to know what erectile difficulties are. A rudely asser- tive penis can be a shrinking violet when you take it out in company.

That is when a fellow can use a very knowing and sympathetic girl. I don't say an Older Woman; I don't say an accomplished call girl. But just a human female who likes men and knows a little about sexual functioning. She might even be a virgin—but probably not a totally ignorant one.

WHY STRONG MEN PANIC

As for *older* males—between twenty and a hundred, say—there is no reason to wish you could remain perpetual- ly at the peak of sexual vigor. It is unrealistic. But among experienced males there are very few who do not know what it is to have a suddenly uninterested penis. This can cause the beginning of panic.

The male joke goes, "It isn't panic the first time you can't get it up the third time. Panic comes the third time you can't get it up the first time." This gets a big laugh in the locker room because nearly every man in there has felt at least a twinge of panic.

Do men come to a sex therapist because they have an occasional erectile failure? Probably not, though they will phone in to a radio talk show and say, "Dr. Ruth, I have this friend of mine . . ." And that's fine, because we all need friends. What I tell them is not to worry about an occasional failure like that. It just means you're "friend" is tired and "his" penis is being smarter than he is.

In my office I am more likely to see men who have persistent erectile problems. Once in a while I see a man who can't remember ever having had an erection. I send him off to see a urologist before trying any sex therapy with him. If the urologist says there is nothing physically wrong, that reassures me *and* the client. Men who have never had an erection should not give up the idea without consulting a doctor.

DEGREES OF DIFFICULTY

Modern sex therapy doesn't like the word *impotence*. It is too vague, and for so long it has conveyed a sense of hopelessness. We say erectile difficulty, or erectile dysfunction, for a whole class of troubles men have with erections. These troubles include

- having erections when alone but never near a woman;
- having erections near a woman that go down when she offers herself;
- having erections during foreplay that wilt when you try to put it in;
- having erections that go down as soon as they get inside;

- having erections that go down after a few thrusts;
- having erections but not with one's wife;
- having half erections, or soft ones;
- having unreliable erections;
- having erections rarely; and last,
- never having had an erection—the class of erectile difficulty that should be taken to a medical doctor. This extreme kind is called primary erectile dysfunction. All other kinds are called secondary.

CAUSES OF ERECTILE DIFFICULTY

The causes of erectile difficulty are mysterious, like the erection itself, which is a complicated reflex connected with the brain and controlled by the brain.

There are physical causes, which are treated by medical doctors. For instance, the hormone testosterone may be injected. In some cases of persistent erectile difficulty, penile implants may be put into the penis by a surgeon. Alcoholics, drug users and people using certain prescription drugs may have erectile trouble.

The psychic causes are experiential, deep in the hidden recesses of the personality. Psychoanalysis probes to find these causes and remove them. It is a slow process and has not a high rate of success in improving sexual problems.

The more reachable causes of sexual dysfunctions like erectile difficulty are the conditioning processes affecting sexual behavior. These processes can often be reversed by sex therapy, which bypasses the deepest causes. Often a person relieved of a distressing dysfunction goes on into psychoanalysis. Meanwhile the client has a functioning sex life.

A VERY TYPICAL CASE

Here is a case of erectile dysfunction that was *so* typical because more than one thing was going wrong with this couple. And the other things contributed to the man's erectile problem. They were a fairly religious, very conventional couple in their thirties. With all their troubles, they weren't thinking seriously of divorce. This was to the good as far as sex therapy was concerned—I can't do sex therapy as a last-ditch stand against divorce. The couple have to be agreed about wanting to stay together and be willing to try to help each other to a happier sex life. They don't have to be madly in love, but they have to be friendly enough to be mutually helpful.

He worked too hard. His kind of business required it, and it was his ingrained habit. There was no question of his changing his line of work. They had two children, lived in a good neighborhood and had a summer home. He was away at work up to twelve hours a day, sometimes seven days a week. They had had pretty good sex in the early years of marriage but less of it as time passed. Resentments built up between them about various aspects of their life.

FIRST THINGS FIRST

After I had listened for one and a half sessions to their story, I told him, in her presence, "The first thing I want you to do is to go buy yourself a basketball." That startled him! This was sex therapy? Was I going to tell him to have sex with a basketball?

I said, "Look. Six days a week you work late. Once a week you have dinner with your family or your wife's family. You go to PTA, you serve on committees, you help with the scout troop. All that is great. You're a good husband and father, even though your job is exhausting. But what time is there for yourself? You used to play basketball. Go buy yourself a basketball and one morning or afternoon a week I absolutely want you to go shoot baskets."

If I had told him to find himself a hobby he would have put it off. But this assignment was definite. If a ball was in his hands he would go use it. He needed something entirely his own, not for the job or the family or the community, just for him, or he would go on thinking he himself did not exist.

Before you want a sex life for yourself, you have to believe you are a person.

Now, I don't tell every man with an erectile difficulty to buy a basketball!

ONE PROBLEM AT A TIME

Then I discussed their sexual problems, which were first that she had no orgasms and then that he had had no erection for six months.

"One thing at a time," I said. "First we deal with his erections. Then if you still aren't having orgasms, we'll work on that."

THE EXERCISES

For the first week they were to have no intercourse and he was not to be made to ejaculate by any means. He was to lie back and let her pet and caress and nuzzle him from top to toe except for the genitals. And he was just to lie there and feel whatever sensations he felt and take note of them. Then he could do the same for her.

"When you met, you wanted to touch each other," I said. "That came before sex. You have to remember those feelings, and how exciting touching was." It was also to let him react to sensuous touching with no challenge to produce an erection. This usually allows the man to have erections, the burden of producing them being gone.

During that week they found the exercises embarrassing and they were awkward about doing them, but they stuck diligently to the task, making little jokes about its being time for homework, her turn or his to be the playground. The awkwardness disappeared a little at a time, and by week's end it was forgotten and he was having pretty good erections. But he feared he would not if he were ever challenged to produce them.

The next week they did the same thing, with an interesting addition. Now, the tour of the body finished, they could—must, in fact—play gently, teasingly with each other's genitals. She was not to bring him to orgasm.

"I should hope not!" she said.

"But he may bring you to orgasm if you wish it," I said. Which startled her so much she forgot to say anything else.

He suggested that, since they were unused to this sort of thing, we should talk about playing with genitals and how it was to be done. I suggested ways of touching, and said whatever one liked the other was to repeat, and they were to tell each other what was especially teasing and exciting. Again I explained that this was a normal thing to do in foreplay and made for much more exciting coitus.

If at any point he began to worry about losing his erection, he could give up his passive role and pleasure her instead. That usually restores the erection, and it stops his watching his own erection, worrying it out of existence.

By the following week, when they were to take turns pleasuring each other to orgasm, her resistance to the idea had fled. The one question on my mind was, would she allow herself to reach orgasm under his ministrations? She had hinted at having "felt something" during brief masturbation episodes "a long time ago" but might not be willing to be pleasured to the point of ecstasy. My fears were unfounded. That week each of them enjoyed orgasms in each other's company.

During this period he was instructed to think only of his own pleasure when it was his turn to lie back and play the pasha, the fancier of erotic pleasure. At another time he might play the attentive lover to her, but when she was pleasuring him he was to think only of himself. To keep negative thoughts at bay, he was to indulge in any sexual fantasy he liked. They might, if they pleased, tell each other their fantasies, but they were not obliged to do this. This pair chose not to. I think she did not want to be jealous of his.

His erections were strong and reliable during this part of the exercises, except for one night when he was exceptionally tired and fell asleep. That was not important. I took them on to the next step. I had to use my little jointed wooden dolls to explain the female-superior position to her. When he was erect she was to get into this position, straddling his loins, and guide his penis into her vagina. She was to move gently but to disengage before he ejaculated. Then she was to repeat the action and disengage again. This teasing behavior, very arousing to the man, was to be repeated on several occasions until the time came when he wanted very much to thrust and ejaculate. Then she would permit him to do so. In this way his erectile ability and his confidence that he could enter her and continue intercourse would be restored.

TALKING ABOUT FEELINGS

During the sessions in my office we talked about the exercises and the feelings they brought out. The basketball player said it made him feel babyish to lie there and let her pet him all over. At first. But he got to liking it within the protection of the intimacy this behavior built up around them. She had not liked doing this to him, or for him. It seemed as if he ought to want her more and that it was humiliating to have to pleasure him. I described to her a possible relationship where each cared for the other's pleasure, where they shared the responsibility for producing the erections and both of their orgasms. The erection especially was their joint property. This kind of counseling, often dealing with much more stubborn resistances, is a very important part of the sex therapy.

DO-IT-YOURSELF SEX THERAPY?

I realize that these procedures are being publicized widely today. People read the books of Masters and Johnson and of Helen Singer Kaplan and they will try some of these things on their own. This is inevitable and even good. Some people will get stuck at some point without professional guidance, but others will not, and it is a good thing that people should get to realize that the actions used in the exercises are not only permissible but beneficial to good sex. Nothing done in the exercises is harmful. If someone reacts strongly against them, the exercises can be—and I am sure will be—dropped. No irreversible harm can be done.

People in remote areas, far from any sex therapist, may very well try these exercises. I only warn that if the exercises bring on very strong negative reactions, and seem to be worsening the marital relationship, they should be dropped for a while at least. Perhaps until there is an opportunity to get professional help.

The exercises are easy to follow, but sometimes they must be modified for the particular couple. And where the sex therapist really demonstrates skill is in clarifying issues, reassuring the two members of the couple. But I repeat that the exercises are not dangerous. This is not do-it-yourself brain surgery!

GOOD NEWS FROM SLUMBERLAND

A man came to me saying he was sure he would never have an erection again. So why did he come to me at all? Because he really believed someone could help him, of course. He wanted the magic that would bring back his erection. After me he would try powdered rhinoceros horn. (Poor rhino!)

I sent him to a sleep clinic where they taped wires to his penis and tucked him in for the night. In the A.M. the recordings showed that he had produced seven erections during his rapid-eye-movement periods of sleep. Thus he learned that he was still capable of erections. This gave him something positive to build on, and we went ahead to work on his having erections while awake.

FAITHFUL IN FANTASY, EVEN

When the man progresses to trying coitus, he needs fantasies to stave off those doubts, that monitoring of his own erection. But some religious men may not lust after anyone but their wives, not even in fantasy. To them I give this advice: Think back over your courtship, the early days of your marriage. Think of moments when you found your wife especially exciting. Build your fantasies on those memories.

I recall giving this advice to one pious fellow and the way he smiled at it. Somehow this made me uneasy, and I found myself overexplaining the idea to him, and telling him how this would involve no impurity of thought since he would be thinking only of desirable feelings for his given bride. He kept smiling in a fixed way and I realized he was already picturing those delectable moments from his marital past. It made me feel almost indecent, being there while he did it!

Whatever he summonded up, it must have been effective. That couple's sex life made a fine comeback.

27

Premature Ejaculation

*I*F you are a man you have probably experienced it at some time. You were dancing close with a girl and you came in your pants. You were bumbling around trying to have sex with a girl in the backseat of a car and you came before you could get in. Or just after you got in, not giving a very good account of yourself as a Don Juan. It may have been on your wedding night.

But while some men get over premature ejaculation after a few vaginal mishaps, with others it seems to be an ingrained habit. So embarrassing and humiliating! And the man feels so rotten because he is not pleasing his lady, and he wants to. But of all the problems a man may have, this may be the easiest to solve. I can think of only one case that was beyond me.

A DIFFICULT CASE

A man complained to me that he always came too soon in his wet dreams! As far as he was concerned, wet dreams were a big disappointment. I told him if he knew anyone with a real case of premature ejaculation, to send him around and I would definitely get rid of it, but I had no training for slumberland sex problems.

WHAT IT IS

Premature ejaculation is coming before you want to—before you have enjoyed the encounter. Leaving you frustrated. It isn't a question of coming in so many seconds, or minutes, or even before the lady is *ready* to give you a gold medal for your performance. It's before *you* want to. We have to define it that way, or other problems confuse the issue. For instance: Suppose the lady won't let you stimulate her enough with foreplay and insists on beginning coitus long before she is near orgasm. You ejaculate after fifteen minutes and her orgasm is still ten minutes away. After a quarter of an hour, that is not premature ejaculation!

Really, what you want is not to overcome "premature ejaculation" but to learn *control*.

THE COUPLE DOES THE THERAPY

When a man phones my office and says he wants to consult me about his premature ejaculation, I hope that he is married or in a good relationship. A loving partner will make the treatment so much simpler. There is a way of working with unattached men on this problem, but the goal is good intercourse and the best person for the man to work with is the lady who will benefit by his improvement. The lady in his life.

The couple do the therapy; the therapist only guides them. If a couple have a good thing going they can find real sexual pleasure in the exercises the therapist will prescribe. These sexual experiences become part of the couple's story, can be used long afterward in their repertoire. They are based on exercises devised by Masters and Johnson twenty years ago; they include a technique invented by Dr. James

Seman, and they have been modified by Dr. Helen Singer Kaplan, my teacher.

SABOTAGE!

When a couple come to me about their premature ejaculation problem, I tell them that if the man has an erection for any length of time at all, and if he does ejaculate, then we can prolong the erection and control the ejaculation. But *he* has to want the skill in controlling his ejaculation himself. Not just for her, not because she has nagged him into coming to a sex therapist. And she has to want this improvement in their mutual sex life for herself. Otherwise one or the other may work up a resentment against the exercises and find a way to sabotage them.

Why would a man do that, hindering his own cure? Some guys just don't give a damn! All they want, for sex, is a woman to pile on top of, to pump away at so they get an orgasm. The sooner the better, because they *want* it! If she doesn't enjoy sex, let *her* go to a therapist.

As for the woman, she may sabotage the exercises for a number of reasons. She thinks it's humiliating, having to work so hard to get him to make love right. She may get bored because sex doesn't mean that much to her. And she may be afraid that once he can control his orgasms he'll be chasing every woman in sight, whereas now he is a nice shy little husband. There may be trouble in that household calling for marital counseling before we embark on sex therapy. And there is something else I caution them about.

"You have come to me because neither one is satisfied with sex. When we have improved the gentleman's control, which we definitely will do, the lady should start to enjoy sex more. But if she doesn't, it may be that *she* has a problem of her own. But for the time being we won't think of that—right now it has to be gentlemen first."

THE EXERCISES

For two weeks the couple will abstain from intercourse. The husband is to take it easy for a while. Flat on his back, letting her play with his penis, thinking of nothing but the sensations in his groin.

First he has to have an erection, which they can obtain by any means they prefer. Then he is to lie back with eyes closed and let her stimulate him manually. Now, she may know how to do that or not. If not, he can give her directions. Truly a rich man's life—doesn't even do that for himself! He must not worry about her feelings. He is the pasha; she is the harem toy. He's the samurai and she the geisha.

If he doesn't know what to tell her to do, I shall be surprised. She is to masturbate him slowly, gently, and he is to wait for that moment just before it's too late. For a feeling that tells him, "One more stroke and there is no turning back—you're going to come." He has to learn to recognize that premonitory sensation. Then he must ask her to stop.

Now, I know this is tension-building material, and she is not going to like it if he gets in the habit of lying there and barking orders at her. Even a good-natured woman has her limits. When he has that feeling, let him say, "Stop, please." Why shout? She isn't a block away.

Very soon the feeling that he is going to come—is that English, going to come?—will go away. Then let him say nicely, "Start, please." We call this the stop-start exercise.

At this point he may have lost part of his erection, but a little attention will bring it back. He may think it wise to advise, "Faster, please" or "Slower, please." When he feels the premonitory sensation again, once again he says, "Stop, please."

Let her think what a great woman she is—a sex therapist in her own right, a skilled courtesan, a sexual Florence Nightingale.

Once, twice, three times, let her bring him to the brink of orgasm and stop. The fourth time—ah! The fourth time she will keep going for the big one. This time he can ejaculate.

The next night he can pleasure her and give her as many orgasms as she wants. He can hug her, kiss her, massage her—whatever the capricious creature wants. But no intercourse. He can use his fingers, tongue, nose, toes—anything to show how appreciative he is of her efforts. This should keep her from feeling she had to do all the work around the house.

While he is being pleasured, I generally say that he is to let her do all the work and that he is not to thrust. But some men have to thrust a little or they go down and stay down, so let him use discretion here.

The couple continue this for a couple of weeks, or until he has been able to last until the fourth premonitory sensation on at least four occasions. After that she is to use petroleum jelly or some such lubricant on her hand. This stimulates the feeling of the lubricated vagina and is much more exciting than the dry hand—which is why we don't use it from the beginning.

Let them continue with the slithery hand until he has lasted to the fourth premonitory sensation on four occasions.

STOP-START COITUS

Now to try to use the stop-start technique with intercourse. When he is erect and she is ready, lubricated, let her get into the female-superior position, straddling him to take the penis into her vagina. He puts his hands on her hips and guides her movements so that she stops in time. Again, three premonitory signals and then he ejaculates on the fourth. This position gives her excellent control of her movements.

After three or four good sessions in this position, let them go on to a side-lying position, facing each other. They practice with that until they are proficient at it and then go to the male-superior, or missionary, position.

During all this the man learns to control ejaculation

almost indefinitely, though endless copulation is *not* desirable in spite of anything you may have heard about some
sexual athletes' staying power. But he gains confidence, and
in the following months he learns to stop and start so
smoothly, at just the right point, that his performance seems
one long uninterrupted entity.

The man should have obtained good control in anything
from a few weeks to a couple of months, and excellent
control by six months after the first exercise. Once a week,
after the couple have gone on to intercourse, they should
have one session of stop-start manual stimulation.

During this period the lady is never to use oral stimulation. It is far too exciting!

LIMITATIONS

This therapy is not available to every client. Orthodox
Jews, for instance, may not ejaculate outside the vagina.
But the exercise can be adapted for them; after the third
premonitory sensation and the third stop, they can restore
the erection, put the penis into the vagina and let him finish
by thrusting to orgasm.

A man can adapt these exercises to a life in which there is
no helpful regular partner; following the very same exercises, starting with a dry hand and going on in time to a
lubricated one, he can do for himself what the woman is
described as doing. This is not ideal, but a man can learn
good control this way and then put it to use in intercourse.

CAUSES OF PREMATURE EJACULATION

In psychoanalytic theory, some men hate women and get
sex with them over with as soon as they can. Hard for the
man who is anxious to learn to control ejaculation, in order
to please his lady, to give much credit to this.

Masturbation, which is now the cure for the condition,
used to be blamed for it! One theory was that young boys,

masturbating swiftly and furtively, trained themselves to come as soon as possible. Could be.

OTHER METHODS FOR CURING PREMATURE EJACULATION

The original Masters and Johnson method called for the woman not to desist from stroking the penis but to pinch it rather firmly just below the head. This worked, but women were often timid about hurting the organ, on the one hand, or then really *were* hurting it on the other. It seems simpler just to have her stop.

Male folklore: guys used to advise each other to masturbate sometime before intercourse in order to lower sexual tension and energy and last longer. This of course made sex less exciting. I never heard how well it worked.

The silliest method was to think about something boring or off-turning during sex. Instead of thinking about the naked woman in your arms, you were to think about your mother-in-law, your boss, some problem at the office. Or add a column of figures mentally.

There are creams sold to rub on the penis and anesthetize it a little so that it won't come so fast. This can have the effect of putting the erection to sleep, and it dulls the sensations in the vagina too.

Fortunately, the stop-start method is so reliable that in a generation we expect to see premature ejaculation disappear entirely. Except possibly in Iran, where obscene books like this one are forbidden!

28

Retarded Ejaculation

So much seems to depend on ejaculating at just the right time, and the rules are so complicated! A guy could go out of his mind!

Men used to worry about coming in their sleep. It was supposed to drain away their manhood. Thank heaven that idea has disappeared! Then, a generation or so ago, some nudnick put out the idea that the man should ejaculate just when his lady is coming. If sooner or later, the show is a flop. Since this happens no more often than you win a fortune on the slot machines, the idea made armies of men doubtful of their worth as lovers. Really nice fellows—a shame! I think that very few people worry about that now, either. If you both have a good time, that calls for hurrahs.

And then there was the idea that a man should select the moments for the ejaculation with studious care because he has only a limited number of emissions to last his whole life, no more. Something like 1,247 ejaculations—or was it 1,472? If any young boy is reading this, don't let that notion get stuck in your darling head! There is no limit to the number of times you can come, or cream, or whatever you and your friends call it now.

Nowadays men still worry about when to ejaculate. If you come too soon, your erection goes down and the encounter is over and the lady hasn't had her fun yet—so that makes you a miserable flop as a lover. If her habit is to reach orgasm after a minute of thrusting and you come in half a minute, *pfui* on you. And if she needs an hour of thrusting and you come in fifty-nine minutes, you're still a premature ejaculator! Is this sex they all talk about really a pleasure?

THE MAN WHO CAN'T COME IN COMPANY

Of course, if such stringent rules were really applied, sex might have disappeared years ago. Couples come to terms with sexual reality.

There is a rule that almost no one is ready to give up on, even so. You should be able to come *sometime*. And that worries those men who find they just can't ejaculate, no matter how long the sex act lasts. They can thrust for an hour but no go.

When a man whose problem is coming too soon first hears about *retarded* ejaculation, he may think, "Hell, I wish I had that problem." But unfortunately it's no fun. It makes a man very unhappy not to be able to come when he wants to. Yes, he likes being able to last long enough to bring the lady to the point where she is thrusting wildly, and hugging and biting and saying, "Yes, yes, *yes!*" But he would like to have his moment, too, while he is holding her, while he is inside. And he can't. After a while he has to give up. Then he can lie next to her while his erection goes down, or he can get up and go to the bathroom and masturbate to ejaculation—because he *can* ejaculate when he is alone.

That relieves tension but it doesn't leave him feeling happy. He feels guilty, he feels ashamed, because he can't make love "like everybody else."

Just as the preorgasmic woman can't achieve orgasm when she wants to, the man with retarded ejaculation can't come when he wants to. The feelings of shame and anger are much the same, except that while the preorgasmic woman may think, "It's his fault—he's a lousy lover! He's impotent!" the man who can't come nearly aways blames himself.

SIMULATED SHUDDERS

He thinks he is freaky because he can come when he masturbates but he can't do it with a woman. Often he can't even do it in the same room with a woman. He may feel like standing up and swearing on a stack of Bibles that he really goes for women, but the evidence seems to show he fears and hates them.

Of all the sexual dysfunctions, this *seems* the most dramatically connected with the inner feelings of the sufferer. If a man can't get hard, or if he comes almost at once, it does really seem as if he has a faulty set of genitals. Those problems may in truth be connected with the mind, but they don't really *seem* to be. But if you can come in the bathroom but not with your wife—that's *crazy!* You obviously are screwed up. And you can't hide the fact from the woman you have sex with.

I take it back—in a way you can. Just as preorgasmic women can buck and moan and pretend to be having the biggest orgasm in history, a man can thrust and writhe and shudder, and roll off as if totally spent. For this perhaps he deserves an Oscar nomination, but he doesn't fool himself.

Well, I wouldn't have described this misery so vividly if there were no cure for it. But I did want to show that having retarded ejaculation is not a sort of backhanded good luck.

WHEN ENOUGH IS ENOUGH

There are cases of what is called partially retarded ejaculation. The condition is rare, but the man can come after pumping away for a long, long time—long after the woman's vagina has dried up, and she has become tired of the whole thing, it is becoming painful for her, and she wishes they had watched a late movie instead.

It is a mistake to think that a woman can enjoy intercourse indefinitely. She has her limits. There are men who can keep up an erection for hours and who think they can bring any woman to orgasm as long as there is no time limit. This is a simplistic notion of sexual interaction. If it lasts too long, the woman always wishes it were over with.

CAUSES OF RETARDED EJACULATION

The condition is, as I have said, much like female orgasmic dysfunction and the faulty mechanism is similar. The man cannot give himself permission to have an orgasm. Not with a woman. The presence of the woman excites in him some fear of losing control, of letting go.

Why does the woman affect him that way? Psychoanalysts can spend years uncovering the deep roots of such feelings. Don't misunderstand me—psychoanalysis is a profound discipline and everyone in sex therapy has learned from it and respects it. But it is slow and very often has no effect on sexual behavior. And it is safe to say that whatever the deeper causes of the dysfunction may be, the fear of performing badly has become a large part of the problem by the time a man comes into sex therapy.

THERAPY—TALKING ABOUT IT FIRST

The therapist has to spend some time talking to the couple about how the therapy works, what the exercises are, and about the need for both persons to carry out their tasks willingly. As in all these two-person forms of therapy. If a couple want to try this therapy on their own, they must keep this in mind. If the rancher and his wife, a long way from any sex clinic, want to try these exercises, they should first tell each other whatever they feel about them. And talk as long as they need to in order to come to a friendly agreement. But people do marvelous things on their own out in the boondocks—plumbing, car repair, roofing, calf or lamb birthing, minor surgery and so on. So I don't think some home sex therapy, without my guidance or the guidance of another therapist, is impossible. It may not work out perfectly, but it is probably worth trying.

THE EXERCISES

To begin, for three days the couple should indulge in exciting sex play, whatever they like to do, but the man is not to masturbate. This prohibition is not forever! But for the present, no going into the bathroom after sex to ejaculate by himself, and no masturbating anytime during those three days. Let him build up a big yearning to have an orgasm. I want him to have a powerful drive later on.

After that they are to continue having sex, but now, as soon after sex play as can be, he is to bring himself to ejaculate in some way that he knows will work. If he can't do that with her upstairs with him, let her go down and watch late TV or set the breakfast table, and let him masturbate to orgasm. And do it with some strong fantasy. I want him to develop a good one that he can use in the next steps of therapy.

Next let him have sex with her, then masturbate in the next room for a session or two, until he feels very confident about going to the next exercise, which is bringing himself to orgasm in her presence.

She must not show impatience with him at this point. And even if she is sure he won't mind, even if she thinks he's a good sport, no matter how much she feels like doing it, no teasing or kidding! If there are any jokes, let *him* make them. He doesn't need to hear, "Okay, sonny, now go play with yourself." Or "Roll over, Rover, and do your thing." It might seem as if he should be able to take a joke. After all, look what *she* is putting up with! But play it safe. Assume his sensitivity is huge at this time. Let the wife be all love, tact and support.

So, for a few sessions he has sex with her and masturbates afterward, coming closer to her as his confidence builds up. He is beginning to connect her with his pleasant feelings as he climaxes. When he can come to orgasm in bed with her, perhaps with her touching him, he is close to home. The great moment comes when she can reach over and take his penis and bring him to ejaculation. This should be continued until she can do it very confidently, and in the end she should be craftily moving her vagina closer to his penis.

Lying on their sides facing each other, or with her in the female-superior position, or any way that suits them best for this maneuver, let her stimulate him to a point very near ejaculation, then insert the penis just inside the vagina for the climax. When this can be done the couple are in the home stretch. Each time they do it he can get farther into the vagina, starting a little earlier in his stages of excitation. The time will come when he can insert his erect penis and thrust until he comes.

During these exercises he should use whatever fantasies help him to give himself up entirely to the encounter and block out all negative thoughts, all tendency to overcontrol, to hold back orgasm.

You can see that the couple must be on good terms to complete these exercises. Tiresome marital bickering must be avoided. Long-term grudges must be abandoned, or given up for the duration. This can be done. I have never seen these exercises carried out in a fairy tale—they are designed to be used by real human beings, in this world. But ordinary mortal people can succeed in these exercises as in many other serious endeavors.

29

Unresponsive Women

SOMETIMES a man is hurt by being turned down, or because the lady responds to him with very little enthusiasm. And he says, "She's frigid." That conveys a picture of a woman with a bored face, and genitals made of ice.

Now, it is very demoralizing to all men to be turned down, but since it may happen to any of you, try to accept it without calling names. Maybe it's impossible not to feel resentment when somebody ignores all our good qualities, which we have stacked up so neatly in our own minds. But for our own self-respect we should not slander people. If a door is slammed in our face, well, that is rude. If it is just calmly closed—well, just say, "We weren't meant for each other."

It's more complicated when a man finds himself married to a woman who seems to want him around but who does not respond to him sexually. This woman seems to have lots of headaches, to fall asleep when her head touches the pillow and to spread her legs silently if approached with insistence, then to lie there as if she had nothing to do with these goings-on.

Many a man has, after a few months of marriage, decided that he must have married a "frigid" woman. He has heard of such women but couldn't believe he would have the bad luck to marry one. Women who may have breasts and vaginas, who can bear children, but can't share the pleasure of sex.

It used to be universally accepted that some women were "frigid" and some men were "impotent." There was nothing to be done about them—or with them. If you married one it had better be for money. The two words covered almost any sexual difficulty a person might have—and all of those difficulties were considered hopeless.

Sex therapists try to find out which of a variety of problems may be keeping a woman from the full enjoyment of sex. Since there are many causes of apparent indifference or inability to enjoy, the word *frigid* has become useless to us; and to the general public, with wider sexual education, the word is falling out of use. What does it mean? A woman can get bored with sex because it is frustrating. She gets sick of trying to have an orgasm. She can seem really not to want it, or she would not clamp herself shut when a penis comes near. Or, while she likes approval and being made a fuss of and even being hugged and kissed and stroked, she doesn't seem to know that sex is something desirable. Sex therapy has divided psychosexual problems into different types, each calling for different treatment.

There are women who don't respond sexually to sexual opportunities or to the idea of sex. They don't get wet down there when an erotic idea is presented to them. But they do want to have relationships, they do fall in love, and many of them come to sex therapy asking to be helped. They will not be dismissed as frigid.

GENERAL SEXUAL DYSFUNCTION

The unresponsive woman does not send signals from her brain to her vagina. The valves don't shut down there, so there is no vasocongestion—what causes the swelling of the outer lips. The vaginal fluids don't lubricate the vagina. Sometimes, on direct stimulation of the clitoris, she can have an orgasm, just as men sometimes have orgasms without erections. But unresponsive women are not attracted to sex, and if they tolerate intercourse it is uncomfortable. So they tend to avoid it.

Sometimes an unresponsive woman comes to sex therapy at the urging of her husband; sometimes it is her idea. In either case the therapist must have her assurance that she is ready to undertake therapy for herself, with desire and determination.

ONE WOMAN'S STORY

A pretty woman of twenty-eight came to me saying she felt she was missing something and that because of that her husband was unhappy. We talked about what happened in bed and it did seem that this was a case of general unresponsiveness. She loved her husband, but she thought it wasn't in a "grown-up" way. She tried to get sex over as fast as possible because she felt tight and dry, and she never initiated sex but tried to dodge it a lot. Her husband was a mild man, but he had a way of criticizing in a light, unserious way that she felt was insidious, and he would tease her about being a "married nun" and called sex "the cross she has to bear." Recently she had become very angry and told him not to speak of this in front of outsiders. He said if it was too serious to be treated as an acceptable foible, it was serious enough to be treated as a real problem. He suggested that she consult a sex therapist and, after she agreed, nagged her for two weeks until she came to me. She said she really wanted to undertake whatever course was indicated; she had put it off only because she was a procrastinator. I decided that she was willing enough and really wanted to find a way to be happier as a grown-up and a married woman.

I talked to her with her husband and they agreed to the course of treatment.

PLEASANT HOMEWORK

The first week they concentrated on what are called the sensate focus exercises. Both the name and the exercises are inherited from Masters and Johnson, the pioneers of sex therapy. Sensate focus may sound like something you do in a lab with microscopes, but it is really very nice. Once a man told me it was something he always wanted to do but only before he had sex, not after, and since he always felt the urge to gallop to orgasm he never got to do it. He had long—since the age of thirteen or so—dreamed of slowly kissing, smelling, touching a woman all over. He said he wasn't sure any woman would let you do it, unless you had bought her in a slave market, and it was worth having some sexual difficulty to get the chance. He was an amusing guy. This is a common fantasy of men, but generally the strong urge to have sex keeps them from carrying it out.

The husband who had called his wife a nun liked the exercises too, very much, and the wife liked them since there was no intercourse to be afraid of. They took turns petting, stroking, nuzzling each other from top to toe but skipping the genitals. And he was not to touch her nipples that first week. When neither partner has any reaction against the exercise it produces a nice intimacy and some mild erotic feelings. When he was pleasuring her, she had some feelings she seemed to remember but from some distant time—some little thrills along portions of her skin. Although they weren't touched, her nipples got hard and she had some goose bumps that were fun. When she pleasured him, he had erections and that amused her. It made him seem like a live toy she could control. And when he stroked her after that, she had stronger reactions, a sort of tingling in the vagina. And she loved being "worshiped." The notion of being a little pagan goddess appealed to her.

The second week they continued the exercises with a difference. Now he could touch, gently pinch and nibble her nipples and play lightly with her genitals—but no trying to bring her to high excitement or orgasm. Just teasing, light caressing. This gave him very hard erections, and when it was his turn she was allowed to bring him to orgasm. She felt tense about being touched genitally, but this was balanced by the amusement she found in masturbating him. She began to have aggressive sexual feelings toward him that amused them both. This triggered something in her and she reported getting wet late in the week.

That was a good sign. The next step was what we call nondemand coitus. It helps when the woman gets wet down there, but if she doesn't the man is to lubricate his penis with petroleum jelly—or, if condoms are their contraceptive, K-Y jelly. Or, if you prefer, the woman may use a brand of lubricating suppository.

They were to indulge in foreplay until he had an erection and she, if possible, was vasocongested and lubricated. Then she was to straddle him and gently lower herself onto his penis, move gently and withdraw. He was not to thrust, or at least not to do so vigorously. She was to withdraw before he came, rest and pet a little and bring back his erection. He could touch her genitally. Then again they were to do the teasing, slow, nondemand coitus. After several such engagements she could finish by bringing him to orgasm.

Once in a great while the woman is overwhelmed with sexual desire during this part of the exercises and finds herself thrusting to orgasm. But that is rare, and it did not happen with this couple. But she was becoming aroused, vasocongesting and lubricating, very regularly.

At this point I felt that further sex therapy was not needed. The specific problem was solved—her hating sex because she was tight and dry, and getting no fun out of it at all. But now she could lubricate and she had a desire to make him have erections and to make him go through the enjoyable throes of orgasm. Before their last session with me they had been "naughty" and gone beyond instructions. He had thrust to orgasm inside her, and she had told him to "do" her right away and he went down on her. Of course that was fun, especially since it was disobeying Teacher. At that point I could hardly resent it, since it was a sign of great improvement. I told them to go away and have fun. They might try this: getting her closer and closer to orgasm and then finishing up with his penis inside, to try to bring her to orgasm coitally—something everybody would like to be able to do, though it isn't the only thing in the world. I recommended a sex manual that they could read together to find ways to combine foreplay, intercourse and afterplay excitingly. And perhaps positions that might work better to bring her to orgasm coitally.

Sometime later I found a postcard from Bermuda in my office mail. There was a picture of a sailboat and I couldn't remember who belonged to the two first names right away, but I guessed who it must be. The only message was this: BINGO! It could only mean that she had enjoyed an orgasm at last while they were having intercourse. That kind of thing often happens on a good vacation. They didn't say, "Wish you were here," and I didn't expect them to.

THAT WAS AN EASY CASE

They had a lot that made what happened under my tutelage easy. For instance, though he had that tendency to criticize in a sneaky way, passing it off as whimsical teasing, he was a gentle fellow without macho hang-ups. He could go along with being pleasured and with "worshiping" her. She was so desirable to him that he could supply erections when they were needed. They got a special break in her suddenly discovering the pleasure of being a vamp and making him react sexually. That opened up a way of being playfully demanding, of asserting her needs.

It is rare to have so few reactions against the therapy. While the therapeutic exercises are pleasant for people who accept them, I do spend a lot of time talking to people about accepting each other and accepting the mutuality of sex. Where they are both hung up on rigid ideas about what is manly or what is indecent, we have to talk that out. A man may refuse to spend all that time pleasuring his wife. The wife may suddenly scream at him to stop, because she is sure he is ugly and she is ugly or what they are doing is ugly—negative ideas coming from long-ingrained attitudes and feelings. They may really not like each other and for that reason resent the intimacy the exercises develop. Then we have to stop the exercises for marital counseling—which often works but not always.

SITUATIONAL UNRESPONSIVENESS

A woman who has had good sexual responses in the past may become unresponsive after certain experiences, such as childbirth. She may be unresponsive just to the man she is now with, no matter how long he tries to arouse her. In fact, his efforts may really turn her off. They reinforce her dislike—he seems like such a "wimp." At the same time, other men may arouse her by a touch. She may have had good responses in an earlier marriage or in premarital sex with other men. She may be very responsive when they are on repeated honeymoons—away on vacation, in exotic or luxurious surroundings—but turned off in the domestic scene. When this is the case, improving her responsiveness in the situation that turns her off may be harder than working with the woman who has never been responsive. Marital therapy, psychoanalysis or some change in the lifestyle of the couple may improve things. Sometimes I can even get somewhere with sensate focus and the rest of the exercises! But it must be said that divorce is often the outcome of stubborn disagreement, and it may be better than continual domestic cold war.

GOING ON TO THE SEARCH FOR ORGASM

Improving the responsiveness of the wife may lead to other needs for therapy. The man may have developed erectile difficulty in this relationship. And the woman may still be stopping short of the full pleasure of orgasm. Then we have to go on, if the couple wants it, to sex therapy dealing with those other issues. These are described in other chapters.

30

Preorgasmic Women

*T*HE loveliest woman you see in a month of Sundays may be preorgasmic. That is the word for having no orgasms, or having them rarely, with difficulty, or not having them the way you want to have them. It is a very common problem and it afflicts women of every kind. Just because a woman turns men on doesn't mean she has great orgasms.

Consider that gorgeous creature you see on television, using some tooth gel and telling you to use it so you can look like her. Or suffering for love every afternoon on a soap opera. She could very well be suffering in real life, much less elegantly, from a complaint that links her with housewives and regular working women all over the world—a secret shortage of what may have been oversold to us as life's greatest reward.

ORGASM ISN'T EVERYTHING

Orgasm has been overemphasized so much lately; one reason why so many women have trouble attaining it. So it may be a good idea to put it in a realistic perspective. Consider that TV beauty who can't have an orgasm. Still, she has a lot out of life. Wherever she goes men fall over themselves to help. Headwaiters, stewards on cruise ships, personnel managers where she looks for work, all jump to help the pretty woman. If she is a TV star, she has money, jewels for thieves to steal, luxury cars that cost a fortune to keep up. Her divorces are examined in detail in sleazy newspapers. She has all that! If she has to get up in the night, her toilet has a golden handle. She eats her starvation diet lunch in expensive restaurants. And so on.

So the earth doesn't move for her! Who needs it? If she wants the earth to move she can live in Los Angeles!

Let us talk about what a nice life you can have without orgasms. Even if you aren't so striking-looking that you cause traffic jams, you can have a real life without orgasms. You can sing, play tennis, tap dance, go on great vacations, have babies, have a career, all without orgasms. You can even love a man, enjoy sex with him and give him great pleasure without orgasms.

That is something people have lost hold of—the knowledge that physical closeness with a loved one is enjoyable apart from orgasms. A good deal of sex therapy goes into teaching people how to get back to that simple knowledge.

Orgasms are wonderful. People who have them enjoy them. Everyone is entitled to search for great orgasms. But they don't replace all the other good things in life, and if you exaggerate their importance or the effect they may have on you, that is a mistake. And, ironically, it may be what is keeping you from having the orgasms you want.

You were born a sexual being and will live so all your life. You are entitled to orgasms. But if you let the thought of them get too big, you are placing too high a value on them. That can hinder good sexual functioning.

PERMISSION WITHHELD

Millions of women are forbidding themselves to have orgasms. Or, to put it the way we usually do, they won't permit themselves to have them. They have erotic feelings, they lubricate, they come close to orgasm—and they hold back. The holding back seems to be involuntary. In the theory of sex therapy they are unconsciously holding back. They can't let go.

They do want the orgasm, but are afraid of it. They are perhaps not totally committed to the present relationship and don't want to lose control of themselves in it. They fear losing control for the brief moment of ecstasy they have heard about. They think that orgasm will change them entirely, that they will become totally enthralled by sex and become promiscuous. The are afraid of becoming animalistic and ugly in the eyes of their partners during the throes of orgasm.

Those are some of the feelings holding women back from abandon. But the fact is that if you have an orgasm, you lose control briefly and assume control shortly afterward. The experience will not change you into someone else. You will still know yourself. The next morning it will still be you in the checkout line at the supermarket, or waiting your turn at the office Xerox machine. You will feel wonderfully up, but still in control.

WAS THAT AN ORGASM?

Initial experiences with orgasms sometimes make women ask, "Is that what all the fuss is about?" It isn't always that there was no orgasm. The first one just may have been one of the little ones. In a lifetime of orgasms, a woman will find that some are big and some little. Even the little ones are nice if you know them for what they are—just nice little orgasms. If you know there will be big ones like the *1812 Overture* coming along.

There is a thing called a missed orgasm. Some women have orgasms but don't recognize them as great pleasures.

With the development of more appreciation of sensuous feelings, there can come greater awareness of the pleasure to be taken in orgasm. Without that awareness the orgasm may just be an odd fluttering sensation in the vagina.

HOW CAN I TELL HER WHAT IT'S LIKE?

A man phoned in to my radio show one Sunday night asking how he could describe orgasm to his girl, who had sex with him but didn't know what an orgasm was. I said he might try to tell her what his orgasms felt like, but that in truth there was no way to convey to her the feeling. When she had one she would know it, unless she had a missed orgasm.

We compare it to a sneeze. Some people rather enjoy sneezing, as a matter of fact.

In orgasmic women, the sexual sensations are much like a man's. Sexual images on the receptors in the brain cause messages to be sent to the genitals. Valves close; blood congests the tissues; lubrication takes place. Stimulation of nerve endings brings on higher and higher erotic feelings, muscles contract, and in these contractions are produced the releasing throbs of pleasure. In the release from sexual tension comes a release from many other tensions the woman is experiencing at the time. The postorgasmic relaxation is as great a pleasure as the orgasm. Some people like it better.

FAKING IT

Here is a letter from a radio listener.

Dear Dr. Ruth: I have been married two years and now I am in a bad fix. My husband thinks I have orgasms but I don't. I have pretended to have them by pretending to act the way he does when he comes. I feel very horny when we have sex, and I wish I could have orgasms. I like it when he enters me, and it never hurts. I know he could make me have an orgasm, but how can I tell him I have been pretending? Does my not having an orgasm mean I don't love him?—E.R.

This is what I wrote back.

Dear E.R.: I don't remember how many times I have dealt with the situation you describe. You know you can't just blunder up to him and say, "You don't give me orgasms. I have to fake them to spare your feelings. You've got to do something about it. I'm tired of faking and not getting the pleasure I want." Instead, write him a note and say you want to have a talk with him and you want him to be prepared to be the wonderful husband you know he is. If he weren't that kind you couldn't make the confession you want to make. Tell him in the note that it isn't a dented fender, that you haven't lost all the money in the bank account, and you haven't had an affair with another man—it is something just between you and him. When you talk to him, say you were brought up always to be polite at parties. A nice girl always acts as if she enjoys. So you have not acted as if you weren't getting everything out of sex that you want. For one thing, you aren't sure just what sexual pleasure is like. You know you enjoy the closeness and giving him pleasure, but you think there is something you are missing and you want the two of you to get a good sex book and read it together and talk about it. Please write me and tell me how things work out.

You see, I don't know why she isn't having orgasms. Maybe all they need is some more foreplay before they begin to have intercourse. Maybe she has to have direct stimulation of the clitoris to reach orgasm. But if they read and discuss the subject together, they will have a much better idea of what is going on. If she writes back, I may suggest going to a sex clinic.

The very people who do not talk about sex together are the ones who don't know that though the instinct to want sex may be natural, the successful carrying out of sexual encounters has to be learned. The first step is for them to begin talking about it, to begin confiding their needs to each other.

HER HUSBAND'S IDEA

A young woman phoned my office saying she had seen my TV show and wanted to consult me privately. I made an appointment and in the first hour I learned that she had never had an orgasm. She had not concealed this from her husband. She was not even much upset by it herself, but he had suggested to her that she should see a therapist. I told her that his idea might be right, but if she was doing this only to please him, I couldn't do much for her. She had to have a strong wish for sexual fulfillment for herself.

"But I *am* doing it to please him," she said.

We went around and around about that. Finally I decided that what she meant was that she was willing to go to some lengths to please her husband. That was a motivation in itself. She told me (in answer to my question, of course) that she had little idea of masturbation, that she had "sort of tried it" but it didn't seem to do anything for her. That was in college, where her roommate had told her about masturbating in the shower to relax so she could study.

A SORT OF SWEET EXPERIENCE

Her first real sexual experience was petting with her boyfriend and then going the whole way with him. She had not enjoyed either very much, but "they were sorta sweet experiences because I liked him." This was the fellow she married. They had been married two years. I made another appointment to see both of them. He told me their marriage was placid, but that they differed on certain points. He liked going out and socializing a lot, and she dreamed of living far out in the country and hardly ever seeing anyone. But she accepted entertaining his friends. She was affectionate but sexually limp. He enjoyed having sex with her but wanted her to enjoy it too. He agreed that it probably would be more exciting if she got into it more.

She had told me that she got wet and wanted to have an

orgasm but was more or less resigned to accepting less than the glorious experience everyone was talking about.

They had heard about foreplay, and bringing the woman close to orgasm before commencing intercourse. And he did do that but it was not very arousing for her.

"Do you tell him what you like?"

But of course she really didn't *know* what she liked. She hadn't really liked anything yet.

"What you were doing to her, with your fingers," I said to him. "That was manual stimulation of the clitoris. But it seemed to miss with her. How would you feel if she were to try doing that for herself, to explore her own reactions?" We talked about having the woman learn to please herself, then teaching her husband to do it. He said it would upset him, he would feel excluded. But he could see the point of it. How would she feel? She said she had no idea. The thought of masturbating was strange and unattractive. When she had tried it at college it only seemed like something she really didn't want to do. But she would try it.

LEARNING TO MASTURBATE

People look at me funny when I say that not everyone knows how to do this. They think people are lying if they say they don't. But I knew that this placid young woman was truly puzzled by what she was asked to do. The first time she did it she lay back on her bed and explored her lips and vagina with her second finger. I had not told her to examine herself with a mirror, as some other therapists do, but just to gently explore and locate her clitoris and the vaginal entrance and see if her finger in there created any sensations different from putting her finger in her mouth, for instance. She was to touch her clitoris, stroke the shaft, make little round movements in the area near it. This she did. She reported that she almost felt something but it might have been her imagination.

That week she dutifully tried this exercise four times, at odd moments in the day. She had a morning job in an architect's office, so her afternoons were free. She tried thinking up fantasies of being with a certain movie actor. She imagined running naked from the shower to turn off the gas on the overcooked broccoli. Now she noticed that she had left her handbag on the lawn outside the back door. Her husband would scold her if he saw that, so she just slipped out quickly—no one could see her here—to get the bag. But the door banged shut behind her and the lock clicked. There she was, naked, locked out, when this movie star came around the corner of the house. He smiled at her and came toward her. She covered her pubic area with the handbag and her nipples with her other hand and forearm, and turned halfway toward the house, asking him to please go away. But he came to her and took her chin and made her look into his eyes and smiled that famous smile and she had to smile back, though she was ashamed to smile under the circumstances. Then he began to pinch her nipples (that's right—with no more introduction than that) and to slide his hands over her buttocks and into her crotch—

She told me she didn't know where all that came from but that she did get wet when she thought of that. But the sensations in her clitoral area were so vague she hardly believed they were really there.

I thought perhaps the fantasy was too mild, but I was unwilling to think she would not improve on it. However, she seemed a bit impoverished as far as fantasies went! They all involved her being caught undressed rather than seeking anything sexual. Fantasies of being caught undressed frequently produced no more than shame and feelings of inadequacy (everyone can see through me, I can't even dress myself, etc.). But in the following week the movie-actor fantasy developed into quite an affair. Always smiling, he came around finally with his gang of bad guys and they all made her go into her room and undress and lie down and masturbate. If she did that, they wouldn't hurt her—for a while. She lay on the bed and they leered at her and took out their penises, the size of salamis, and rubbed them on her. She just kept trying to masturbate and that time she really became excited and thought something big was going to happen, but it didn't.

TRYING A VIBRATOR

I could see that her fantasies were getting somewhere, but she was only coming close to orgasm and not getting there, and she seemed to be discouraged, so I suggested a vibrator.

People often wonder why we don't just start with a vibrator. The reason is that women can become so dependent on the strong vibrations that they refuse to accept lesser stimulation. Then they have to be "weaned" from the vibrator. It is a roundabout way to go, but in this lady's case I thought it would be best, if she would accept the idea. She bought one, and inside the week she had her first orgasm. In the company of her fantasy movie actor and his bad guys.

I told her to use the vibrator, but every other time, just before she was going to have an orgasm, to stop the vibrator and finish with her finger. After a while she got so that she could masturbate to orgasm with only her hand, but she used the vibrator sometimes too.

The next step was to include the husband in her orgasms. After all, it had all been his idea. We discussed this next step, all three together, and they went off understanding, I felt sure, what they were going to do and why. They had sex together, then he held her in his arms and she masturbated to orgasm. He kept his hand over hers while she did it. The next time they had sex he stimulated her first, very slowly and gently, with her hand over his, and with her telling him now and then just what to do. When she was highly aroused they had intercourse, but she did not come, so he continued to stimulate her until she nearly made it. In the end she finished herself.

They continued experimenting in this way on their own and I believe that they may ultimately have found a way to bring her to orgasm in the act of coitus, after much foreplay. But this is a goal that some couples never reach. In this case I believe the husband was truly happy to have his wife enjoying orgasms during their encounters. And the idea of it excited him.

THE KEGEL EXERCISES

Very often the woman client can have orgasms masturbating but not from having her husband's penis thrusting repeatedly, or moving in a grinding movement, or even from the pressure of his pubic bone over her clitoris. The fact is that clitoral stimulation is much easier by other means than by coitus. In coitus the clitoris is moved somewhat as the inner lips pull the clitoral hood with them, but this stimulation is weak compared to direct touching or rubbing in the clitoral area.

The sensations leading to orgasm during coitus are much stronger in women who can tense their vaginal muscles, gripping the penis with them. Women are therefore told to use the Kegel exercises to strengthen the muscles and to learn how to use them.

When a man has an orgasm there are muscular spasms at the base of the penis; the effect of this involuntary muscle clenching on the local nerve endings is, most men agree, the most intense physical pleasure in male existence. Men do no exercises to acquire good muscle tone in that area. Those muscles just seem to be there, ready to do the job, whether the guy is an athlete or a ninety-seven-pound weakling! But in women the corresponding pleasure muscle often seems to be very lazy, and to need regular workouts.

The muscle involved is called the pubococcygeus (pronounced *pyoo-bo-coxxi*-jee-*us,* with the strong accent on the *jee*), nicknamed the pleasure muscle. This long muscle is anchored at one end to the pubic bone, the one under the pubic hair. The other end is attached to the coccyx, the tail end of the spine. The muscle surrounds the urethra, the outer genitals and the anus and controls everything in that area—stops urine flow, helps evacuate the bowel, helps push a baby through the birth channel—and when a woman knows how to use it, the pubococcygeus plays an important part in intercourse and in achieving orgasm.

More than fifty years ago, Dr. Arnold Kegel developed an exercise for women designed to strengthen the pubococcygeus muscle to help them contain their urine. The Kegel exercises are as simple as can be. To learn how to do them, the woman sits on the toilet and urinates a little, stops the flow, urinates a little, stops, and repeats until she has emptied her bladder. That teaches her where the muscle is and how to contract and relax it rhythmically to strengthen it.

The exercises can be done sitting at a desk, waiting for a stoplight to change while driving—whenever there is a moment to concentrate. Contract the pubococcygeus, count ten, relax. Repeat ten times. Take a break.

After ten days of this you should be very good at it. Then for something trickier: in fluttery succession, try to contract-relax-contract-relax-contract-relax. When you are in the act of coitus, getting near your goal of orgasm, this action can help immensely. Especially if you bear down at the same time, like a woman in childbirth.

Women masturbating, with fingers or with the vibrator, find this muscle clenching a terrific aid to orgasm—with or without some penislike object contained in the vagina to grip on; perhaps better with some such object in place. A dildo may be used; if you don't own one of these, a cucumber or banana will do!

SOLO OR DUO?

Masters and Johnson created the techniques of modern sex therapy that have been adapted by all the rest of us. They recommend having the wife explore her vagina while leaning back against her husband, as if the two were leaning back in a chaise longue. This has a nice togetherness about it, but those of us who were taught by Helen Singer Kaplan lean to the notion that a woman makes more progress learning to masturbate on her own. She is not being watched, and she *feels* that she is not being watched. No one is holding a stopwatch to see how soon she finds a hint of a sensation in her clitoral area. When she herself knows what touches and movements are good, she can pass this knowledge on to her man.

But we are not rigid. I can imagine a woman, one who feels lonely and discouraged by herself, who might prefer the companionship of the man's arms around her as she begins to explore herself.

MASTURBATION AND MARRIAGE

They go together very nicely; masturbation is a good friend. Physically, the distinction between expert foreplay and masturbation is nonexistent. Masturbation should be part of the couple's repertoire; to be held in the arms of your loved one understandingly as you bring yourself to sexual release is to have a distinctly married feeling.

Masturbation techniques are used in foreplay, and for bringing orgasm after coitus sometimes. And masturbation is for times when one partner needs sexual release and the other is not available. Not available in the sense of being out of town or, on some occasions, tired or not in the mood. It is a fortunate thing when the couple are not upset by each other's autoeroticism.

There is a way for men to feel good about their women's masturbation. The woman is mistress of many skills and mysteries. She is a mystery herself, with her ability to take his seed and create and hold life within her body. Her knowledge of being female has many facets. Her ability to walk and move like a woman, to sit and lie in female ways, to brush her hair like a woman, to put on makeup artfully if that is her style. Not least is her knowledge of her own female body, which she is willing to share with him.

What she teaches him and what they learn together, exploring love's anatomy, trying many acts of love and many positions, can lead to mutual release through intercourse, bodies entwined, his male organ held in her female

one. That is a lovely thing, and some couples do it success-
fully right away and some after years of intimacy.

There is a very exciting way to make love, combining
intercourse and manual stimulation of the clitoris. The
couple must find a position in which her hand or his can
reach her clitoris while they are engaged in coitus. For the
woman this is very satisfying as she gets strong stimulation
of the clitoris while holding his penis within her.

LAST THOUGHTS ABOUT ORGASM

Women who do not have orgasms from intercourse are in
the majority. Is this a gloomy fact? Look at it this way—if
you have orgasms from intercourse, fabulous. If not, you
are with the majority and not singled out by a cruel fate
through some fault of your own.

Statistics in this area are not up to date, and are constantly
changing anyway. Suffice it to say that some women have
orgasms through intercourse, some only through masturbation or other direct stimulation of the clitoris and some
report having never had an orgasm.

There is also a small percentage so orgasmic that they can
think themselves into an orgasm and a small percentage who
may be physically incapable of orgasm.

Whatever the numbers, and whatever category you fall
into, sex should still be a cherished and special part of your
life.

31

Vaginismus

TALK about one end not knowing what the other is doing! What about a wife in bed with her husband, and she wants to have sex with him very badly, but her vagina won't let him in? Seems to have a mind of its own, and truly a penis-hating one. The muscles at the entrance, the introitus, are clamped tight as a vase. And she has no idea on earth what is going on down there.

Some people say that women who have vaginismus really hate men—deep down underneath. But sex therapists say that when women are cured of this condition they are very much relieved. This has been my experience.

Vaginismus shows up the first time a couple try to have intercourse (coitus), and sometimes it goes on for weeks after the wedding. Months. Years. The married pair tell nobody about it because—well, how would *you* feel? All the hoopla on the wedding day, then you ride off in the Just Married car, tin cans banging and making everyone turn around expecting an accident, and, comes the wedding night—nothing. Just shame and embarrassment and discomfort to remember.

A SECRET UNHAPPINESS

Neither one wants to admit they couldn't do it. Does she want to say, "All those miles you traveled to the wedding, all those presents, people making toasts in champagne, and I can't even open up to let my poor husband in"?

Does he want to admit he can't get into his wife?

Often they haven't even heard of vaginismus. They think very often that she has a hymen made of steel plate. Or that his manly member is a weakling.

Everywhere they go, as the weeks go by, they see sexual heroes and heroines. People going around smiling and confident and joking with each other as if everything must be all right everywhere, not a cloud of sexual anxiety in the sky. People who obviously can Do It. She sees an anchorwoman on TV. An Indian woman in a sari selling soft pretzels in the subway. She is sure they can Do It, and probably did last night. They all have wide-open vaginas. Butterflies and bluebirds flying in and out.

He sees the office manager, who he used to think was an old fuddy. Now he imagines this virile white-haired man as going through his wife, three secretaries and a call girl every day. He glances curiously at every man he passes. In a hardware-store window he stares a long time at a power drill, thinking how easily it goes through wood and even metal.

"How's married life?" the fresh mailroom boy asks him.

They go to dinner at her family's. How they smile at everyone, so that nobody should guess. How their jaws ache!

ALL SO AVOIDABLE

It would all be so much easier if they had heard of this before, if they knew that lots of people had gone through it. If they knew that there is a sensible way to deal with it.

I have had clients who have struggled with vaginismus a

long, long time. Very seldom do they come to someone for help in the beginning. I have helped people whose marriages have been unconsummated for three years. The first thing I tell them is that we are going to get the marriage consummated very soon, without the slightest doubt. Definitely. I have no reason to believe otherwise, and at this point they need a big dose of optimism.

TO CLEAR A FEW THINGS UP

To clear a few things up—vaginismus (what a word!) is not the same as vaginitis. A great many people get the two mixed up. Vaginitis is an itchy, burning inflammation of the lining of the vagina. You get a prescription for it from a doctor and usually it goes right away. Vaginismus is a muscle clamped shut with some fear that the woman doesn't really understand. After all, she may be a little fearful of this initiation into sex, but not *that* fearful.

The theory is that she has been frightened sometime in the past about being penetrated. Some story reached her about rape or painful doing away with the hymen. Or she just heard about intercourse when she was too little to understand. She didn't know that a grown woman has room in there for a penis. She got the idea of something hard being pushed right inside where there was only room for a little stream of urine, and hurting the woman badly.

Or, according to another theory, she is envious of men for having penises, and this is her way of getting revenge. The bride who desperately wants to get past this stage in her marriage can really resent that theory.

What else about vaginismus? There are a number of interesting facts. Sexual response: You might think the woman with vaginismus would be so much afraid of sex that she could not lubricate, but very often she can. And many women with vaginismus know what it is to have an orgasm. They have masturbated and had orgasms that way, or they have had them during heavy petting. Sometimes she can insert a tampon to absorb menstrual fluid. Either the opening is large enough for the tampon but not a penis, or the emotional situations are different and she is not tense when inserting the tampon. I would suppose the latter.

Not every woman with vaginismus is a virgin. The condition can develop after she has had intercourse many times. Some painful condition in the vagina can bring it on. Women sometimes have it after childbirth, fearing that they are not healed entirely and that coitus will be painful.

Like many other sexual problems, this has been blamed on misdirected religious teaching, and sometimes the histories of the women involved seem to bear this out. But the condition exists in very modern, broad-minded women too. Getting rid of your religion will not cure your vaginismus.

Some surgeons have severed the muscle involved surgically to try to cure the condition. Don't do it! That muscle serves a purpose and should not be damaged. Contracting that muscle during orgasm can add much to the pleasure of it, especially when the muscle grips a hard penis. And that gripping is very pleasing to the man as well.

NEEDED: A LOVING COUPLE

Vaginismus can be relieved by a very simple procedure to be carried out by husband and wife together, patiently and lovingly, over a short period of time.

During this period it will be wonderful if the couple have a little repertoire of sexual activities for bringing each other to orgasm. Manual stimulation and oral sex are available to this couple and will take the tension out of overcoming vaginismus.

When a woman comes to me with this problem, the first thing I have her do is visit a gynecologist in order to reassure both of us that there is no abnormal physical condition in the vagina. This idea of a physical abnormality is very strong in the woman's mind, and she must be assured that there is nothing wrong in there behind that stubborn muscle. It helps the husband to know that too. They both must feel quite safe about using the simple, gentle technique they are going to use to decondition the muscle. In my office I show them a picture of the vagina so that they will see that there is plenty of room in there for anything they intend to put there. The vagina when empty is limp, but it is very elastic and will stretch easily to contain any penis. Only at the entrance are there strong muscles that for the present are resisting intromission. I assure them that soon they will be making love in the way all their ancestors did.

Little by little we are going to persuade that muscle to accept the presence of harmless objects in the vagina. Not by stretching the muscle, only by getting it to relax.

THE EXERCISES

This is what I tell them to do. Lying side by side, or in any position they find comfortable, with no idea of having sex just now, she is to take his little finger and put the tip against the entrance to the vagina. I have shown them where. So many people have no idea! It is a little more than halfway down from the top of the genital opening.

The man is to let her do that, she being in control of the finger. Let the finger stay there at the lips a little while, then let her push it in a very little bit until she feels just a little discomfort. Let the finger stay like that and let her become accustomed to the feeling. While she is allowing this the discomfort may go away. If not, after a while let her remove his finger and put her own there awhile. This continues (not so long at any one session as to let really strong feelings of boredom or annoyance build up) until the feeling of discomfort disappears. Little by little, fingers go farther into the vagina. The feeling of discomfort eases at each stage of insertion. The nerves and muscles in there must be shown, very patiently, that this thing the couple want to do doesn't hurt. After a period of a week or so, usually, the couple can insert the whole pinkie and move it in and out easily. Then larger fingers are tried, patiently, and then two fingers.

When two fingers go in easily, can be moved in and out and then rotated, it is time for the next big step.

Although the muscle is recalcitrant in the beginning, the vagina is usually lubricating in response to the attention it is getting. Actually, the woman's brain is sending conflicting messages to the area—one to get wet, the other to defend the entrance. She should not put a finger to those lips until she has some sensation that means getting wet down there, and he should not push in until he is aware of some wetness. Not gushing out, just enough to feel. I might, in some rare cases, suggest using a lubricant on the fingers.

During this period I like the couple to be relaxed and chatting easily while they conduct these gentle intrusions. Couples report giggling a good deal, which is natural enough. Some soft radio music during this deconditioning may be soothing. I shouldn't think hard rock or disco would set the right mood, but the couple know best how they react to it.

Now they are ready to try—guess what? To try putting the penis in there little by little, at the woman's pace. I suggest the female-superior position, with him on his back and her straddling him. When he is good and hard, let her lower herself onto the penis a little. No thrusting or attempt to have anything like intercourse. Getting the whole penis into the vagina easily may take a few sessions, but the end is clearly in view at this point. Every stage calls for mutual congratulations! Halfway down the penis calls for soft hurrahs. All the way down calls for hip, hip, hurrahs! And when they feel impelled to move up and down, to encourage him to thrust enough for him to ejaculate, that is a red-letter day that they can celebrate annually. The marriage is consummated!

It takes a while before they can effect intromission and totally uninhibited thrusting. But that day does come. While he is supplying patient erections the couple may sometimes have to pay attention to his penis and pet it hard again. And he should be given orgasms manually or orally throughout the deconditioning period.

DON'T DO IT IN A HAMMOCK!

One couple had an awkward time when it came to the first partial insertion of the penis. The bed was so springy that she had little control. Straddling him, she felt as though she were on one of those tippy rubber horses people try to ride in the water. She was gripping the penis like the pommel of a Western saddle. When the penis was pointing due west, her vagina was heading northeast. She reported to me that the session had been a hopeless defeat.

I suggested, thinking fast, that they continue the attempts on the floor. That would be a more stable platform. Things went very smoothly after that. The idea may be Dr. Ruth's own great contribution to sex therapy, first published right here!

KEEPING PEACE IN THE FAMILY

The severity of this problem varies widely, but where there is good feeling between husband and wife there is every reason to believe that the vaginismus will be relieved. All the while the couple should make special efforts to keep peace in the family. The problem tends to make the man feel inadequate, and the woman too. Both should be aware of these feelings, irrational though they may be. Often the therapist has to intervene. Remember that the husband, having to supply erections on demand, needs all the support the wife can give. One husband timidly snitched on his wife to me. He was so upset to be doing that! But he was right. During little spats they had, she would tell him he was impotent. I said that neither of them was ever to say anything like that to the other, *ever.* That was sabotaging all our work, and I would have to stop trying to help them. The wife stopped calling him that and things progressed very well.

In sex therapy we can't have the couple yelling "Impotent!" and "Frigid!" at each other! The whole theory of sex therapy is that, seeing any sex problem as mutual, the couple can improve things together.

I do think that a couple could work this problem through on their own, using good sense and mutual kindness. Actually, many couples relieve mild vaginismus without ever going near a sex manual or a therapist—just by being gentle and unhurried in their early lovemaking. But I think some society should put sex manuals on every desert island, for the romantic pairs who get stranded there.

32

Openness and Honesty

"WE agreed from the beginning that we would be totally open with each other," the very young woman told me. The story of her deteriorating relationship with a young man was very familiar to me. She and the young man were attracted to each other. Fairly soon they were sharing an apartment. They had a notion that the thing to be in a relationship is totally open—meaning free, uninhibited and without reticence. This idea is in the air—as I said, I have heard it so often.

Now, it seemed, as the young woman told me her troubles, she did not want quite so much openness. The case in point was his casual evening of sex with another young woman, which he freely told her about. Instead of being so open, she would, after six months with him, like him to keep a few things in. She would rather not hear about every passing sexual fantasy he had about every passing female. She would like him to control his feelings for passing females and she would like him to shut up about those he had and she would like him to make a commitment to her instead of being so free and to stop telling her things that

252

made her feel awful. In short, she was sick of what she called openness.

I advised her to have a talk with her young man, to explain that she had tried six months of total openness and now she wanted to negotiate for something else that he did not seem mature enough to accept—some commitment, loyalty, consideration. I asked her if she weren't really more inclined to break off with him than to try to get him in line with her revised ideas. She said she was, she just wanted someone to tell her it was all right to do that instead of bleeding in the cause of openness.

But now, having said this, we must again consider the world of the '90s in light of the AIDS epidemic—and if you don't think that it is an epidemic, you are wrong and cannot afford to gamble that I am wrong—and question the legitimacy of casual sex. Whether this is what you do, or this is what you and your partner have agreed each is permitted to do, or this is what you know your partner does and you do not care—this cannot be condoned at a time when a mistake can mean a horrific disease leading to death for you or your partner. This is not an issue any longer of morality of whether one must curtail sex for moral or religious reasons, but simply that we live in a terrible time when we have to use common sense to reduce the possibility of exposure to someone with AIDS. When the time comes, God willing, when we no longer have to worry about contracting a death-dealing virus, then we can again engage in the luxury of innovative and experimental relationships for those of you who want to try this. In the meantime, use your common sense and practice safer sex in all aspects of your joyous and monogamous sex life.

ANOTHER KIND OF OPENNESS

I am all for openness of another kind—I mean being open to each other, ready to accept each other's wants and needs and feelings within the framework of a loyal and considerate relationship. That openness has a place in every home.

People often join together out of a strong mutual attraction, having little idea what kind of real person the other is. When surprising needs and desires begin to surface, one or both may be quite annoyed at these unwanted emotions.

It may develop, for instance, that a couple who thrilled each other while showing off to each other during the courtship period will find on longer acquaintance that they are really uncongenial. The man who acted like a party boy and man-about-town is actually clever (enough to put on a courtship act for long enough to interest her) but by nature and long-established habit very shy, retiring and wanting a rather solitary existence—only, with her sharing it. She is outgoing, exuberant, always happiest with a crowd around. He admired her vivacity but never realized what it meant or that she would want a life full of noise and company.

Now they see each other for the first time, and each is threatened and angered by what is seen. He wants his way and refuses to understand her at all; the simple fact that she is a person separate from him, and not the embodiment of a dream he had about a girl who existed just to please him with her pretty ways—that he refuses to understand. She sees that a man who used to be fun and ready for anything she wanted has turned into a selfish grouch who wants to stay by himself and read—and force her to have a rotten time being all alone with him.

These two close themselves to each other. They refuse to accept or share each other's feelings about life in any way. A major readjustment has to come or they will break up, which is what people do now instead of living on in soured unions.

Perhaps in a later relationship with someone else, each of these people will realize the importance of learning about the real person one is with before plunging into a rash commitment. And the importance of listening to the other person when he or she seems totally unsympathetic—listening, being open, discovering the reality of another human being.

Actually, many people have married, gone through some very rough early years because of major disagreements, then learned to understand each other along with those strange feelings and needs that were at first so unwelcome.

SHEDDING THAT ARMOR

Even without major misunderstandings, people in a new relationship carry into it an invisible suit of armor. This is the protection they wear against threats and invasions by others—people in business, on the street, in crowded stores, in forced situations like high-school classes. One needs some protection against the human race at large, but in marriage there must be a readiness to accept the other person's tender spots, and accept loving gestures, touches, kindnesses. And in the night, when lovers lie together, sexual passion spent, wanting something softer and more protective for a while, it helps if each is open to the other's offerings and needs.

AND THEN THERE IS HONESTY

What many people call openness in a relationship is in fact not only being closed to each other but actually being hostile and harmful. It would be less confusing if they called it honesty rather than openness. The idea of a harmful rough honesty is understandable; a harmful emotional openness, or receptivity, makes no sense.

Many young people engage in rebellion against what they see as hypocrisy, and take the stand that in their relationships they will always be honest. The honesty they take such pride in showing is egotistical, harsh, hostile, and when it comes to "honesty" in disregarding any human need for fidelity, it is simply uninformed about what human relationships are and what feeds them and keeps them alive.

The idea that there are no feelings of possessiveness, no fears of being supplanted, no jealousy, no wanting to be treated protectively and regarded as very special and valuable, and that two people with no exclusive claim on each other can maintain a loving relationship, is a complete misunderstanding of the human heart and soul.

As a youthful misunderstanding, born out of ardor and idealism, that is forgivable—though we hope it will not persist too long.

There is, however, a very harmful honesty running around loose these days that is not confined to the young. Among people who have spent fortunes learning to express themselves, to assert themselves, to avoid "playing games" and to live with everyone on terms of a boring and uncharming "honesty"—behaving in a way our parents would say was simply very rude—among these people a totally destructive honesty lives on and men and women of forty and fifty solemnly adhere to it.

A woman tells me, about a cactus in a bowl someone gave me, "I hate that bowl. You'll have to excuse me, but what I feel I have to say." What about me? If I had to say what I felt, I'd say she is a boring and stupid woman with fifth-rate, worn-out junk for ideas. Now, I will not tell her that because, God forgive me, it is the truth. I see only cruelty and destructiveness in telling her that truth. So I jolly along about the offending bowl, and say she has fine feelings, the sensitivity (sensitivity! Forgive me that lie, O Lord!) of a true esthete.

In marriages and relationships, I say it is a pointless cruelty to confess or brag about your sexual past to a spouse or partner. And if you slip and commit an infidelity, that is yours to swallow and digest, and do not burden your loving partner with it if it can be avoided.

But remember—and I know what you are now thinking: "Here comes the warning about AIDS"—it is a terrible thing if you do not reveal to your loving partner that you have strayed from the monogamous path and for all you know you may have been exposed to AIDS with someone other than he or she. Even if you used a condom during this "slip" can you be sure that you did not also engage in some sexual activity that would have allowed the virus to pass from your temporary lover to you? In these times, it is far better—pardon the platitude—to be safe than sorry. Stay at home.

A NICE KIND OF HONESTY

That's the honesty of a man who, wishing always to be honest in his marriage, resists a very strong temptation to go to bed with another woman. Later his wife teases him. "I saw you looking at Doris at the Browners' cookout. Be careful, sonny; she'll eat you up." He laughs and says something acknowledging a foolish wandering eye—something innocuous, the remark of a childishly innocent may. He doesn't bother his wife with a tale against this neighborhood temptress. His wife can meet the woman and never feel the strain of an enmity. That is a helpful, genuine honesty, kept in shape at some cost, tempered with real humility.

Another helpful kind of honesty. A wife gives him his favorite dish, which she doesn't like. He asks, "Why the bribe? What am I in for—another party at the Waymans' pool?" She says no, it's because he was right and she was wrong in that fight in the car on Sunday. At least he wasn't *so* wrong. Not enough to be yelled at. She has actually thought it over and concluded that there was something to his point of view, and she has told him. He is touched by her kindness and by her serious and thoughtful character. And her honesty, which he prizes.

A woman has been faking orgasms for years. Never ever having a genuine orgasm. She wants to learn how to have one with him, a long-range goal, but this means admitting that she has been faking, that she hasn't been really overwhelmed by his bedroom mastery. Of course he is hurt, but in the cause of making the sex between them genuine, so she will no longer have to fake what she feels so bitter about not having. This confession caused her shame and pain too, but she has risked his anger to let him know something about herself and her deepest desires.

As two people grow in knowledge of each other, fewer and fewer pretenses survive between them. They grow more and more into expressing their true feelings to each other. This exchange of philosophical truth pleases them both as they care less and less about pretense. But they spare each other, with increasing skill, those little outbursts of "frankness" that they used to wound each other with in the quarrels of their early years together. That is a wonderful honesty between a loving couple.

33

Last Words about Long Loving

*A*S a last few words: If you have read all the advice in this book about how to be part of a loving couple, getting to be wiser and better at loving every month and every year, and helping your life's companion to light your common path—in that case I don't see how you can possibly fail as a lover. Perhaps you deserve a medal right now. In any case, you have my blessing, which is easier to bestow.

Realistically speaking, this book can help you—I really think so—if you are already disposed to be a good partner in love, if you have that certain knack of loving. Your prospects were good before you picked up the book. I don't claim to have invented love or even good sex—I just try to promote them. Loving couples were around before the first expert adviser on loving and coupling appeared. But the beginning couple and even some veteran couples will make use of any good advice that seems right to them.

Still speaking realistically, some marriages are doomed from the beginning. But I have seen others, not doomed but in deep trouble, that have been turned around. I have even loaned a hand. That has been a very great satisfaction to me.

If at any point I seem to have implied that something you have done is a fatal error and will destroy your happiness inevitably, well, forget it. People and good relationships are resilient.

If anything I have passed on to you ever turns out to be of use to you, do write me a letter telling me what a wise woman I am. I love that kind of letter.

SOME RELATIONSHIPS RIPEN SOONER

If you are a young person starting a relationship, you may think all the talk about lasting relationships, rewarding relationships, substantial ones, is about couples who have grown gray together and more or less stuck with each other anyway.

Well, there are lots of elderly people who are very glad to have each other's company—and having very enjoyable sex too, as I like to report to the world.

I am very much interested in getting more health-care professionals to see that handicapped people, institutionalized people and the very elderly do have the warmth and comfort and joy that sexual companionship can give them.

But the mature marriage or relationship isn't necessarily one involving senior citizens or even the middle-aged. It is quite usual to have a sturdy, established life companionship going while relatively young, if you have any aptitude for it and if you can take the time to give your marriage or relationship regular attention.

And the rewards of a ripening relationship are not all in the security, the sentiment or the philosophy. With care and attention the sex in that relationship gets better and better. The very best sex is what a long-loving couple design for themselves, that only they know how to give each other, that is tailored to their special desires and needs.

Trust, communicate, share, work at your marriage, think

about it, ask for help if you need help. Be realistic and always loving. Talk about your feelings but don't make them a burden. Stay together, realize that you're in this together. I have faith in you.

Index

ABOUT THE AUTHOR

Author, psychologist, and media personality, DR. RUTH WESTHEIMER is America's best-known and best-loved psychosexual therapist. She pioneered the field of media psychology with her nationally syndicated radio call-in show, *Sexually Speaking*. She continues to offer advice on love and relationships to millions through her syndicated television show, *Ask Dr. Ruth*, and her newspaper column of the same name. Dr. Westheimer, who earned her doctorate in the Interdisciplinary Study of Family from Columbia University, is currently Adjunct Associate Professor at New York University and lecturer in geriatrics at Brookdale Hospital in New York City.